Deep Soul Cleansing
12 STEP WORKBOOK

Passing on the Program . . .

THE 12 STEPS

STEP 1. We admitted we were powerless over our addition- that our lives have become unmanageable.

A SPONSOR'S GUIDE

Forms Created from and Used with AA's Literature

Pan Fellowship

First Edition

This edition printed in the United Kingdom

ISBN 978-0-9556930-2-1

To *All* my Sponsees
including those that speak to me and still consider me their
Sponsor and they that don't speak to me or consider me their
Sponsor anymore.

To my Sponsor George F.
who taught me through his example that a commitment to
Sponsor is for life.

Our thanks and gratitude to Alcoholics Anonymous for the gift they have given to the world of the Twelve Steps. This volume has been compiled using quotes from some of the 13 of AA's copyrighted books for use in life both in and out of Alcoholics Anonymous and the use in living experience of the "Program," which we recognise as the Steps. This material has been reprinted for the ease and speed of study during a Pan-Fellowship Retreat.

WE STRONGLY SUGGEST THAT EACH INDIVIDUAL WISHING TO BETTER UNDERSTAND THE 12 STEPS DO AS WE HAVE DONE AND PURCHASE AND STUDY ALL THE BOOKS OF ALCOHOLICS ANONYMOUS:

Alcoholics Anonymous
The Twelve Steps and Twelve Traditions
As Bill Sees It
The Language of the Heart
Came to Believe
The Best of the Grapevine
Dr. Bob and the Good Oldtimers
Experience, Strength, and Hope
Pass it On—Bill Wilson and the AA Message
Daily Reflections
The Home Group: Heartbeat of AA
AA Comes of Age
Living Sober

ALL THAT WE HAVE ATTEMPTED TO DO IS, TO FIND, AND "PULL OUT," THE EXPERIENCE OF THE 12 STEPS IN THE MANY LIVES OF THOSE WHO CONTRIBUTED TO THOSE 13 BOOKS.

In an attempt to honour and accent the lessons and information found in these texts we have often **bolded**, *italicized*, and <u>underlined</u> these 1,000 quotes from that material. In a further attempt to keep the material true to its original writing the use of these quotes often cause this written material to switch personal pronoun. Often the writing will switch from first person, to second person, to third person and back again; all within the same paragraph. Besides the text changes gender rather frequently. We trust this will not be too distracting from the objective of the Step work involved. It is our intention to increase our own and the reader's depth of understanding of this amazing programme the 12 Steps of Alcoholics Anonymous.

Quotes printed without permission of Alcoholics Anonymous

Table of Contents

Introduction

It is our desire that as many people as possible realise the power and wisdom encapsulated in the Twelve Steps. We have been using these methods for many years now. They have never failed to bring about relief for those of us who have looked deep within our souls to see our part in the creation of our life's problems. Our mental, emotional, psychological, and spiritual relief has been immense. We trust the reader who chooses this path will find the same. We can choose to be *"happy, joyous and free"*. [1]

The ability to work the Programme in the meetings of the various Twelve Step programmes is easier than outside the rooms. It is much easier than in our Relationships, Family, and Work lives. The Buddhists call this cloistered virtue. It does not create a *"bridge to normal living"*.

The use of this material was originally designed for use by alcoholics but as time has gone on there seems to have been the creation of a Pan-Fellowship.[i] Here members have found that once one addiction was "handled" with the Steps another would rear its ugly head. *"Very effective answers to problems other than freedom from alcohol have always been found through special purpose groups, some of them operating within AA and some on the outside."* [2]

This *Pan-Fellowship* came about by "accident." When holding a retreat using the AA material it gradually expanded to assist other *"troubled"* souls *"of this very troubled world."* [3] We have struggled with the whole idea of this work and after long investigation find nothing "wrong" in what we are doing, either in the Traditions or anywhere in AA's literature. We trust if anyone has a problem they will do as exhaustive an investigation as we have. You will find much of that research on these pages.

"Shall we reflect that the roads to recovery are many; that any story or theory of recovery from one who has trod the highway is bound to contain much truth." [4] We believe you'll find by using this workbook you will gain that truth about yourself.

This material is founded on basic information from the book *Alcoholics Anonymous, Twelve Steps and Twelve Traditions* and other 12 Step and spiritual literature. All other material is based on practical experience from the lives of fellow addicts. They have found

---

[i] Pan Fellowship means a group where all Twelve Step Fellowships are welcome to work the Steps on multiple problems.

peace of mind and contented sanity and sobriety by the planned way of spiritual life set forth originally in the literature of Alcoholics Anonymous.

Spiritual concepts must be embraced, but these do not involve organised religion. Although we must believe in a Higher Power, it is our privilege to interpret it according to our own understanding.

We must acquire honesty, humility and appreciation and eliminate self-centredness to keep our peace and sobriety. For those who are willing to accept the Twelve Step Programme as a means of recovery from any addiction, we recommend a close study of the books **"Alcoholics Anonymous (...the Big Book (AA members' fond nickname for this volume))"** [5] and the *Twelve Steps and Twelve Traditions*. Don't just read them; study them *repeatedly*. These books were written by alcoholics for alcoholics, though they have proven to work for any addiction and are based on the trials and experience of members.

Our experience shows that the programme of these Twelve Steps works no matter what the "addiction." *We further suggest the definition of addiction as, "anything that we do that we cannot seem to stop doing on our own steam."* This would include things like overeating, smoking, gambling, co-dependence, worrying, etc, not forgetting sexual behaviour, anger or rage and many other things.

When you are ready to do *anything* suggested, going "to any lengths," then you are ready to work the Steps. *Many are not ready until they have suffered greatly. Others may never be ready.* The spiritual path laid out in the pages of *Alcoholics Anonymous* and the *Twelve Steps and Twelve Traditions* is available to all spiritual beliefs. **"Clergyman of practically every denomination has given AA their blessing."** [6]

The programme **"can be achieved in any walk of life...because the achievement is not ours but God's. ...There is no situation too difficult, none too desperate, no unhappiness too great to be overcome in this great fellowship..."** [7] And it's many Twelve Step offspring.

As is said at the end of many meetings after the closing prayer, this program *"Works if you work it. So, work it you're worth it!"* **"With the tools and guideposts of Alcoholics Anonymous, we can learn a little of this precious gift—our gateway to human spirituality."** [8]

The Twelve Steps

THE TWELVE STEPS

Let us begin... *"Here are the Steps we took, which are suggested as a program of recovery:*

1) *We admitted we were powerless over alcohol* (our addiction)—*that our lives had become unmanageable.*

2) *Came to believe that a Power greater than ourselves could restore us to sanity.*

3) *Made a decision to turn our will and our lives over to the care of God as we understood Him.*

4) *Made a searching and fearless moral inventory of ourselves.*

5) *Admitted to God, to ourselves, and to another human being the exact nature of our wrongs.*

6) *Were entirely ready to have God remove all these defects of character.*

7) *Humbly asked Him to remove our shortcomings.*

8) *Made a list of persons we had harmed, and became willing to make amends to them all.*

9) *Made direct amends to such people wherever possible, except when to do so would injure them or others.*

10) *Continued to take personal inventory and when we were wrong promptly admitted it.*

11) *Sought through prayer and meditation to improve our conscious contact with God as we understood Him, praying only for knowledge of His will for us and the power to carry that out.*

12) *Having had a spiritual awakening as the result of these steps, we tried to carry this message to alcoholics, and to practice these principles in all our affairs."* [9]

The Twelve Steps are a *"marvellous way of life so simple in structure, so profound in practice."* [10]

Opening Prayer*

We are here to develop and maintain a conscious contact with a *Power Greater than Ourselves*. It has been said that where two or more are gathered together in the name of Good, there this Higher Power would be in the midst. We believe that It is here with us now. We believe this is something It would have us do, and that we have It's blessing.

We pledge our honesty, open mindedness, and willingness to work these steps, searching our hearts and minds for weaknesses and errors that we may be free.

We believe that within each of us there is a unique connection to God and that we are real partners with It in this business of living, *accepting our full responsibilities* and certain that the rewards are freedom and growth and happiness.

For this we are grateful. We ask at all times to be guided, as we maintain conscious contact with God, finding new ways of living our gratitude.

And so it is. Amen

This opening prayer is taken from what was called the "Ala-non Prayer" in Southern California. It is updated in more current language and gender removed for a more acceptable presentation and specifically pointed at the Steps.

Step One

STEP ONE – THE FOUNDATION – DEFEAT
Worksheet for the First Half
"We Admitted We Were Powerless Over (Our Addiction)- ...*"*[11]

READ IN PREPARATION:

"Big Book" of Alcoholics Anonymous – from the...
                                        Preface through Page 43
Twelve Steps and Twelve Traditions
                                        Pages 21-24 *(Read 21-22–daily)*

- -

First Half – Suggested work

Complete the following items giving *specific examples for each,* giving dates, times and the people involved. Please write a *paragraph rather than a sentence* for each example of your drinking/addictive behaviour.

1) Loss of control because of your using/addictive behaviour, i.e. blackouts, overdoses, bingeing, ruined plans, etc.

2) Behaviour of a destructive nature.

3) Situations where you put yourself or others in danger and/or had accidents due to your addiction.

4) Attempts to control or stop your addiction.

5) Substitution of other addictive substances and/or behaviour.

6) Broken promises to stop or moderate your drinking/addiction to yourself, family, friends and/or employers.

7) Examples of denial of addictions represented in my life.

8) What is the three fold nature of your dis-ease and what does that mean to you?

9) Do I truly feel hopeless without help? And what does that look like?

STEP ONE – THE FOUNDATION –DEFEAT
Worksheet for the "Second Half"
"...That Our Lives Had Become Unmanageable." [12]

READ IN PREPARATION:

"Big Book" of *Alcoholics Anonymous* – Preface through Page 43

Twelve Steps and Twelve Traditions – Pages 21-24 *(Read 21-22–daily)*

Second Half – Suggested work

Complete the following items giving *specific examples for each,* giving dates, times and the people involved. Please write a *paragraph rather than a sentence* for each example of your ...ism*. We are talking about our ...ism not your wasm.

1) The effects of your ...ism* on family, friends and/or employers and other personal relationships.

2) Your loss, due to your ...ism*, of relationships, including marriages, partnerships and/or friendships, etc.

3) Your loss, due to your ...ism*, of jobs, education, employment, and other opportunities, etc.

4) Situations, which have led to breaking the law and/or convictions.

5) Physical damage; i.e. Weight gain/loss, illness, broken bones and types of treatment.

6) Loss of physical freedom and/or freedom to choose.

7) Loss of interest in hobbies, sports, people, social activities, etc.

    ...ism =   *trouble controlling emotions, experiencing misery, depression, trouble earning, feelings of uselessness, full of fear, unhappiness and trouble giving or receiving.*

12 STEP WORKBOOK

STEP ONE – THE FOUNDATION – DEFEAT

Worksheet for the 'Second Half'

"...That Our Lives Had Become Unmanageable"

READ IN PREPARATION!

Big Book of Alcoholics Anonymous – Preface through Page 43

Twelve Steps and Twelve Traditions – Pages 21-24 (Step One only)

Second Half – Page 1 of Work

Compare the following lists, giving examples of how the sense of being defeated, and the people around you. Please write a sentence or two for each example of your list. We're interested in how you feel.

The effects of... on the family, the community, members and your friends, classmates.

1) ....

2) ....

3) ....

4) ....

5) ....

6) Loss of spiritual freedom and/or freedom to choose.

Those of interest in hobbies, sports, trips, social activities, etc.

> Result: controlling emotions experiencing unrest, depression, inappropriate caring, feeling, boredom or restless, full of fear, unhappiness and discouraging or declining.

A SPONSOR'S GUIDE

5

Step Two

STEP TWO – THE ANSWER – OPEN-MINDEDNESS

Worksheet for Step Two

"*Came To Believe* That A Power Greater Than Ourselves *Could* Restore Us *To Sanity*." [13]

READ IN PREPARATION:

In the "Big Book" of *Alcoholics Anonymous*   Pages 44-57

And, in the *Twelve Steps and Twelve Traditions* – Step Two
                                                            Pages 25-34

- -

SUGGESTED WORK

"A Power greater than ourselves"

Please **write a paragraph** rather than a sentence for this question. Complete all of the following items giving **specific examples** for each, giving dates, times and people involved. In each suggested assignments try to come up with different examples then in past writing.

1)   What does this phrase **"a Power greater than ourselves**" mean to you?

2)   Give an example of a "Power" working in your life or others that you have seen. (E.g. coincidences, through other people, AA, etc.)

3)   How does the possibility of finding the presence of a "Power greater than yourself" working in your life give you hope? The possibility of trust and lack of fear?

...could restore us to "sanity".

4)   Where and when could behaviour (drunk or sober) in your past (or not so past) be classified as "insane"?

5)   Write about "insane" behaviour (drunk or sober) that has affected your relationships, your education, your work or hopes for work, your freedom.

6)   Regarding the above, why do you think we wrote in brackets "drunk or sober?"

Step Three

'God I offer myself to Thee—to build with me and to do with me as Thou wilt. Relieve me of the bondage of self that I may better do Thy will. Take away my difficulties, that victory over them may bear witness to those I would help of Thy Power, Thy Love, and Thy Way of life. May I do Thy will always!'"

14

STEP THREE – THE DECISION – SURRENDER

"Made A _Decision_ To Turn Our _Will_ And Our _Lives_ Over To The _Care_ Of God, As We Understood Him" [15]

READ IN PREPARATION:

"Big Book" of _Alcoholics Anonymous_   Pages 58-63

And, _Twelve Steps and Twelve Traditions_ – Step Three

                                                       Pages 35-42

SUGGESTED WORK

Complete the following items giving _specific examples for each,_ giving dates, times and the people involved. Please write a _paragraph rather than a sentence_ for each example.

1)   What evidence is there that you are willing to change your behaviour? And, what behaviour do you want to give up?

2)   How do you think that, with the help of the program and Members of AA, you will be able to change? How can you use the help available?

3)   Define "the Program."

4)   How does your <u>will</u> relate to you carrying out your <u>thoughts</u> (beliefs)?

5)   How does your <u>life</u> relate to your <u>actions</u>?

6)   What are you doing today to turn over your "will and your life" to each of the following:
     a) Your Higher Power
     b) The program (the steps)

7)   How are you an active or passive person? How have you gotten things done or put them off?

8)   How have you accepted or evaded responsibility in your life?

9)   What does the word decision mean? And, is this an active process? And, explain your answer.

Step Four

STEP FOUR – CLEANING HOUSE – HONESTY
Made A Searching and Fearless Moral Inventory Of Ourselves [16]

READ IN PREPARATION:

"Alcoholics Anonymous – **"Next we launched...** (cont. to)...*truth about yourself."* –   Pages 63-71

And, *Twelve Steps and Twelve Traditions* – Step Four
                                                      Pages 43-55

I'm Resentful at or Fear: (1)	The Cause (2)	Affects my: (3) (Check below)
		❑ Self-Esteem ❑ Security ❑ Ambitions ❑ Personal Relations ❑ Sex Relations ❑ Pride/Shame ❑ Fear

List Major "Character Defects" in preparation for STEPS 6 & 7

AMENDS		STEP 8
		❑ Now ❑ Later ❑ Never

I'm Resentful at or Fear: (1)	The Cause (2)	Affects my: (3) (Check below)
		❑ Self-Esteem ❑ Security ❑ Ambitions ❑ Personal Relations ❑ Sex Relations ❑ Pride/Shame ❑ Fear

List Major "Character Defects" in preparation for STEPS 6 & 7

AMENDS		STEP 8
		❑ Now ❑ Later ❑ Never

I'm Resentful at or Fear: (1)	The Cause (2)	Affects my: (3) (Check below)
		❑ Self-Esteem ❑ Security ❑ Ambitions ❑ Personal Relations ❑ Sex Relations ❑ Pride/Shame ❑ Fear

List Major "Character Defects" in preparation for STEPS 6 & 7

AMENDS		STEP 8
		❑ Now ❑ Later ❑ Never

Ask yourself: ** (AA 67.3) * (AA 62.2)	*Putting out of our minds the wrongs others had done, we resolutely looked for our own mistakes... We admitted our wrongs honestly...* ** Column (4)
Where had (I) been selfish, self-centred or self-seeking?**	
Where had (I) been dishonest?**	
Where had (I) been frightened?**	
Where had (I) been (responsible) to blame?**	
What decisions did I make based on self that later placed me in a position to be hurt?*	
When in the past can I remember making this decision?* (Early memory.)	
Where was I wrong?** **What was my part?**	

Ask yourself: ** (AA 67.3) * (AA 62.2)	*Putting out of our minds the wrongs others had done, we resolutely looked for our own mistakes... We admitted our wrongs honestly...* ** Column (4)
Where had (I) been selfish, self-centred or self-seeking?**	
Where had (I) been dishonest?**	
Where had (I) been frightened?**	
Where had (I) been (responsible) to blame?**	
What decisions did I make based on self that later placed me in a position to be hurt?*	
When in the past can I remember making this decision?* (Early memory.)	
Where was I wrong?** **What was my part?**	

Ask yourself: ** (AA 67.3) * (AA 62.2)	*Putting out of our minds the wrongs others had done, we resolutely looked for our own mistakes... We admitted our wrongs honestly...* ** Column (4)
Where had (I) been selfish, self-centred or self-seeking?**	
Where had (I) been dishonest?**	
Where had (I) been frightened?**	
Where had (I) been (responsible) to blame?**	
What decisions did I make based on self that later placed me in a position to be hurt?*	
When in the past can I remember making this decision?* (Early memory.)	
Where was I wrong?** **What was my part?**	

I'm Resentful at or Fear: (1)	The Cause (2)	Affects my: (3) (Check below)
		☐ Self-Esteem ☐ Security ☐ Ambitions ☐ Personal Relations ☐ Sex Relations ☐ Pride/Shame ☐ Fear

List Major "Character Defects" in preparation for STEPS 6 & 7

AMENDS		STEP 8
		☐ Now ☐ Later ☐ Never

I'm Resentful at or Fear: (1)	The Cause (2)	Affects my: (3) (Check below)
		☐ Self-Esteem ☐ Security ☐ Ambitions ☐ Personal Relations ☐ Sex Relations ☐ Pride/Shame ☐ Fear

List Major "Character Defects" in preparation for STEPS 6 & 7

AMENDS		STEP 8
		☐ Now ☐ Later ☐ Never

I'm Resentful at or Fear: (1)	The Cause (2)	Affects my: (3) (Check below)
		☐ Self-Esteem ☐ Security ☐ Ambitions ☐ Personal Relations ☐ Sex Relations ☐ Pride/Shame ☐ Fear

List Major "Character Defects" in preparation for STEPS 6 & 7

AMENDS		STEP 8
		☐ Now ☐ Later ☐ Never

Ask yourself: ** (AA 67.3) * (AA 62.2)	Putting out of our minds the wrongs others had done, we resolutely looked for our own mistakes... We admitted our wrongs honestly...** Column (4)
Where had (I) been selfish, self-centred or self-seeking?**	
Where had (I) been dishonest?**	
Where had (I) been frightened?**	
Where had (I) been (responsible) to blame?**	
What decisions did I make based on self that later placed me in a position to be hurt?*	
When in the past can I remember making this decision?* (Early memory.)	
Where was I wrong?** **What was my part?**	

Ask yourself: ** (AA 67.3) * (AA 62.2)	Putting out of our minds the wrongs others had done, we resolutely looked for our own mistakes... We admitted our wrongs honestly...** Column (4)
Where had (I) been selfish, self-centred or self-seeking?**	
Where had (I) been dishonest?**	
Where had (I) been frightened?**	
Where had (I) been (responsible) to blame?**	
What decisions did I make based on self that later placed me in a position to be hurt?*	
When in the past can I remember making this decision?* (Early memory.)	
Where was I wrong?** **What was my part?**	

Ask yourself: ** (AA 67.3) * (AA 62.2)	Putting out of our minds the wrongs others had done, we resolutely looked for our own mistakes... We admitted our wrongs honestly...** Column (4)
Where had (I) been selfish, self-centred or self-seeking?**	
Where had (I) been dishonest?**	
Where had (I) been frightened?**	
Where had (I) been (responsible) to blame?**	
What decisions did I make based on self that later placed me in a position to be hurt?*	
When in the past can I remember making this decision?* (Early memory.)	
Where was I wrong?** **What was my part?**	

I'm Resentful at or Fear: (1)	The Cause (2)	Affects my: (3) (Check below)
		☐ Self-Esteem ☐ Security ☐ Ambitions ☐ Personal Relations ☐ Sex Relations ☐ Pride/Shame ☐ Fear

List Major "Character Defects" in preparation for STEPS 6 & 7

AMENDS		STEP 8
		☐ Now ☐ Later ☐ Never

I'm Resentful at or Fear: (1)	The Cause (2)	Affects my: (3) (Check below)
		☐ Self-Esteem ☐ Security ☐ Ambitions ☐ Personal Relations ☐ Sex Relations ☐ Pride/Shame ☐ Fear

List Major "Character Defects" in preparation for STEPS 6 & 7

AMENDS		STEP 8
		☐ Now ☐ Later ☐ Never

I'm Resentful at or Fear: (1)	The Cause (2)	Affects my: (3) (Check below)
		☐ Self-Esteem ☐ Security ☐ Ambitions ☐ Personal Relations ☐ Sex Relations ☐ Pride/Shame ☐ Fear

List Major "Character Defects" in preparation for STEPS 6 & 7

AMENDS		STEP 8
		☐ Now ☐ Later ☐ Never

Ask yourself: ** (AA 67.3) * (AA 62.2)	Putting out of our minds the wrongs others had done, we resolutely looked for our own mistakes… We admitted our wrongs honestly…** Column (4)
Where had (I) been selfish, self-centred or self-seeking?**	
Where had (I) been dishonest?**	
Where had (I) been frightened?**	
Where had (I) been (responsible) to blame?**	
What decisions did I make based on self that later placed me in a position to be hurt?*	
When in the past can I remember making this decision?* (Early memory.)	
Where was I wrong?** **What was my part?**	

Ask yourself: ** (AA 67.3) * (AA 62.2)	Putting out of our minds the wrongs others had done, we resolutely looked for our own mistakes… We admitted our wrongs honestly…** Column (4)
Where had (I) been selfish, self-centred or self-seeking?**	
Where had (I) been dishonest?**	
Where had (I) been frightened?**	
Where had (I) been (responsible) to blame?**	
What decisions did I make based on self that later placed me in a position to be hurt?*	
When in the past can I remember making this decision?* (Early memory.)	
Where was I wrong?** **What was my part?**	

Ask yourself: ** (AA 67.3) * (AA 62.2)	Putting out of our minds the wrongs others had done, we resolutely looked for our own mistakes… We admitted our wrongs honestly…** Column (4)
Where had (I) been selfish, self-centred or self-seeking?**	
Where had (I) been dishonest?**	
Where had (I) been frightened?**	
Where had (I) been (responsible) to blame?**	
What decisions did I make based on self that later placed me in a position to be hurt?*	
When in the past can I remember making this decision?* (Early memory.)	
Where was I wrong?** **What was my part?**	

I'm Resentful at or Fear: (1)	The Cause (2)	Affects my: (3) (Check below)
		☐ Self-Esteem ☐ Security ☐ Ambitions ☐ Personal Relations ☐ Sex Relations ☐ Pride/Shame ☐ Fear

List Major "Character Defects" in preparation for STEPS 6 & 7

AMENDS		STEP 8
		☐ Now ☐ Later ☐ Never

I'm Resentful at or Fear: (1)	The Cause (2)	Affects my: (3) (Check below)
		☐ Self-Esteem ☐ Security ☐ Ambitions ☐ Personal Relations ☐ Sex Relations ☐ Pride/Shame ☐ Fear

List Major "Character Defects" in preparation for STEPS 6 & 7

AMENDS		STEP 8
		☐ Now ☐ Later ☐ Never

I'm Resentful at or Fear: (1)	The Cause (2)	Affects my: (3) (Check below)
		☐ Self-Esteem ☐ Security ☐ Ambitions ☐ Personal Relations ☐ Sex Relations ☐ Pride/Shame ☐ Fear

List Major "Character Defects" in preparation for STEPS 6 & 7

AMENDS		STEP 8
		☐ Now ☐ Later ☐ Never

Ask yourself: ** (AA 67.3) * (AA 62.2)	Putting out of our minds the wrongs others had done, we resolutely looked for our own mistakes... We admitted our wrongs honestly...** Column (4)
Where had (I) been selfish, self-centred or self-seeking?**	
Where had (I) been dishonest?**	
Where had (I) been frightened?**	
Where had (I) been (responsible) to blame?**	
What decisions did I make based on self that later placed me in a position to be hurt?*	
When in the past can I remember making this decision?* (Early memory.)	
Where was I wrong?** What was my part?	

Ask yourself: ** (AA 67.3) * (AA 62.2)	Putting out of our minds the wrongs others had done, we resolutely looked for our own mistakes... We admitted our wrongs honestly...** Column (4)
Where had (I) been selfish, self-centred or self-seeking?**	
Where had (I) been dishonest?**	
Where had (I) been frightened?**	
Where had (I) been (responsible) to blame?**	
What decisions did I make based on self that later placed me in a position to be hurt?*	
When in the past can I remember making this decision?* (Early memory.)	
Where was I wrong?** What was my part?	

Ask yourself: ** (AA 67.3) * (AA 62.2)	Putting out of our minds the wrongs others had done, we resolutely looked for our own mistakes... We admitted our wrongs honestly...** Column (4)
Where had (I) been selfish, self-centred or self-seeking?**	
Where had (I) been dishonest?**	
Where had (I) been frightened?**	
Where had (I) been (responsible) to blame?**	
What decisions did I make based on self that later placed me in a position to be hurt?*	
When in the past can I remember making this decision?* (Early memory.)	
Where was I wrong?** What was my part?	

I'm Resentful at or Fear: (1)	The Cause (2)	Affects my: (3) (Check below)
		☐ Self-Esteem ☐ Security ☐ Ambitions ☐ Personal Relations ☐ Sex Relations ☐ Pride/Shame ☐ Fear

List Major "Character Defects" in preparation for STEPS 6 & 7

AMENDS		STEP 8
		☐ Now ☐ Later ☐ Never

I'm Resentful at or Fear: (1)	The Cause (2)	Affects my: (3) (Check below)
		☐ Self-Esteem ☐ Security ☐ Ambitions ☐ Personal Relations ☐ Sex Relations ☐ Pride/Shame ☐ Fear

List Major "Character Defects" in preparation for STEPS 6 & 7

AMENDS		STEP 8
		☐ Now ☐ Later ☐ Never

I'm Resentful at or Fear: (1)	The Cause (2)	Affects my: (3) (Check below)
		☐ Self-Esteem ☐ Security ☐ Ambitions ☐ Personal Relations ☐ Sex Relations ☐ Pride/Shame ☐ Fear

List Major "Character Defects" in preparation for STEPS 6 & 7

AMENDS		STEP 8
		☐ Now ☐ Later ☐ Never

Ask yourself: ** (AA 67.3) * (AA 62.2)	Putting out of our minds the wrongs others had done, we resolutely looked for our own mistakes... We admitted our wrongs honestly...** Column (4)
Where had (I) been selfish, self-centred or self-seeking?**	
Where had (I) been dishonest?**	
Where had (I) been frightened?**	
Where had (I) been (responsible) to blame?**	
What decisions did I make based on self that later placed me in a position to be hurt?*	
When in the past can I remember making this decision?* (Early memory.)	
Where was I wrong?** **What was my part?**	

Ask yourself: ** (AA 67.3) * (AA 62.2)	Putting out of our minds the wrongs others had done, we resolutely looked for our own mistakes... We admitted our wrongs honestly...** Column (4)
Where had (I) been selfish, self-centred or self-seeking?**	
Where had (I) been dishonest?**	
Where had (I) been frightened?**	
Where had (I) been (responsible) to blame?**	
What decisions did I make based on self that later placed me in a position to be hurt?*	
When in the past can I remember making this decision?* (Early memory.)	
Where was I wrong?** **What was my part?**	

Ask yourself: ** (AA 67.3) * (AA 62.2)	Putting out of our minds the wrongs others had done, we resolutely looked for our own mistakes... We admitted our wrongs honestly...** Column (4)
Where had (I) been selfish, self-centred or self-seeking?**	
Where had (I) been dishonest?**	
Where had (I) been frightened?**	
Where had (I) been (responsible) to blame?**	
What decisions did I make based on self that later placed me in a position to be hurt?*	
When in the past can I remember making this decision?* (Early memory.)	
Where was I wrong?** **What was my part?**	

I'm Resentful at or Fear: (1)	The Cause (2)	Affects my: (3) (Check below)
		❑ Self-Esteem ❑ Security ❑ Ambitions ❑ Personal Relations ❑ Sex Relations ❑ Pride/Shame ❑ Fear

List Major "Character Defects" in preparation for STEPS 6 & 7

AMENDS		STEP 8
		❑ Now ❑ Later ❑ Never

I'm Resentful at or Fear: (1)	The Cause (2)	Affects my: (3) (Check below)
		❑ Self-Esteem ❑ Security ❑ Ambitions ❑ Personal Relations ❑ Sex Relations ❑ Pride/Shame ❑ Fear

List Major "Character Defects" in preparation for STEPS 6 & 7

AMENDS		STEP 8
		❑ Now ❑ Later ❑ Never

I'm Resentful at or Fear: (1)	The Cause (2)	Affects my: (3) (Check below)
		❑ Self-Esteem ❑ Security ❑ Ambitions ❑ Personal Relations ❑ Sex Relations ❑ Pride/Shame ❑ Fear

List Major "Character Defects" in preparation for STEPS 6 & 7

AMENDS		STEP 8
		❑ Now ❑ Later ❑ Never

Ask yourself: ** (AA 67.3) * (AA 62.2)	Putting out of our minds the wrongs others had done, we resolutely looked for our own mistakes... We admitted our wrongs honestly...** Column (4)
Where had (I) been selfish, self-centred or self-seeking?**	
Where had (I) been dishonest?**	
Where had (I) been frightened?**	
Where had (I) been (responsible) to blame?**	
What decisions did I make based on self that later placed me in a position to be hurt?*	
When in the past can I remember making this decision?* (Early memory.)	
Where was I wrong?** **What was my part?**	

Ask yourself: ** (AA 67.3) * (AA 62.2)	Putting out of our minds the wrongs others had done, we resolutely looked for our own mistakes... We admitted our wrongs honestly...** Column (4)
Where had (I) been selfish, self-centred or self-seeking?**	
Where had (I) been dishonest?**	
Where had (I) been frightened?**	
Where had (I) been (responsible) to blame?**	
What decisions did I make based on self that later placed me in a position to be hurt?*	
When in the past can I remember making this decision?* (Early memory.)	
Where was I wrong?** **What was my part?**	

Ask yourself: ** (AA 67.3) * (AA 62.2)	Putting out of our minds the wrongs others had done, we resolutely looked for our own mistakes... We admitted our wrongs honestly...** Column (4)
Where had (I) been selfish, self-centred or self-seeking?**	
Where had (I) been dishonest?**	
Where had (I) been frightened?**	
Where had (I) been (responsible) to blame?**	
What decisions did I make based on self that later placed me in a position to be hurt?*	
When in the past can I remember making this decision?* (Early memory.)	
Where was I wrong?** **What was my part?**	

I'm Resentful at or Fear: (1)	The Cause (2)	Affects my: (3) (Check below)
		❑ Self-Esteem ❑ Security ❑ Ambitions ❑ Personal Relations ❑ Sex Relations ❑ Pride/Shame ❑ Fear

List Major "Character Defects" in preparation for STEPS 6 & 7

AMENDS		STEP 8
		❑ Now ❑ Later ❑ Never

I'm Resentful at or Fear: (1)	The Cause (2)	Affects my: (3) (Check below)
		❑ Self-Esteem ❑ Security ❑ Ambitions ❑ Personal Relations ❑ Sex Relations ❑ Pride/Shame ❑ Fear

List Major "Character Defects" in preparation for STEPS 6 & 7

AMENDS		STEP 8
		❑ Now ❑ Later ❑ Never

I'm Resentful at or Fear: (1)	The Cause (2)	Affects my: (3) (Check below)
		❑ Self-Esteem ❑ Security ❑ Ambitions ❑ Personal Relations ❑ Sex Relations ❑ Pride/Shame ❑ Fear

List Major "Character Defects" in preparation for STEPS 6 & 7

AMENDS		STEP 8
		❑ Now ❑ Later ❑ Never

Ask yourself: ** (AA 67.3) * (AA 62.2)	Putting out of our minds the wrongs others had done, we resolutely looked for our own mistakes... We admitted our wrongs honestly...** Column (4)
Where had (I) been selfish, self-centred or self-seeking?**	
Where had (I) been dishonest?**	
Where had (I) been frightened?**	
Where had (I) been (responsible) to blame?**	
What decisions did I make based on self that later placed me in a position to be hurt?*	
When in the past can I remember making this decision?* (Early memory.)	
Where was I wrong?** **What was my part?**	

Ask yourself: ** (AA 67.3) * (AA 62.2)	Putting out of our minds the wrongs others had done, we resolutely looked for our own mistakes... We admitted our wrongs honestly...** Column (4)
Where had (I) been selfish, self-centred or self-seeking?**	
Where had (I) been dishonest?**	
Where had (I) been frightened?**	
Where had (I) been (responsible) to blame?**	
What decisions did I make based on self that later placed me in a position to be hurt?*	
When in the past can I remember making this decision?* (Early memory.)	
Where was I wrong?** **What was my part?**	

Ask yourself: ** (AA 67.3) * (AA 62.2)	Putting out of our minds the wrongs others had done, we resolutely looked for our own mistakes... We admitted our wrongs honestly...** Column (4)
Where had (I) been selfish, self-centred or self-seeking?**	
Where had (I) been dishonest?**	
Where had (I) been frightened?**	
Where had (I) been (responsible) to blame?**	
What decisions did I make based on self that later placed me in a position to be hurt?*	
When in the past can I remember making this decision?* (Early memory.)	
Where was I wrong?** **What was my part?**	

I'm Resentful at or Fear: (1)	The Cause (2)	Affects my: (3) (Check below)
		☐ Self-Esteem ☐ Security ☐ Ambitions ☐ Personal Relations ☐ Sex Relations ☐ Pride/Shame ☐ Fear

List Major "Character Defects" in preparation for STEPS 6 & 7

AMENDS		STEP 8
		☐ Now ☐ Later ☐ Never

I'm Resentful at or Fear: (1)	The Cause (2)	Affects my: (3) (Check below)
		☐ Self-Esteem ☐ Security ☐ Ambitions ☐ Personal Relations ☐ Sex Relations ☐ Pride/Shame ☐ Fear

List Major "Character Defects" in preparation for STEPS 6 & 7

AMENDS		STEP 8
		☐ Now ☐ Later ☐ Never

I'm Resentful at or Fear: (1)	The Cause (2)	Affects my: (3) (Check below)
		☐ Self-Esteem ☐ Security ☐ Ambitions ☐ Personal Relations ☐ Sex Relations ☐ Pride/Shame ☐ Fear

List Major "Character Defects" in preparation for STEPS 6 & 7

AMENDS		STEP 8
		☐ Now ☐ Later ☐ Never

12 STEP WORKBOOK

Ask yourself: ** (AA 67.3) * (AA 62.2)	Putting out of our minds the wrongs others had done, we resolutely looked for our own mistakes... We admitted our wrongs honestly...** Column (4)
Where had (I) been selfish, self-centred or self-seeking?**	
Where had (I) been dishonest?**	
Where had (I) been frightened?**	
Where had (I) been (responsible) to blame?**	
What decisions did I make based on self that later placed me in a position to be hurt?*	
When in the past can I remember making this decision?* (Early memory.)	
Where was I wrong?** **What was my part?**	

Ask yourself: ** (AA 67.3) * (AA 62.2)	Putting out of our minds the wrongs others had done, we resolutely looked for our own mistakes... We admitted our wrongs honestly...** Column (4)
Where had (I) been selfish, self-centred or self-seeking?**	
Where had (I) been dishonest?**	
Where had (I) been frightened?**	
Where had (I) been (responsible) to blame?**	
What decisions did I make based on self that later placed me in a position to be hurt?*	
When in the past can I remember making this decision?* (Early memory.)	
Where was I wrong?** **What was my part?**	

Ask yourself: ** (AA 67.3) * (AA 62.2)	Putting out of our minds the wrongs others had done, we resolutely looked for our own mistakes... We admitted our wrongs honestly...** Column (4)
Where had (I) been selfish, self-centred or self-seeking?**	
Where had (I) been dishonest?**	
Where had (I) been frightened?**	
Where had (I) been (responsible) to blame?**	
What decisions did I make based on self that later placed me in a position to be hurt?*	
When in the past can I remember making this decision?* (Early memory.)	
Where was I wrong?** **What was my part?**	

I'm Resentful at or Fear: (1)	The Cause (2)	Affects my: (3) (Check below)
		❑ Self-Esteem ❑ Security ❑ Ambitions ❑ Personal Relations ❑ Sex Relations ❑ Pride/Shame ❑ Fear

List Major "Character Defects" in preparation for STEPS 6 & 7

AMENDS		STEP 8
		❑ Now ❑ Later ❑ Never

I'm Resentful at or Fear: (1)	The Cause (2)	Affects my: (3) (Check below)
		❑ Self-Esteem ❑ Security ❑ Ambitions ❑ Personal Relations ❑ Sex Relations ❑ Pride/Shame ❑ Fear

List Major "Character Defects" in preparation for STEPS 6 & 7

AMENDS		STEP 8
		❑ Now ❑ Later ❑ Never

I'm Resentful at or Fear: (1)	The Cause (2)	Affects my: (3) (Check below)
		❑ Self-Esteem ❑ Security ❑ Ambitions ❑ Personal Relations ❑ Sex Relations ❑ Pride/Shame ❑ Fear

List Major "Character Defects" in preparation for STEPS 6 & 7

AMENDS		STEP 8
		❑ Now ❑ Later ❑ Never

Ask yourself: ** (AA 67.3) * (AA 62.2)	Putting out of our minds the wrongs others had done, we resolutely looked for our own mistakes... We admitted our wrongs honestly...** Column (4)
Where had (I) been selfish, self-centred or self-seeking?**	
Where had (I) been dishonest?**	
Where had (I) been frightened?**	
Where had (I) been (responsible) to blame?**	
What decisions did I make based on self that later placed me in a position to be hurt?*	
When in the past can I remember making this decision?* (Early memory.)	
Where was I wrong?** **What was my part?**	

Ask yourself: ** (AA 67.3) * (AA 62.2)	Putting out of our minds the wrongs others had done, we resolutely looked for our own mistakes... We admitted our wrongs honestly...** Column (4)
Where had (I) been selfish, self-centred or self-seeking?**	
Where had (I) been dishonest?**	
Where had (I) been frightened?**	
Where had (I) been (responsible) to blame?**	
What decisions did I make based on self that later placed me in a position to be hurt?*	
When in the past can I remember making this decision?* (Early memory.)	
Where was I wrong?** **What was my part?**	

Ask yourself: ** (AA 67.3) * (AA 62.2)	Putting out of our minds the wrongs others had done, we resolutely looked for our own mistakes... We admitted our wrongs honestly...** Column (4)
Where had (I) been selfish, self-centred or self-seeking?**	
Where had (I) been dishonest?**	
Where had (I) been frightened?**	
Where had (I) been (responsible) to blame?**	
What decisions did I make based on self that later placed me in a position to be hurt?*	
When in the past can I remember making this decision?* (Early memory.)	
Where was I wrong?** **What was my part?**	

I'm Resentful at or Fear: (1)	The Cause (2)	Affects my: (3) (Check below)
		☐ Self-Esteem ☐ Security ☐ Ambitions ☐ Personal Relations ☐ Sex Relations ☐ Pride/Shame ☐ Fear

List Major "Character Defects" in preparation for STEPS 6 & 7

AMENDS		STEP 8
		☐ Now ☐ Later ☐ Never

I'm Resentful at or Fear: (1)	The Cause (2)	Affects my: (3) (Check below)
		☐ Self-Esteem ☐ Security ☐ Ambitions ☐ Personal Relations ☐ Sex Relations ☐ Pride/Shame ☐ Fear

List Major "Character Defects" in preparation for STEPS 6 & 7

AMENDS		STEP 8
		☐ Now ☐ Later ☐ Never

I'm Resentful at or Fear: (1)	The Cause (2)	Affects my: (3) (Check below)
		☐ Self-Esteem ☐ Security ☐ Ambitions ☐ Personal Relations ☐ Sex Relations ☐ Pride/Shame ☐ Fear

List Major "Character Defects" in preparation for STEPS 6 & 7

AMENDS		STEP 8
		☐ Now ☐ Later ☐ Never

Ask yourself: ** (AA 67.3) * (AA 62.2)	Putting out of our minds the wrongs others had done, we resolutely looked for our own mistakes... We admitted our wrongs honestly...** Column (4)
Where had (I) been selfish, self-centred or self-seeking?**	
Where had (I) been dishonest?**	
Where had (I) been frightened?**	
Where had (I) been (responsible) to blame?**	
What decisions did I make based on self that later placed me in a position to be hurt?*	
When in the past can I remember making this decision?* (Early memory.)	
Where was I wrong?** **What was my part?**	

Ask yourself: ** (AA 67.3) * (AA 62.2)	Putting out of our minds the wrongs others had done, we resolutely looked for our own mistakes... We admitted our wrongs honestly...** Column (4)
Where had (I) been selfish, self-centred or self-seeking?**	
Where had (I) been dishonest?**	
Where had (I) been frightened?**	
Where had (I) been (responsible) to blame?**	
What decisions did I make based on self that later placed me in a position to be hurt?*	
When in the past can I remember making this decision?* (Early memory.)	
Where was I wrong?** **What was my part?**	

Ask yourself: ** (AA 67.3) * (AA 62.2)	Putting out of our minds the wrongs others had done, we resolutely looked for our own mistakes... We admitted our wrongs honestly...** Column (4)
Where had (I) been selfish, self-centred or self-seeking?**	
Where had (I) been dishonest?**	
Where had (I) been frightened?**	
Where had (I) been (responsible) to blame?**	
What decisions did I make based on self that later placed me in a position to be hurt?*	
When in the past can I remember making this decision?* (Early memory.)	
Where was I wrong?** **What was my part?**	

I'm Resentful at or Fear: (1)	The Cause (2)	Affects my: (3) (Check below)
		❑ Self-Esteem ❑ Security ❑ Ambitions ❑ Personal Relations ❑ Sex Relations ❑ Pride/Shame ❑ Fear

List Major "Character Defects" in preparation for STEPS 6 & 7

AMENDS		STEP 8
		❑ Now ❑ Later ❑ Never

I'm Resentful at or Fear: (1)	The Cause (2)	Affects my: (3) (Check below)
		❑ Self-Esteem ❑ Security ❑ Ambitions ❑ Personal Relations ❑ Sex Relations ❑ Pride/Shame ❑ Fear

List Major "Character Defects" in preparation for STEPS 6 & 7

AMENDS		STEP 8
		❑ Now ❑ Later ❑ Never

I'm Resentful at or Fear: (1)	The Cause (2)	Affects my: (3) (Check below)
		❑ Self-Esteem ❑ Security ❑ Ambitions ❑ Personal Relations ❑ Sex Relations ❑ Pride/Shame ❑ Fear

List Major "Character Defects" in preparation for STEPS 6 & 7

AMENDS		STEP 8
		❑ Now ❑ Later ❑ Never

12 STEP WORKBOOK

Ask yourself: ** (AA 67.3) * (AA 62.2)	Putting out of our minds the wrongs others had done, we resolutely looked for our own mistakes... We admitted our wrongs honestly...** Column (4)
Where had (I) been selfish, self-centred or self-seeking?**	
Where had (I) been dishonest?**	
Where had (I) been frightened?**	
Where had (I) been (responsible) to blame?**	
What decisions did I make based on self that later placed me in a position to be hurt?*	
When in the past can I remember making this decision?* (Early memory.)	
Where was I wrong?** **What was my part?**	

Ask yourself: ** (AA 67.3) * (AA 62.2)	Putting out of our minds the wrongs others had done, we resolutely looked for our own mistakes... We admitted our wrongs honestly...** Column (4)
Where had (I) been selfish, self-centred or self-seeking?**	
Where had (I) been dishonest?**	
Where had (I) been frightened?**	
Where had (I) been (responsible) to blame?**	
What decisions did I make based on self that later placed me in a position to be hurt?*	
When in the past can I remember making this decision?* (Early memory.)	
Where was I wrong?** **What was my part?**	

Ask yourself: ** (AA 67.3) * (AA 62.2)	Putting out of our minds the wrongs others had done, we resolutely looked for our own mistakes... We admitted our wrongs honestly...** Column (4)
Where had (I) been selfish, self-centred or self-seeking?**	
Where had (I) been dishonest?**	
Where had (I) been frightened?**	
Where had (I) been (responsible) to blame?**	
What decisions did I make based on self that later placed me in a position to be hurt?*	
When in the past can I remember making this decision?* (Early memory.)	
Where was I wrong?** **What was my part?**	

I'm Resentful at or Fear: (1)	The Cause (2)	Affects my: (3) (Check below)
		☐ Self-Esteem ☐ Security ☐ Ambitions ☐ Personal Relations ☐ Sex Relations ☐ Pride/Shame ☐ Fear

List Major "Character Defects" in preparation for STEPS 6 & 7

AMENDS		STEP 8
		☐ Now ☐ Later ☐ Never

I'm Resentful at or Fear: (1)	The Cause (2)	Affects my: (3) (Check below)
		☐ Self-Esteem ☐ Security ☐ Ambitions ☐ Personal Relations ☐ Sex Relations ☐ Pride/Shame ☐ Fear

List Major "Character Defects" in preparation for STEPS 6 & 7

AMENDS		STEP 8
		☐ Now ☐ Later ☐ Never

I'm Resentful at or Fear: (1)	The Cause (2)	Affects my: (3) (Check below)
		☐ Self-Esteem ☐ Security ☐ Ambitions ☐ Personal Relations ☐ Sex Relations ☐ Pride/Shame ☐ Fear

List Major "Character Defects" in preparation for STEPS 6 & 7

AMENDS		STEP 8
		☐ Now ☐ Later ☐ Never

Ask yourself: ** (AA 67.3) * (AA 62.2)	Putting out of our minds the wrongs others had done, we resolutely looked for our own mistakes... We admitted our wrongs honestly...** Column (4)
Where had (I) been selfish, self-centred or self-seeking?**	
Where had (I) been dishonest?**	
Where had (I) been frightened?**	
Where had (I) been (responsible) to blame?**	
What decisions did I make based on self that later placed me in a position to be hurt?*	
When in the past can I remember making this decision?* (Early memory.)	
Where was I wrong?** **What was my part?**	

Ask yourself: ** (AA 67.3) * (AA 62.2)	Putting out of our minds the wrongs others had done, we resolutely looked for our own mistakes... We admitted our wrongs honestly...** Column (4)
Where had (I) been selfish, self-centred or self-seeking?**	
Where had (I) been dishonest?**	
Where had (I) been frightened?**	
Where had (I) been (responsible) to blame?**	
What decisions did I make based on self that later placed me in a position to be hurt?*	
When in the past can I remember making this decision?* (Early memory.)	
Where was I wrong?** **What was my part?**	

Ask yourself: ** (AA 67.3) * (AA 62.2)	Putting out of our minds the wrongs others had done, we resolutely looked for our own mistakes... We admitted our wrongs honestly...** Column (4)
Where had (I) been selfish, self-centred or self-seeking?**	
Where had (I) been dishonest?**	
Where had (I) been frightened?**	
Where had (I) been (responsible) to blame?**	
What decisions did I make based on self that later placed me in a position to be hurt?*	
When in the past can I remember making this decision?* (Early memory.)	
Where was I wrong?** **What was my part?**	

I'm Resentful at or Fear: (1)	The Cause (2)	Affects my: (3) (Check below)
		❏ Self-Esteem ❏ Security ❏ Ambitions ❏ Personal Relations ❏ Sex Relations ❏ Pride/Shame ❏ Fear

List Major "Character Defects" in preparation for STEPS 6 & 7					

AMENDS		STEP 8
		❏ Now ❏ Later ❏ Never

I'm Resentful at or Fear: (1)	The Cause (2)	Affects my: (3) (Check below)
		❏ Self-Esteem ❏ Security ❏ Ambitions ❏ Personal Relations ❏ Sex Relations ❏ Pride/Shame ❏ Fear

List Major "Character Defects" in preparation for STEPS 6 & 7					

AMENDS		STEP 8
		❏ Now ❏ Later ❏ Never

I'm Resentful at or Fear: (1)	The Cause (2)	Affects my: (3) (Check below)
		❏ Self-Esteem ❏ Security ❏ Ambitions ❏ Personal Relations ❏ Sex Relations ❏ Pride/Shame ❏ Fear

List Major "Character Defects" in preparation for STEPS 6 & 7					

AMENDS		STEP 8
		❏ Now ❏ Later ❏ Never

Ask yourself: ** (AA 67.3) * (AA 62.2)	Putting out of our minds the wrongs others had done, we resolutely looked for our own mistakes... We admitted our wrongs honestly...** Column (4)
Where had (I) been selfish, self-centred or self-seeking?**	
Where had (I) been dishonest?**	
Where had (I) been frightened?**	
Where had (I) been (responsible) to blame?**	
What decisions did I make based on self that later placed me in a position to be hurt?*	
When in the past can I remember making this decision?* (Early memory.)	
Where was I wrong?** **What was my part?**	

Ask yourself: ** (AA 67.3) * (AA 62.2)	Putting out of our minds the wrongs others had done, we resolutely looked for our own mistakes... We admitted our wrongs honestly...** Column (4)
Where had (I) been selfish, self-centred or self-seeking?**	
Where had (I) been dishonest?**	
Where had (I) been frightened?**	
Where had (I) been (responsible) to blame?**	
What decisions did I make based on self that later placed me in a position to be hurt?*	
When in the past can I remember making this decision?* (Early memory.)	
Where was I wrong?** **What was my part?**	

Ask yourself: ** (AA 67.3) * (AA 62.2)	Putting out of our minds the wrongs others had done, we resolutely looked for our own mistakes... We admitted our wrongs honestly...** Column (4)
Where had (I) been selfish, self-centred or self-seeking?**	
Where had (I) been dishonest?**	
Where had (I) been frightened?**	
Where had (I) been (responsible) to blame?**	
What decisions did I make based on self that later placed me in a position to be hurt?*	
When in the past can I remember making this decision?* (Early memory.)	
Where was I wrong?** **What was my part?**	

I'm Resentful at or Fear: (1)	The Cause (2)	Affects my: (3) (Check below)
		☐ Self-Esteem ☐ Security ☐ Ambitions ☐ Personal Relations ☐ Sex Relations ☐ Pride/Shame ☐ Fear

List Major "Character Defects" in preparation for STEPS 6 & 7

AMENDS		STEP 8
		☐ Now ☐ Later ☐ Never

I'm Resentful at or Fear: (1)	The Cause (2)	Affects my: (3) (Check below)
		☐ Self-Esteem ☐ Security ☐ Ambitions ☐ Personal Relations ☐ Sex Relations ☐ Pride/Shame ☐ Fear

List Major "Character Defects" in preparation for STEPS 6 & 7

AMENDS		STEP 8
		☐ Now ☐ Later ☐ Never

I'm Resentful at or Fear: (1)	The Cause (2)	Affects my: (3) (Check below)
		☐ Self-Esteem ☐ Security ☐ Ambitions ☐ Personal Relations ☐ Sex Relations ☐ Pride/Shame ☐ Fear

List Major "Character Defects" in preparation for STEPS 6 & 7

AMENDS		STEP 8
		☐ Now ☐ Later ☐ Never

12 STEP WORKBOOK

Ask yourself: ** (AA 67.3) * (AA 62.2)	Putting out of our minds the wrongs others had done, we resolutely looked for our own mistakes... We admitted our wrongs honestly...** Column (4)
Where had (I) been selfish, self-centred or self-seeking?**	
Where had (I) been dishonest?**	
Where had (I) been frightened?**	
Where had (I) been (responsible) to blame?**	
What decisions did I make based on self that later placed me in a position to be hurt?*	
When in the past can I remember making this decision?* (Early memory.)	
Where was I wrong?** **What was my part?**	

Ask yourself: ** (AA 67.3) * (AA 62.2)	Putting out of our minds the wrongs others had done, we resolutely looked for our own mistakes... We admitted our wrongs honestly...** Column (4)
Where had (I) been selfish, self-centred or self-seeking?**	
Where had (I) been dishonest?**	
Where had (I) been frightened?**	
Where had (I) been (responsible) to blame?**	
What decisions did I make based on self that later placed me in a position to be hurt?*	
When in the past can I remember making this decision?* (Early memory.)	
Where was I wrong?** **What was my part?**	

Ask yourself: ** (AA 67.3) * (AA 62.2)	Putting out of our minds the wrongs others had done, we resolutely looked for our own mistakes... We admitted our wrongs honestly...** Column (4)
Where had (I) been selfish, self-centred or self-seeking?**	
Where had (I) been dishonest?**	
Where had (I) been frightened?**	
Where had (I) been (responsible) to blame?**	
What decisions did I make based on self that later placed me in a position to be hurt?*	
When in the past can I remember making this decision?* (Early memory.)	
Where was I wrong?** **What was my part?**	

I'm Resentful at or Fear: (1)	The Cause (2)	Affects my: (3) (Check below)
		❑ Self-Esteem ❑ Security ❑ Ambitions ❑ Personal Relations ❑ Sex Relations ❑ Pride/Shame ❑ Fear

List Major "Character Defects" in preparation for STEPS 6 & 7

AMENDS		STEP 8
		❑ Now ❑ Later ❑ Never

I'm Resentful at or Fear: (1)	The Cause (2)	Affects my: (3) (Check below)
		❑ Self-Esteem ❑ Security ❑ Ambitions ❑ Personal Relations ❑ Sex Relations ❑ Pride/Shame ❑ Fear

List Major "Character Defects" in preparation for STEPS 6 & 7

AMENDS		STEP 8
		❑ Now ❑ Later ❑ Never

I'm Resentful at or Fear: (1)	The Cause (2)	Affects my: (3) (Check below)
		❑ Self-Esteem ❑ Security ❑ Ambitions ❑ Personal Relations ❑ Sex Relations ❑ Pride/Shame ❑ Fear

List Major "Character Defects" in preparation for STEPS 6 & 7

AMENDS		STEP 8
		❑ Now ❑ Later ❑ Never

Ask yourself: ** (AA 67.3) * (AA 62.2)	Putting out of our minds the wrongs others had done, we resolutely looked for our own mistakes... We admitted our wrongs honestly...** Column (4)
Where had (I) been selfish, self-centred or self-seeking?**	
Where had (I) been dishonest?**	
Where had (I) been frightened?**	
Where had (I) been (responsible) to blame?**	
What decisions did I make based on self that later placed me in a position to be hurt?*	
When in the past can I remember making this decision?* (Early memory.)	
Where was I wrong?** What was my part?	

Ask yourself: ** (AA 67.3) * (AA 62.2)	Putting out of our minds the wrongs others had done, we resolutely looked for our own mistakes... We admitted our wrongs honestly...** Column (4)
Where had (I) been selfish, self-centred or self-seeking?**	
Where had (I) been dishonest?**	
Where had (I) been frightened?**	
Where had (I) been (responsible) to blame?**	
What decisions did I make based on self that later placed me in a position to be hurt?*	
When in the past can I remember making this decision?* (Early memory.)	
Where was I wrong?** What was my part?	

Ask yourself: ** (AA 67.3) * (AA 62.2)	Putting out of our minds the wrongs others had done, we resolutely looked for our own mistakes... We admitted our wrongs honestly...** Column (4)
Where had (I) been selfish, self-centred or self-seeking?**	
Where had (I) been dishonest?**	
Where had (I) been frightened?**	
Where had (I) been (responsible) to blame?**	
What decisions did I make based on self that later placed me in a position to be hurt?*	
When in the past can I remember making this decision?* (Early memory.)	
Where was I wrong?** What was my part?	

I'm Resentful at or Fear: (1)	The Cause (2)	Affects my: (3) (Check below)
		☐ Self-Esteem ☐ Security ☐ Ambitions ☐ Personal Relations ☐ Sex Relations ☐ Pride/Shame ☐ Fear

List Major "Character Defects" in preparation for STEPS 6 & 7

AMENDS		STEP 8
		☐ Now ☐ Later ☐ Never

I'm Resentful at or Fear: (1)	The Cause (2)	Affects my: (3) (Check below)
		☐ Self-Esteem ☐ Security ☐ Ambitions ☐ Personal Relations ☐ Sex Relations ☐ Pride/Shame ☐ Fear

List Major "Character Defects" in preparation for STEPS 6 & 7

AMENDS		STEP 8
		☐ Now ☐ Later ☐ Never

I'm Resentful at or Fear: (1)	The Cause (2)	Affects my: (3) (Check below)
		☐ Self-Esteem ☐ Security ☐ Ambitions ☐ Personal Relations ☐ Sex Relations ☐ Pride/Shame ☐ Fear

List Major "Character Defects" in preparation for STEPS 6 & 7

AMENDS		STEP 8
		☐ Now ☐ Later ☐ Never

Ask yourself: ** (AA 67.3) * (AA 62.2)	Putting out of our minds the wrongs others had done, we resolutely looked for our own mistakes... We admitted our wrongs honestly...** Column (4)
Where had (I) been selfish, self-centred or self-seeking?**	
Where had (I) been dishonest?**	
Where had (I) been frightened?**	
Where had (I) been (responsible) to blame?**	
What decisions did I make based on self that later placed me in a position to be hurt?*	
When in the past can I remember making this decision?* (Early memory.)	
Where was I wrong?** What was my part?	

Ask yourself: ** (AA 67.3) * (AA 62.2)	Putting out of our minds the wrongs others had done, we resolutely looked for our own mistakes... We admitted our wrongs honestly...** Column (4)
Where had (I) been selfish, self-centred or self-seeking?**	
Where had (I) been dishonest?**	
Where had (I) been frightened?**	
Where had (I) been (responsible) to blame?**	
What decisions did I make based on self that later placed me in a position to be hurt?*	
When in the past can I remember making this decision?* (Early memory.)	
Where was I wrong?** What was my part?	

Ask yourself: ** (AA 67.3) * (AA 62.2)	Putting out of our minds the wrongs others had done, we resolutely looked for our own mistakes... We admitted our wrongs honestly...** Column (4)
Where had (I) been selfish, self-centred or self-seeking?**	
Where had (I) been dishonest?**	
Where had (I) been frightened?**	
Where had (I) been (responsible) to blame?**	
What decisions did I make based on self that later placed me in a position to be hurt?*	
When in the past can I remember making this decision?* (Early memory.)	
Where was I wrong?** What was my part?	

I'm Resentful at or Fear: (1)	The Cause (2)	Affects my: (3) (Check below)
		❑ Self-Esteem ❑ Security ❑ Ambitions ❑ Personal Relations ❑ Sex Relations ❑ Pride/Shame ❑ Fear

List Major "Character Defects" in preparation for STEPS 6 & 7					

AMENDS		STEP 8
		❑ Now ❑ Later ❑ Never

I'm Resentful at or Fear: (1)	The Cause (2)	Affects my: (3) (Check below)
		❑ Self-Esteem ❑ Security ❑ Ambitions ❑ Personal Relations ❑ Sex Relations ❑ Pride/Shame ❑ Fear

List Major "Character Defects" in preparation for STEPS 6 & 7					

AMENDS		STEP 8
		❑ Now ❑ Later ❑ Never

I'm Resentful at or Fear: (1)	The Cause (2)	Affects my: (3) (Check below)
		❑ Self-Esteem ❑ Security ❑ Ambitions ❑ Personal Relations ❑ Sex Relations ❑ Pride/Shame ❑ Fear

List Major "Character Defects" in preparation for STEPS 6 & 7					

AMENDS		STEP 8
		❑ Now ❑ Later ❑ Never

Ask yourself: ** (AA 67.3) * (AA 62.2)	Putting out of our minds the wrongs others had done, we resolutely looked for our own mistakes... We admitted our wrongs honestly...** Column (4)
Where had (I) been selfish, self-centred or self-seeking?**	
Where had (I) been dishonest?**	
Where had (I) been frightened?**	
Where had (I) been (responsible) to blame?**	
What decisions did I make based on self that later placed me in a position to be hurt?*	
When in the past can I remember making this decision?* (Early memory.)	
Where was I wrong?** **What was my part?**	

Ask yourself: ** (AA 67.3) * (AA 62.2)	Putting out of our minds the wrongs others had done, we resolutely looked for our own mistakes... We admitted our wrongs honestly...** Column (4)
Where had (I) been selfish, self-centred or self-seeking?**	
Where had (I) been dishonest?**	
Where had (I) been frightened?**	
Where had (I) been (responsible) to blame?**	
What decisions did I make based on self that later placed me in a position to be hurt?*	
When in the past can I remember making this decision?* (Early memory.)	
Where was I wrong?** **What was my part?**	

Ask yourself: ** (AA 67.3) * (AA 62.2)	Putting out of our minds the wrongs others had done, we resolutely looked for our own mistakes... We admitted our wrongs honestly...** Column (4)
Where had (I) been selfish, self-centred or self-seeking?**	
Where had (I) been dishonest?**	
Where had (I) been frightened?**	
Where had (I) been (responsible) to blame?**	
What decisions did I make based on self that later placed me in a position to be hurt?*	
When in the past can I remember making this decision?* (Early memory.)	
Where was I wrong?** **What was my part?**	

I'm Resentful at or Fear: (1)	The Cause (2)	Affects my: (3) (Check below)
		☐ Self-Esteem ☐ Security ☐ Ambitions ☐ Personal Relations ☐ Sex Relations ☐ Pride/Shame ☐ Fear

List Major "Character Defects" in preparation for STEPS 6 & 7

AMENDS		STEP 8
		☐ Now ☐ Later ☐ Never

I'm Resentful at or Fear: (1)	The Cause (2)	Affects my: (3) (Check below)
		☐ Self-Esteem ☐ Security ☐ Ambitions ☐ Personal Relations ☐ Sex Relations ☐ Pride/Shame ☐ Fear

List Major "Character Defects" in preparation for STEPS 6 & 7

AMENDS		STEP 8
		☐ Now ☐ Later ☐ Never

I'm Resentful at or Fear: (1)	The Cause (2)	Affects my: (3) (Check below)
		☐ Self-Esteem ☐ Security ☐ Ambitions ☐ Personal Relations ☐ Sex Relations ☐ Pride/Shame ☐ Fear

List Major "Character Defects" in preparation for STEPS 6 & 7

AMENDS		STEP 8
		☐ Now ☐ Later ☐ Never

Ask yourself: ** (AA 67.3) * (AA 62.2)	Putting out of our minds the wrongs others had done, we resolutely looked for our own mistakes... We admitted our wrongs honestly...** Column (4)
Where had (I) been selfish, self-centred or self-seeking?**	
Where had (I) been dishonest?**	
Where had (I) been frightened?**	
Where had (I) been (responsible) to blame?**	
What decisions did I make based on self that later placed me in a position to be hurt?*	
When in the past can I remember making this decision?* (Early memory.)	
Where was I wrong?** **What was my part?**	

Ask yourself: ** (AA 67.3) * (AA 62.2)	Putting out of our minds the wrongs others had done, we resolutely looked for our own mistakes... We admitted our wrongs honestly...** Column (4)
Where had (I) been selfish, self-centred or self-seeking?**	
Where had (I) been dishonest?**	
Where had (I) been frightened?**	
Where had (I) been (responsible) to blame?**	
What decisions did I make based on self that later placed me in a position to be hurt?*	
When in the past can I remember making this decision?* (Early memory.)	
Where was I wrong?** **What was my part?**	

Ask yourself: ** (AA 67.3) * (AA 62.2)	Putting out of our minds the wrongs others had done, we resolutely looked for our own mistakes... We admitted our wrongs honestly...** Column (4)
Where had (I) been selfish, self-centred or self-seeking?**	
Where had (I) been dishonest?**	
Where had (I) been frightened?**	
Where had (I) been (responsible) to blame?**	
What decisions did I make based on self that later placed me in a position to be hurt?*	
When in the past can I remember making this decision?* (Early memory.)	
Where was I wrong?** **What was my part?**	

I'm Resentful at or Fear: (1)	The Cause (2)	Affects my: (3) (Check below)

Affects my: (3) (Check below)
- ❑ Self-Esteem
- ❑ Security
- ❑ Ambitions
- ❑ Personal Relations
- ❑ Sex Relations
- ❑ Pride/Shame
- ❑ Fear

List Major "Character Defects" in preparation for STEPS 6 & 7

AMENDS | | **STEP 8**

STEP 8
- ❑ Now
- ❑ Later
- ❑ Never

I'm Resentful at or Fear: (1)	The Cause (2)	Affects my: (3) (Check below)

Affects my: (3) (Check below)
- ❑ Self-Esteem
- ❑ Security
- ❑ Ambitions
- ❑ Personal Relations
- ❑ Sex Relations
- ❑ Pride/Shame
- ❑ Fear

List Major "Character Defects" in preparation for STEPS 6 & 7

AMENDS | | **STEP 8**

STEP 8
- ❑ Now
- ❑ Later
- ❑ Never

I'm Resentful at or Fear: (1)	The Cause (2)	Affects my: (3) (Check below)

Affects my: (3) (Check below)
- ❑ Self-Esteem
- ❑ Security
- ❑ Ambitions
- ❑ Personal Relations
- ❑ Sex Relations
- ❑ Pride/Shame
- ❑ Fear

List Major "Character Defects" in preparation for STEPS 6 & 7

AMENDS | | **STEP 8**

STEP 8
- ❑ Now
- ❑ Later
- ❑ Never

Ask yourself: ** (AA 67.3) * (AA 62.2)	Putting out of our minds the wrongs others had done, we resolutely looked for our own mistakes... We admitted our wrongs honestly...** Column (4)
Where had (I) been selfish, self-centred or self-seeking?**	
Where had (I) been dishonest?**	
Where had (I) been frightened?**	
Where had (I) been (responsible) to blame?**	
What decisions did I make based on self that later placed me in a position to be hurt?*	
When in the past can I remember making this decision?* (Early memory.)	
Where was I wrong?** **What was my part?**	

Ask yourself: ** (AA 67.3) * (AA 62.2)	Putting out of our minds the wrongs others had done, we resolutely looked for our own mistakes... We admitted our wrongs honestly...** Column (4)
Where had (I) been selfish, self-centred or self-seeking?**	
Where had (I) been dishonest?**	
Where had (I) been frightened?**	
Where had (I) been (responsible) to blame?**	
What decisions did I make based on self that later placed me in a position to be hurt?*	
When in the past can I remember making this decision?* (Early memory.)	
Where was I wrong?** **What was my part?**	

Ask yourself: ** (AA 67.3) * (AA 62.2)	Putting out of our minds the wrongs others had done, we resolutely looked for our own mistakes... We admitted our wrongs honestly...** Column (4)
Where had (I) been selfish, self-centred or self-seeking?**	
Where had (I) been dishonest?**	
Where had (I) been frightened?**	
Where had (I) been (responsible) to blame?**	
What decisions did I make based on self that later placed me in a position to be hurt?*	
When in the past can I remember making this decision?* (Early memory.)	
Where was I wrong?** **What was my part?**	

I'm Resentful at or Fear: (1)	The Cause (2)	Affects my: (3) (Check below)
		☐ Self-Esteem ☐ Security ☐ Ambitions ☐ Personal Relations ☐ Sex Relations ☐ Pride/Shame ☐ Fear

List Major "Character Defects" in preparation for STEPS 6 & 7

AMENDS		STEP 8
		☐ Now ☐ Later ☐ Never

I'm Resentful at or Fear: (1)	The Cause (2)	Affects my: (3) (Check below)
		☐ Self-Esteem ☐ Security ☐ Ambitions ☐ Personal Relations ☐ Sex Relations ☐ Pride/Shame ☐ Fear

List Major "Character Defects" in preparation for STEPS 6 & 7

AMENDS		STEP 8
		☐ Now ☐ Later ☐ Never

I'm Resentful at or Fear: (1)	The Cause (2)	Affects my: (3) (Check below)
		☐ Self-Esteem ☐ Security ☐ Ambitions ☐ Personal Relations ☐ Sex Relations ☐ Pride/Shame ☐ Fear

List Major "Character Defects" in preparation for STEPS 6 & 7

AMENDS		STEP 8
		☐ Now ☐ Later ☐ Never

Ask yourself: ** (AA 67.3) * (AA 62.2)	Putting out of our minds the wrongs others had done, we resolutely looked for our own mistakes... We admitted our wrongs honestly...** Column (4)
Where had (I) been selfish, self-centred or self-seeking?**	
Where had (I) been dishonest?**	
Where had (I) been frightened?**	
Where had (I) been (responsible) to blame?**	
What decisions did I make based on self that later placed me in a position to be hurt?*	
When in the past can I remember making this decision?* (Early memory.)	
Where was I wrong?** **What was my part?**	

Ask yourself: ** (AA 67.3) * (AA 62.2)	Putting out of our minds the wrongs others had done, we resolutely looked for our own mistakes... We admitted our wrongs honestly...** Column (4)
Where had (I) been selfish, self-centred or self-seeking?**	
Where had (I) been dishonest?**	
Where had (I) been frightened?**	
Where had (I) been (responsible) to blame?**	
What decisions did I make based on self that later placed me in a position to be hurt?*	
When in the past can I remember making this decision?* (Early memory.)	
Where was I wrong?** **What was my part?**	

Ask yourself: ** (AA 67.3) * (AA 62.2)	Putting out of our minds the wrongs others had done, we resolutely looked for our own mistakes... We admitted our wrongs honestly...** Column (4)
Where had (I) been selfish, self-centred or self-seeking?**	
Where had (I) been dishonest?**	
Where had (I) been frightened?**	
Where had (I) been (responsible) to blame?**	
What decisions did I make based on self that later placed me in a position to be hurt?*	
When in the past can I remember making this decision?* (Early memory.)	
Where was I wrong?** **What was my part?**	

I'm Resentful at or Fear: (1)	The Cause (2)	Affects my: (3) (Check below)
		☐ Self-Esteem ☐ Security ☐ Ambitions ☐ Personal Relations ☐ Sex Relations ☐ Pride/Shame ☐ Fear

List Major "Character Defects" in preparation for STEPS 6 & 7

AMENDS		STEP 8
		☐ Now ☐ Later ☐ Never

I'm Resentful at or Fear: (1)	The Cause (2)	Affects my: (3) (Check below)
		☐ Self-Esteem ☐ Security ☐ Ambitions ☐ Personal Relations ☐ Sex Relations ☐ Pride/Shame ☐ Fear

List Major "Character Defects" in preparation for STEPS 6 & 7

AMENDS		STEP 8
		☐ Now ☐ Later ☐ Never

I'm Resentful at or Fear: (1)	The Cause (2)	Affects my: (3) (Check below)
		☐ Self-Esteem ☐ Security ☐ Ambitions ☐ Personal Relations ☐ Sex Relations ☐ Pride/Shame ☐ Fear

List Major "Character Defects" in preparation for STEPS 6 & 7

AMENDS		STEP 8
		☐ Now ☐ Later ☐ Never

12 STEP WORKBOOK

Ask yourself: ** (AA 67.3) * (AA 62.2)	Putting out of our minds the wrongs others had done, we resolutely looked for our own mistakes... We admitted our wrongs honestly...** Column (4)
Where had (I) been selfish, self-centred or self-seeking?**	
Where had (I) been dishonest?**	
Where had (I) been frightened?**	
Where had (I) been (responsible) to blame?**	
What decisions did I make based on self that later placed me in a position to be hurt?*	
When in the past can I remember making this decision?* (Early memory.)	
Where was I wrong?** **What was my part?**	

Ask yourself: ** (AA 67.3) * (AA 62.2)	Putting out of our minds the wrongs others had done, we resolutely looked for our own mistakes... We admitted our wrongs honestly...** Column (4)
Where had (I) been selfish, self-centred or self-seeking?**	
Where had (I) been dishonest?**	
Where had (I) been frightened?**	
Where had (I) been (responsible) to blame?**	
What decisions did I make based on self that later placed me in a position to be hurt?*	
When in the past can I remember making this decision?* (Early memory.)	
Where was I wrong?** **What was my part?**	

Ask yourself: ** (AA 67.3) * (AA 62.2)	Putting out of our minds the wrongs others had done, we resolutely looked for our own mistakes... We admitted our wrongs honestly...** Column (4)
Where had (I) been selfish, self-centred or self-seeking?**	
Where had (I) been dishonest?**	
Where had (I) been frightened?**	
Where had (I) been (responsible) to blame?**	
What decisions did I make based on self that later placed me in a position to be hurt?*	
When in the past can I remember making this decision?* (Early memory.)	
Where was I wrong?** **What was my part?**	

I'm Resentful at or Fear: (1)	The Cause (2)	Affects my: (3) (Check below)
		☐ Self-Esteem ☐ Security ☐ Ambitions ☐ Personal Relations ☐ Sex Relations ☐ Pride/Shame ☐ Fear

List Major "Character Defects" in preparation for STEPS 6 & 7

AMENDS		STEP 8
		☐ Now ☐ Later ☐ Never

I'm Resentful at or Fear: (1)	The Cause (2)	Affects my: (3) (Check below)
		☐ Self-Esteem ☐ Security ☐ Ambitions ☐ Personal Relations ☐ Sex Relations ☐ Pride/Shame ☐ Fear

List Major "Character Defects" in preparation for STEPS 6 & 7

AMENDS		STEP 8
		☐ Now ☐ Later ☐ Never

I'm Resentful at or Fear: (1)	The Cause (2)	Affects my: (3) (Check below)
		☐ Self-Esteem ☐ Security ☐ Ambitions ☐ Personal Relations ☐ Sex Relations ☐ Pride/Shame ☐ Fear

List Major "Character Defects" in preparation for STEPS 6 & 7

AMENDS		STEP 8
		☐ Now ☐ Later ☐ Never

Ask yourself: ** (AA 67.3) * (AA 62.2)	Putting out of our minds the wrongs others had done, we resolutely looked for our own mistakes... We admitted our wrongs honestly...** Column (4)
Where had (I) been selfish, self-centred or self-seeking?**	
Where had (I) been dishonest?**	
Where had (I) been frightened?**	
Where had (I) been (responsible) to blame?**	
What decisions did I make based on self that later placed me in a position to be hurt?*	
When in the past can I remember making this decision?* (Early memory.)	
Where was I wrong?** **What was my part?**	

Ask yourself: ** (AA 67.3) * (AA 62.2)	Putting out of our minds the wrongs others had done, we resolutely looked for our own mistakes... We admitted our wrongs honestly...** Column (4)
Where had (I) been selfish, self-centred or self-seeking?**	
Where had (I) been dishonest?**	
Where had (I) been frightened?**	
Where had (I) been (responsible) to blame?**	
What decisions did I make based on self that later placed me in a position to be hurt?*	
When in the past can I remember making this decision?* (Early memory.)	
Where was I wrong?** **What was my part?**	

Ask yourself: ** (AA 67.3) * (AA 62.2)	Putting out of our minds the wrongs others had done, we resolutely looked for our own mistakes... We admitted our wrongs honestly...** Column (4)
Where had (I) been selfish, self-centred or self-seeking?**	
Where had (I) been dishonest?**	
Where had (I) been frightened?**	
Where had (I) been (responsible) to blame?**	
What decisions did I make based on self that later placed me in a position to be hurt?*	
When in the past can I remember making this decision?* (Early memory.)	
Where was I wrong?** **What was my part?**	

I'm Resentful at or Fear: (1)	The Cause (2)	Affects my: (3) (Check below)
		❑ Self-Esteem ❑ Security ❑ Ambitions ❑ Personal Relations ❑ Sex Relations ❑ Pride/Shame ❑ Fear

List Major "Character Defects" in preparation for STEPS 6 & 7

AMENDS		STEP 8
		❑ Now ❑ Later ❑ Never

I'm Resentful at or Fear: (1)	The Cause (2)	Affects my: (3) (Check below)
		❑ Self-Esteem ❑ Security ❑ Ambitions ❑ Personal Relations ❑ Sex Relations ❑ Pride/Shame ❑ Fear

List Major "Character Defects" in preparation for STEPS 6 & 7

AMENDS		STEP 8
		❑ Now ❑ Later ❑ Never

I'm Resentful at or Fear: (1)	The Cause (2)	Affects my: (3) (Check below)
		❑ Self-Esteem ❑ Security ❑ Ambitions ❑ Personal Relations ❑ Sex Relations ❑ Pride/Shame ❑ Fear

List Major "Character Defects" in preparation for STEPS 6 & 7

AMENDS		STEP 8
		❑ Now ❑ Later ❑ Never

Ask yourself: ** (AA 67.3) * (AA 62.2)	Putting out of our minds the wrongs others had done, we resolutely looked for our own mistakes... We admitted our wrongs honestly...** Column (4)
Where had (I) been selfish, self-centred or self-seeking?**	
Where had (I) been dishonest?**	
Where had (I) been frightened?**	
Where had (I) been (responsible) to blame?**	
What decisions did I make based on self that later placed me in a position to be hurt?*	
When in the past can I remember making this decision?* (Early memory.)	
Where was I wrong?** **What was my part?**	

Ask yourself: ** (AA 67.3) * (AA 62.2)	Putting out of our minds the wrongs others had done, we resolutely looked for our own mistakes... We admitted our wrongs honestly...** Column (4)
Where had (I) been selfish, self-centred or self-seeking?**	
Where had (I) been dishonest?**	
Where had (I) been frightened?**	
Where had (I) been (responsible) to blame?**	
What decisions did I make based on self that later placed me in a position to be hurt?*	
When in the past can I remember making this decision?* (Early memory.)	
Where was I wrong?** **What was my part?**	

Ask yourself: ** (AA 67.3) * (AA 62.2)	Putting out of our minds the wrongs others had done, we resolutely looked for our own mistakes... We admitted our wrongs honestly...** Column (4)
Where had (I) been selfish, self-centred or self-seeking?**	
Where had (I) been dishonest?**	
Where had (I) been frightened?**	
Where had (I) been (responsible) to blame?**	
What decisions did I make based on self that later placed me in a position to be hurt?*	
When in the past can I remember making this decision?* (Early memory.)	
Where was I wrong?** **What was my part?**	

I'm Resentful at or Fear: (1)	The Cause (2)	Affects my: (3) (Check below)
		☐ Self-Esteem ☐ Security ☐ Ambitions ☐ Personal Relations ☐ Sex Relations ☐ Pride/Shame ☐ Fear

List Major "Character Defects" in preparation for STEPS 6 & 7

AMENDS		STEP 8
		☐ Now ☐ Later ☐ Never

I'm Resentful at or Fear: (1)	The Cause (2)	Affects my: (3) (Check below)
		☐ Self-Esteem ☐ Security ☐ Ambitions ☐ Personal Relations ☐ Sex Relations ☐ Pride/Shame ☐ Fear

List Major "Character Defects" in preparation for STEPS 6 & 7

AMENDS		STEP 8
		☐ Now ☐ Later ☐ Never

I'm Resentful at or Fear: (1)	The Cause (2)	Affects my: (3) (Check below)
		☐ Self-Esteem ☐ Security ☐ Ambitions ☐ Personal Relations ☐ Sex Relations ☐ Pride/Shame ☐ Fear

List Major "Character Defects" in preparation for STEPS 6 & 7

AMENDS		STEP 8
		☐ Now ☐ Later ☐ Never

Ask yourself: ** (AA 67.3) * (AA 62.2)	Putting out of our minds the wrongs others had done, we resolutely looked for our own mistakes... We admitted our wrongs honestly...** Column (4)
Where had (I) been selfish, self-centred or self-seeking?**	
Where had (I) been dishonest?**	
Where had (I) been frightened?**	
Where had (I) been (responsible) to blame?**	
What decisions did I make based on self that later placed me in a position to be hurt?*	
When in the past can I remember making this decision?* (Early memory.)	
Where was I wrong?** **What was my part?**	

Ask yourself: ** (AA 67.3) * (AA 62.2)	Putting out of our minds the wrongs others had done, we resolutely looked for our own mistakes... We admitted our wrongs honestly...** Column (4)
Where had (I) been selfish, self-centred or self-seeking?**	
Where had (I) been dishonest?**	
Where had (I) been frightened?**	
Where had (I) been (responsible) to blame?**	
What decisions did I make based on self that later placed me in a position to be hurt?*	
When in the past can I remember making this decision?* (Early memory.)	
Where was I wrong?** **What was my part?**	

Ask yourself: ** (AA 67.3) * (AA 62.2)	Putting out of our minds the wrongs others had done, we resolutely looked for our own mistakes... We admitted our wrongs honestly...** Column (4)
Where had (I) been selfish, self-centred or self-seeking?**	
Where had (I) been dishonest?**	
Where had (I) been frightened?**	
Where had (I) been (responsible) to blame?**	
What decisions did I make based on self that later placed me in a position to be hurt?*	
When in the past can I remember making this decision?* (Early memory.)	
Where was I wrong?** **What was my part?**	

I'm Resentful at or Fear: (1)	The Cause (2)	Affects my: (3) (Check below)
		❑ Self-Esteem ❑ Security ❑ Ambitions ❑ Personal Relations ❑ Sex Relations ❑ Pride/Shame ❑ Fear

List Major "Character Defects" in preparation for STEPS 6 & 7

AMENDS		STEP 8
		❑ Now ❑ Later ❑ Never

I'm Resentful at or Fear: (1)	The Cause (2)	Affects my: (3) (Check below)
		❑ Self-Esteem ❑ Security ❑ Ambitions ❑ Personal Relations ❑ Sex Relations ❑ Pride/Shame ❑ Fear

List Major "Character Defects" in preparation for STEPS 6 & 7

AMENDS		STEP 8
		❑ Now ❑ Later ❑ Never

I'm Resentful at or Fear: (1)	The Cause (2)	Affects my: (3) (Check below)
		❑ Self-Esteem ❑ Security ❑ Ambitions ❑ Personal Relations ❑ Sex Relations ❑ Pride/Shame ❑ Fear

List Major "Character Defects" in preparation for STEPS 6 & 7

AMENDS		STEP 8
		❑ Now ❑ Later ❑ Never

Ask yourself: ** (AA 67.3) * (AA 62.2)	Putting out of our minds the wrongs others had done, we resolutely looked for our own mistakes... We admitted our wrongs honestly...** Column (4)
Where had (I) been selfish, self-centred or self-seeking?**	
Where had (I) been dishonest?**	
Where had (I) been frightened?**	
Where had (I) been (responsible) to blame?**	
What decisions did I make based on self that later placed me in a position to be hurt?*	
When in the past can I remember making this decision?* (Early memory.)	
Where was I wrong?** **What was my part?**	

Ask yourself: ** (AA 67.3) * (AA 62.2)	Putting out of our minds the wrongs others had done, we resolutely looked for our own mistakes... We admitted our wrongs honestly...** Column (4)
Where had (I) been selfish, self-centred or self-seeking?**	
Where had (I) been dishonest?**	
Where had (I) been frightened?**	
Where had (I) been (responsible) to blame?**	
What decisions did I make based on self that later placed me in a position to be hurt?*	
When in the past can I remember making this decision?* (Early memory.)	
Where was I wrong?** **What was my part?**	

Ask yourself: ** (AA 67.3) * (AA 62.2)	Putting out of our minds the wrongs others had done, we resolutely looked for our own mistakes... We admitted our wrongs honestly...** Column (4)
Where had (I) been selfish, self-centred or self-seeking?**	
Where had (I) been dishonest?**	
Where had (I) been frightened?**	
Where had (I) been (responsible) to blame?**	
What decisions did I make based on self that later placed me in a position to be hurt?*	
When in the past can I remember making this decision?* (Early memory.)	
Where was I wrong?** **What was my part?**	

I'm Resentful at or Fear: (1)	The Cause (2)	Affects my: (3) (Check below)
		❑ Self-Esteem ❑ Security ❑ Ambitions ❑ Personal Relations ❑ Sex Relations ❑ Pride/Shame ❑ Fear

List Major "Character Defects" in preparation for STEPS 6 & 7

AMENDS		STEP 8
		❑ Now ❑ Later ❑ Never

I'm Resentful at or Fear: (1)	The Cause (2)	Affects my: (3) (Check below)
		❑ Self-Esteem ❑ Security ❑ Ambitions ❑ Personal Relations ❑ Sex Relations ❑ Pride/Shame ❑ Fear

List Major "Character Defects" in preparation for STEPS 6 & 7

AMENDS		STEP 8
		❑ Now ❑ Later ❑ Never

I'm Resentful at or Fear: (1)	The Cause (2)	Affects my: (3) (Check below)
		❑ Self-Esteem ❑ Security ❑ Ambitions ❑ Personal Relations ❑ Sex Relations ❑ Pride/Shame ❑ Fear

List Major "Character Defects" in preparation for STEPS 6 & 7

AMENDS		STEP 8
		❑ Now ❑ Later ❑ Never

Ask yourself: ** (AA 67.3) * (AA 62.2)	Putting out of our minds the wrongs others had done, we resolutely looked for our own mistakes... We admitted our wrongs honestly...** Column (4)
Where had (I) been selfish, self-centred or self-seeking?**	
Where had (I) been dishonest?**	
Where had (I) been frightened?**	
Where had (I) been (responsible) to blame?**	
What decisions did I make based on self that later placed me in a position to be hurt?*	
When in the past can I remember making this decision?* (Early memory.)	
Where was I wrong?** **What was my part?**	

Ask yourself: ** (AA 67.3) * (AA 62.2)	Putting out of our minds the wrongs others had done, we resolutely looked for our own mistakes... We admitted our wrongs honestly...** Column (4)
Where had (I) been selfish, self-centred or self-seeking?**	
Where had (I) been dishonest?**	
Where had (I) been frightened?**	
Where had (I) been (responsible) to blame?**	
What decisions did I make based on self that later placed me in a position to be hurt?*	
When in the past can I remember making this decision?* (Early memory.)	
Where was I wrong?** **What was my part?**	

Ask yourself: ** (AA 67.3) * (AA 62.2)	Putting out of our minds the wrongs others had done, we resolutely looked for our own mistakes... We admitted our wrongs honestly...** Column (4)
Where had (I) been selfish, self-centred or self-seeking?**	
Where had (I) been dishonest?**	
Where had (I) been frightened?**	
Where had (I) been (responsible) to blame?**	
What decisions did I make based on self that later placed me in a position to be hurt?*	
When in the past can I remember making this decision?* (Early memory.)	
Where was I wrong?** **What was my part?**	

I'm Resentful at or Fear: (1)	The Cause (2)	Affects my: (3) (Check below)
		☐ Self-Esteem ☐ Security ☐ Ambitions ☐ Personal Relations ☐ Sex Relations ☐ Pride/Shame ☐ Fear

List Major "Character Defects" in preparation for STEPS 6 & 7

AMENDS		STEP 8
		☐ Now ☐ Later ☐ Never

I'm Resentful at or Fear: (1)	The Cause (2)	Affects my: (3) (Check below)
		☐ Self-Esteem ☐ Security ☐ Ambitions ☐ Personal Relations ☐ Sex Relations ☐ Pride/Shame ☐ Fear

List Major "Character Defects" in preparation for STEPS 6 & 7

AMENDS		STEP 8
		☐ Now ☐ Later ☐ Never

I'm Resentful at or Fear: (1)	The Cause (2)	Affects my: (3) (Check below)
		☐ Self-Esteem ☐ Security ☐ Ambitions ☐ Personal Relations ☐ Sex Relations ☐ Pride/Shame ☐ Fear

List Major "Character Defects" in preparation for STEPS 6 & 7

AMENDS		STEP 8
		☐ Now ☐ Later ☐ Never

Ask yourself: ** (AA 67.3) * (AA 62.2)	Putting out of our minds the wrongs others had done, we resolutely looked for our own mistakes... We admitted our wrongs honestly...** Column (4)
Where had (I) been selfish, self-centred or self-seeking?**	
Where had (I) been dishonest?**	
Where had (I) been frightened?**	
Where had (I) been (responsible) to blame?**	
What decisions did I make based on self that later placed me in a position to be hurt?*	
When in the past can I remember making this decision?* (Early memory.)	
Where was I wrong?** What was my part?	

Ask yourself: ** (AA 67.3) * (AA 62.2)	Putting out of our minds the wrongs others had done, we resolutely looked for our own mistakes... We admitted our wrongs honestly...** Column (4)
Where had (I) been selfish, self-centred or self-seeking?**	
Where had (I) been dishonest?**	
Where had (I) been frightened?**	
Where had (I) been (responsible) to blame?**	
What decisions did I make based on self that later placed me in a position to be hurt?*	
When in the past can I remember making this decision?* (Early memory.)	
Where was I wrong?** What was my part?	

Ask yourself: ** (AA 67.3) * (AA 62.2)	Putting out of our minds the wrongs others had done, we resolutely looked for our own mistakes... We admitted our wrongs honestly...** Column (4)
Where had (I) been selfish, self-centred or self-seeking?**	
Where had (I) been dishonest?**	
Where had (I) been frightened?**	
Where had (I) been (responsible) to blame?**	
What decisions did I make based on self that later placed me in a position to be hurt?*	
When in the past can I remember making this decision?* (Early memory.)	
Where was I wrong?** What was my part?	

I'm Resentful at or Fear: (1)	The Cause (2)	Affects my: (3) (Check below)
		☐ Self-Esteem ☐ Security ☐ Ambitions ☐ Personal Relations ☐ Sex Relations ☐ Pride/Shame ☐ Fear

List Major "Character Defects" in preparation for STEPS 6 & 7

AMENDS		STEP 8
		☐ Now ☐ Later ☐ Never

I'm Resentful at or Fear: (1)	The Cause (2)	Affects my: (3) (Check below)
		☐ Self-Esteem ☐ Security ☐ Ambitions ☐ Personal Relations ☐ Sex Relations ☐ Pride/Shame ☐ Fear

List Major "Character Defects" in preparation for STEPS 6 & 7

AMENDS		STEP 8
		☐ Now ☐ Later ☐ Never

I'm Resentful at or Fear: (1)	The Cause (2)	Affects my: (3) (Check below)
		☐ Self-Esteem ☐ Security ☐ Ambitions ☐ Personal Relations ☐ Sex Relations ☐ Pride/Shame ☐ Fear

List Major "Character Defects" in preparation for STEPS 6 & 7

AMENDS		STEP 8
		☐ Now ☐ Later ☐ Never

Ask yourself: ** (AA 67.3) * (AA 62.2)	Putting out of our minds the wrongs others had done, we resolutely looked for our own mistakes... We admitted our wrongs honestly...** Column (4)
Where had (I) been selfish, self-centred or self-seeking?**	
Where had (I) been dishonest?**	
Where had (I) been frightened?**	
Where had (I) been (responsible) to blame?**	
What decisions did I make based on self that later placed me in a position to be hurt?*	
When in the past can I remember making this decision?* (Early memory.)	
Where was I wrong?** **What was my part?**	

Ask yourself: ** (AA 67.3) * (AA 62.2)	Putting out of our minds the wrongs others had done, we resolutely looked for our own mistakes... We admitted our wrongs honestly...** Column (4)
Where had (I) been selfish, self-centred or self-seeking?**	
Where had (I) been dishonest?**	
Where had (I) been frightened?**	
Where had (I) been (responsible) to blame?**	
What decisions did I make based on self that later placed me in a position to be hurt?*	
When in the past can I remember making this decision?* (Early memory.)	
Where was I wrong?** **What was my part?**	

Ask yourself: ** (AA 67.3) * (AA 62.2)	Putting out of our minds the wrongs others had done, we resolutely looked for our own mistakes... We admitted our wrongs honestly...** Column (4)
Where had (I) been selfish, self-centred or self-seeking?**	
Where had (I) been dishonest?**	
Where had (I) been frightened?**	
Where had (I) been (responsible) to blame?**	
What decisions did I make based on self that later placed me in a position to be hurt?*	
When in the past can I remember making this decision?* (Early memory.)	
Where was I wrong?** **What was my part?**	

I'm Resentful at or Fear: (1)	The Cause (2)	Affects my: (3) (Check below)
		❑ Self-Esteem ❑ Security ❑ Ambitions ❑ Personal Relations ❑ Sex Relations ❑ Pride/Shame ❑ Fear

List Major "Character Defects" in preparation for STEPS 6 & 7

AMENDS		STEP 8
		❑ Now ❑ Later ❑ Never

I'm Resentful at or Fear: (1)	The Cause (2)	Affects my: (3) (Check below)
		❑ Self-Esteem ❑ Security ❑ Ambitions ❑ Personal Relations ❑ Sex Relations ❑ Pride/Shame ❑ Fear

List Major "Character Defects" in preparation for STEPS 6 & 7

AMENDS		STEP 8
		❑ Now ❑ Later ❑ Never

I'm Resentful at or Fear: (1)	The Cause (2)	Affects my: (3) (Check below)
		❑ Self-Esteem ❑ Security ❑ Ambitions ❑ Personal Relations ❑ Sex Relations ❑ Pride/Shame ❑ Fear

List Major "Character Defects" in preparation for STEPS 6 & 7

AMENDS		STEP 8
		❑ Now ❑ Later ❑ Never

Ask yourself: ** (AA 67.3) * (AA 62.2)	*Putting out of our minds the wrongs others had done, we resolutely looked for our own mistakes... We admitted our wrongs honestly...** Column (4)*
Where had (I) been selfish, self-centred or self-seeking?**	
Where had (I) been dishonest?**	
Where had (I) been frightened?**	
Where had (I) been (responsible) to blame?**	
What decisions did I make based on self that later placed me in a position to be hurt?*	
When in the past can I remember making this decision?* (Early memory.)	
Where was I wrong?** **What was my part?**	

Ask yourself: ** (AA 67.3) * (AA 62.2)	*Putting out of our minds the wrongs others had done, we resolutely looked for our own mistakes... We admitted our wrongs honestly...** Column (4)*
Where had (I) been selfish, self-centred or self-seeking?**	
Where had (I) been dishonest?**	
Where had (I) been frightened?**	
Where had (I) been (responsible) to blame?**	
What decisions did I make based on self that later placed me in a position to be hurt?*	
When in the past can I remember making this decision?* (Early memory.)	
Where was I wrong?** **What was my part?**	

Ask yourself: ** (AA 67.3) * (AA 62.2)	*Putting out of our minds the wrongs others had done, we resolutely looked for our own mistakes... We admitted our wrongs honestly...** Column (4)*
Where had (I) been selfish, self-centred or self-seeking?**	
Where had (I) been dishonest?**	
Where had (I) been frightened?**	
Where had (I) been (responsible) to blame?**	
What decisions did I make based on self that later placed me in a position to be hurt?*	
When in the past can I remember making this decision?* (Early memory.)	
Where was I wrong?** **What was my part?**	

I'm Resentful at or Fear: (1)	The Cause (2)	Affects my: (3) (Check below)
		☐ Self-Esteem ☐ Security ☐ Ambitions ☐ Personal Relations ☐ Sex Relations ☐ Pride/Shame ☐ Fear

List Major "Character Defects" in preparation for STEPS 6 & 7

AMENDS		STEP 8
		☐ Now ☐ Later ☐ Never

I'm Resentful at or Fear: (1)	The Cause (2)	Affects my: (3) (Check below)
		☐ Self-Esteem ☐ Security ☐ Ambitions ☐ Personal Relations ☐ Sex Relations ☐ Pride/Shame ☐ Fear

List Major "Character Defects" in preparation for STEPS 6 & 7

AMENDS		STEP 8
		☐ Now ☐ Later ☐ Never

I'm Resentful at or Fear: (1)	The Cause (2)	Affects my: (3) (Check below)
		☐ Self-Esteem ☐ Security ☐ Ambitions ☐ Personal Relations ☐ Sex Relations ☐ Pride/Shame ☐ Fear

List Major "Character Defects" in preparation for STEPS 6 & 7

AMENDS		STEP 8
		☐ Now ☐ Later ☐ Never

Ask yourself: ** (AA 67.3) * (AA 62.2)	Putting out of our minds the wrongs others had done, we resolutely looked for our own mistakes... We admitted our wrongs honestly... ** Column (4)
Where had (I) been selfish, self-centred or self-seeking?**	
Where had (I) been dishonest?**	
Where had (I) been frightened?**	
Where had (I) been (responsible) to blame?**	
What decisions did I make based on self that later placed me in a position to be hurt?*	
When in the past can I remember making this decision?* (Early memory.)	
Where was I wrong?** **What was my part?**	

Ask yourself: ** (AA 67.3) * (AA 62.2)	Putting out of our minds the wrongs others had done, we resolutely looked for our own mistakes... We admitted our wrongs honestly... ** Column (4)
Where had (I) been selfish, self-centred or self-seeking?**	
Where had (I) been dishonest?**	
Where had (I) been frightened?**	
Where had (I) been (responsible) to blame?**	
What decisions did I make based on self that later placed me in a position to be hurt?*	
When in the past can I remember making this decision?* (Early memory.)	
Where was I wrong?** **What was my part?**	

Ask yourself: ** (AA 67.3) * (AA 62.2)	Putting out of our minds the wrongs others had done, we resolutely looked for our own mistakes... We admitted our wrongs honestly... ** Column (4)
Where had (I) been selfish, self-centred or self-seeking?**	
Where had (I) been dishonest?**	
Where had (I) been frightened?**	
Where had (I) been (responsible) to blame?**	
What decisions did I make based on self that later placed me in a position to be hurt?*	
When in the past can I remember making this decision?* (Early memory.)	
Where was I wrong?** **What was my part?**	

I'm Resentful at or Fear: (1)	The Cause (2)	Affects my: (3) (Check below)
		❑ Self-Esteem ❑ Security ❑ Ambitions ❑ Personal Relations ❑ Sex Relations ❑ Pride/Shame ❑ Fear

List Major "Character Defects" in preparation for STEPS 6 & 7

AMENDS		STEP 8
		❑ Now ❑ Later ❑ Never

I'm Resentful at or Fear: (1)	The Cause (2)	Affects my: (3) (Check below)
		❑ Self-Esteem ❑ Security ❑ Ambitions ❑ Personal Relations ❑ Sex Relations ❑ Pride/Shame ❑ Fear

List Major "Character Defects" in preparation for STEPS 6 & 7

AMENDS		STEP 8
		❑ Now ❑ Later ❑ Never

I'm Resentful at or Fear: (1)	The Cause (2)	Affects my: (3) (Check below)
		❑ Self-Esteem ❑ Security ❑ Ambitions ❑ Personal Relations ❑ Sex Relations ❑ Pride/Shame ❑ Fear

List Major "Character Defects" in preparation for STEPS 6 & 7

AMENDS		STEP 8
		❑ Now ❑ Later ❑ Never

Ask yourself: ** (AA 67.3) * (AA 62.2)	Putting out of our minds the wrongs others had done, we resolutely looked for our own mistakes... We admitted our wrongs honestly...** Column (4)
Where had (I) been selfish, self-centred or self-seeking?**	
Where had (I) been dishonest?**	
Where had (I) been frightened?**	
Where had (I) been (responsible) to blame?**	
What decisions did I make based on self that later placed me in a position to be hurt?*	
When in the past can I remember making this decision?* (Early memory.)	
Where was I wrong?** **What was my part?**	

Ask yourself: ** (AA 67.3) * (AA 62.2)	Putting out of our minds the wrongs others had done, we resolutely looked for our own mistakes... We admitted our wrongs honestly...** Column (4)
Where had (I) been selfish, self-centred or self-seeking?**	
Where had (I) been dishonest?**	
Where had (I) been frightened?**	
Where had (I) been (responsible) to blame?**	
What decisions did I make based on self that later placed me in a position to be hurt?*	
When in the past can I remember making this decision?* (Early memory.)	
Where was I wrong?** **What was my part?**	

Ask yourself: ** (AA 67.3) * (AA 62.2)	Putting out of our minds the wrongs others had done, we resolutely looked for our own mistakes... We admitted our wrongs honestly...** Column (4)
Where had (I) been selfish, self-centred or self-seeking?**	
Where had (I) been dishonest?**	
Where had (I) been frightened?**	
Where had (I) been (responsible) to blame?**	
What decisions did I make based on self that later placed me in a position to be hurt?*	
When in the past can I remember making this decision?* (Early memory.)	
Where was I wrong?** **What was my part?**	

I'm Resentful at or Fear: (1)	The Cause (2)	Affects my: (3) (Check below)
		☐ Self-Esteem ☐ Security ☐ Ambitions ☐ Personal Relations ☐ Sex Relations ☐ Pride/Shame ☐ Fear

List Major "Character Defects" in preparation for STEPS 6 & 7

AMENDS		STEP 8
		☐ Now ☐ Later ☐ Never

I'm Resentful at or Fear: (1)	The Cause (2)	Affects my: (3) (Check below)
		☐ Self-Esteem ☐ Security ☐ Ambitions ☐ Personal Relations ☐ Sex Relations ☐ Pride/Shame ☐ Fear

List Major "Character Defects" in preparation for STEPS 6 & 7

AMENDS		STEP 8
		☐ Now ☐ Later ☐ Never

I'm Resentful at or Fear: (1)	The Cause (2)	Affects my: (3) (Check below)
		☐ Self-Esteem ☐ Security ☐ Ambitions ☐ Personal Relations ☐ Sex Relations ☐ Pride/Shame ☐ Fear

List Major "Character Defects" in preparation for STEPS 6 & 7

AMENDS		STEP 8
		☐ Now ☐ Later ☐ Never

12 STEP WORKBOOK

Ask yourself: ** (AA 67.3) * (AA 62.2)	Putting out of our minds the wrongs others had done, we resolutely looked for our own mistakes... We admitted our wrongs honestly...** Column (4)
Where had (I) been selfish, self-centred or self-seeking?**	
Where had (I) been dishonest?**	
Where had (I) been frightened?**	
Where had (I) been (responsible) to blame?**	
What decisions did I make based on self that later placed me in a position to be hurt?*	
When in the past can I remember making this decision?* (Early memory.)	
Where was I wrong?** **What was my part?**	

Ask yourself: ** (AA 67.3) * (AA 62.2)	Putting out of our minds the wrongs others had done, we resolutely looked for our own mistakes... We admitted our wrongs honestly...** Column (4)
Where had (I) been selfish, self-centred or self-seeking?**	
Where had (I) been dishonest?**	
Where had (I) been frightened?**	
Where had (I) been (responsible) to blame?**	
What decisions did I make based on self that later placed me in a position to be hurt?*	
When in the past can I remember making this decision?* (Early memory.)	
Where was I wrong?** **What was my part?**	

Ask yourself: ** (AA 67.3) * (AA 62.2)	Putting out of our minds the wrongs others had done, we resolutely looked for our own mistakes... We admitted our wrongs honestly...** Column (4)
Where had (I) been selfish, self-centred or self-seeking?**	
Where had (I) been dishonest?**	
Where had (I) been frightened?**	
Where had (I) been (responsible) to blame?**	
What decisions did I make based on self that later placed me in a position to be hurt?*	
When in the past can I remember making this decision?* (Early memory.)	
Where was I wrong?** **What was my part?**	

I'm Resentful at or Fear: (1)	The Cause (2)	Affects my: (3) (Check below)
		❑ Self-Esteem ❑ Security ❑ Ambitions ❑ Personal Relations ❑ Sex Relations ❑ Pride/Shame ❑ Fear

List Major "Character Defects" in preparation for STEPS 6 & 7

AMENDS		STEP 8
		❑ Now ❑ Later ❑ Never

I'm Resentful at or Fear: (1)	The Cause (2)	Affects my: (3) (Check below)
		❑ Self-Esteem ❑ Security ❑ Ambitions ❑ Personal Relations ❑ Sex Relations ❑ Pride/Shame ❑ Fear

List Major "Character Defects" in preparation for STEPS 6 & 7

AMENDS		STEP 8
		❑ Now ❑ Later ❑ Never

I'm Resentful at or Fear: (1)	The Cause (2)	Affects my: (3) (Check below)
		❑ Self-Esteem ❑ Security ❑ Ambitions ❑ Personal Relations ❑ Sex Relations ❑ Pride/Shame ❑ Fear

List Major "Character Defects" in preparation for STEPS 6 & 7

AMENDS		STEP 8
		❑ Now ❑ Later ❑ Never

12 STEP WORKBOOK

Ask yourself: ** (AA 67.3) * (AA 62.2)	Putting out of our minds the wrongs others had done, we resolutely looked for our own mistakes... We admitted our wrongs honestly...** Column (4)
Where had (I) been selfish, self-centred or self-seeking?**	
Where had (I) been dishonest?**	
Where had (I) been frightened?**	
Where had (I) been (responsible) to blame?**	
What decisions did I make based on self that later placed me in a position to be hurt?*	
When in the past can I remember making this decision?* (Early memory.)	
Where was I wrong?** **What was my part?**	

Ask yourself: ** (AA 67.3) * (AA 62.2)	Putting out of our minds the wrongs others had done, we resolutely looked for our own mistakes... We admitted our wrongs honestly...** Column (4)
Where had (I) been selfish, self-centred or self-seeking?**	
Where had (I) been dishonest?**	
Where had (I) been frightened?**	
Where had (I) been (responsible) to blame?**	
What decisions did I make based on self that later placed me in a position to be hurt?*	
When in the past can I remember making this decision?* (Early memory.)	
Where was I wrong?** **What was my part?**	

Ask yourself: ** (AA 67.3) * (AA 62.2)	Putting out of our minds the wrongs others had done, we resolutely looked for our own mistakes... We admitted our wrongs honestly...** Column (4)
Where had (I) been selfish, self-centred or self-seeking?**	
Where had (I) been dishonest?**	
Where had (I) been frightened?**	
Where had (I) been (responsible) to blame?**	
What decisions did I make based on self that later placed me in a position to be hurt?*	
When in the past can I remember making this decision?* (Early memory.)	
Where was I wrong?** **What was my part?**	

I'm Resentful at or Fear: (1)	The Cause (2)	Affects my: (3) (Check below)
		❑ Self-Esteem ❑ Security ❑ Ambitions ❑ Personal Relations ❑ Sex Relations ❑ Pride/Shame ❑ Fear

List Major "Character Defects" in preparation for STEPS 6 & 7				

AMENDS		STEP 8
		❑ Now ❑ Later ❑ Never

I'm Resentful at or Fear: (1)	The Cause (2)	Affects my: (3) (Check below)
		❑ Self-Esteem ❑ Security ❑ Ambitions ❑ Personal Relations ❑ Sex Relations ❑ Pride/Shame ❑ Fear

List Major "Character Defects" in preparation for STEPS 6 & 7				

AMENDS		STEP 8
		❑ Now ❑ Later ❑ Never

I'm Resentful at or Fear: (1)	The Cause (2)	Affects my: (3) (Check below)
		❑ Self-Esteem ❑ Security ❑ Ambitions ❑ Personal Relations ❑ Sex Relations ❑ Pride/Shame ❑ Fear

List Major "Character Defects" in preparation for STEPS 6 & 7				

AMENDS		STEP 8
		❑ Now ❑ Later ❑ Never

Ask yourself: ** (AA 67.3) * (AA 62.2)	Putting out of our minds the wrongs others had done, we resolutely looked for our own mistakes… We admitted our wrongs honestly…** Column (4)
Where had (I) been selfish, self-centred or self-seeking?**	
Where had (I) been dishonest?**	
Where had (I) been frightened?**	
Where had (I) been (responsible) to blame?**	
What decisions did I make based on self that later placed me in a position to be hurt?*	
When in the past can I remember making this decision?* (Early memory.)	
Where was I wrong?** What was my part?	

Ask yourself: ** (AA 67.3) * (AA 62.2)	Putting out of our minds the wrongs others had done, we resolutely looked for our own mistakes… We admitted our wrongs honestly…** Column (4)
Where had (I) been selfish, self-centred or self-seeking?**	
Where had (I) been dishonest?**	
Where had (I) been frightened?**	
Where had (I) been (responsible) to blame?**	
What decisions did I make based on self that later placed me in a position to be hurt?*	
When in the past can I remember making this decision?* (Early memory.)	
Where was I wrong?** What was my part?	

Ask yourself: ** (AA 67.3) * (AA 62.2)	Putting out of our minds the wrongs others had done, we resolutely looked for our own mistakes… We admitted our wrongs honestly…** Column (4)
Where had (I) been selfish, self-centred or self-seeking?**	
Where had (I) been dishonest?**	
Where had (I) been frightened?**	
Where had (I) been (responsible) to blame?**	
What decisions did I make based on self that later placed me in a position to be hurt?*	
When in the past can I remember making this decision?* (Early memory.)	
Where was I wrong?** What was my part?	

I'm Resentful at or Fear: (1)	The Cause (2)	Affects my: (3) (Check below)
		❑ Self-Esteem ❑ Security ❑ Ambitions ❑ Personal Relations ❑ Sex Relations ❑ Pride/Shame ❑ Fear

List Major "Character Defects" in preparation for STEPS 6 & 7

AMENDS		STEP 8
		❑ Now ❑ Later ❑ Never

I'm Resentful at or Fear: (1)	The Cause (2)	Affects my: (3) (Check below)
		❑ Self-Esteem ❑ Security ❑ Ambitions ❑ Personal Relations ❑ Sex Relations ❑ Pride/Shame ❑ Fear

List Major "Character Defects" in preparation for STEPS 6 & 7

AMENDS		STEP 8
		❑ Now ❑ Later ❑ Never

I'm Resentful at or Fear: (1)	The Cause (2)	Affects my: (3) (Check below)
		❑ Self-Esteem ❑ Security ❑ Ambitions ❑ Personal Relations ❑ Sex Relations ❑ Pride/Shame ❑ Fear

List Major "Character Defects" in preparation for STEPS 6 & 7

AMENDS		STEP 8
		❑ Now ❑ Later ❑ Never

12 STEP WORKBOOK

Ask yourself: ** (AA 67.3) * (AA 62.2)	Putting out of our minds the wrongs others had done, we resolutely looked for our own mistakes... We admitted our wrongs honestly...** Column (4)
Where had (I) been selfish, self-centred or self-seeking?**	
Where had (I) been dishonest?**	
Where had (I) been frightened?**	
Where had (I) been (responsible) to blame?**	
What decisions did I make based on self that later placed me in a position to be hurt?*	
When in the past can I remember making this decision?* (Early memory.)	
Where was I wrong?** **What was my part?**	

Ask yourself: ** (AA 67.3) * (AA 62.2)	Putting out of our minds the wrongs others had done, we resolutely looked for our own mistakes... We admitted our wrongs honestly...** Column (4)
Where had (I) been selfish, self-centred or self-seeking?**	
Where had (I) been dishonest?**	
Where had (I) been frightened?**	
Where had (I) been (responsible) to blame?**	
What decisions did I make based on self that later placed me in a position to be hurt?*	
When in the past can I remember making this decision?* (Early memory.)	
Where was I wrong?** **What was my part?**	

Ask yourself: ** (AA 67.3) * (AA 62.2)	Putting out of our minds the wrongs others had done, we resolutely looked for our own mistakes... We admitted our wrongs honestly...** Column (4)
Where had (I) been selfish, self-centred or self-seeking?**	
Where had (I) been dishonest?**	
Where had (I) been frightened?**	
Where had (I) been (responsible) to blame?**	
What decisions did I make based on self that later placed me in a position to be hurt?*	
When in the past can I remember making this decision?* (Early memory.)	
Where was I wrong?** **What was my part?**	

I'm Resentful at or Fear: (1)	The Cause (2)	Affects my: (3) (Check below)
		☐ Self-Esteem ☐ Security ☐ Ambitions ☐ Personal Relations ☐ Sex Relations ☐ Pride/Shame ☐ Fear

List Major "Character Defects" in preparation for STEPS 6 & 7

AMENDS		STEP 8
		☐ Now ☐ Later ☐ Never

I'm Resentful at or Fear: (1)	The Cause (2)	Affects my: (3) (Check below)
		☐ Self-Esteem ☐ Security ☐ Ambitions ☐ Personal Relations ☐ Sex Relations ☐ Pride/Shame ☐ Fear

List Major "Character Defects" in preparation for STEPS 6 & 7

AMENDS		STEP 8
		☐ Now ☐ Later ☐ Never

I'm Resentful at or Fear: (1)	The Cause (2)	Affects my: (3) (Check below)
		☐ Self-Esteem ☐ Security ☐ Ambitions ☐ Personal Relations ☐ Sex Relations ☐ Pride/Shame ☐ Fear

List Major "Character Defects" in preparation for STEPS 6 & 7

AMENDS		STEP 8
		☐ Now ☐ Later ☐ Never

Ask yourself: ** (AA 67.3) * (AA 62.2)	Putting out of our minds the wrongs others had done, we resolutely looked for our own mistakes... We admitted our wrongs honestly...** Column (4)
Where had (I) been selfish, self-centred or self-seeking?**	
Where had (I) been dishonest?**	
Where had (I) been frightened?**	
Where had (I) been (responsible) to blame?**	
What decisions did I make based on self that later placed me in a position to be hurt?*	
When in the past can I remember making this decision?* (Early memory.)	
Where was I wrong?** **What was my part?**	

Ask yourself: ** (AA 67.3) * (AA 62.2)	Putting out of our minds the wrongs others had done, we resolutely looked for our own mistakes... We admitted our wrongs honestly...** Column (4)
Where had (I) been selfish, self-centred or self-seeking?**	
Where had (I) been dishonest?**	
Where had (I) been frightened?**	
Where had (I) been (responsible) to blame?**	
What decisions did I make based on self that later placed me in a position to be hurt?*	
When in the past can I remember making this decision?* (Early memory.)	
Where was I wrong?** **What was my part?**	

Ask yourself: ** (AA 67.3) * (AA 62.2)	Putting out of our minds the wrongs others had done, we resolutely looked for our own mistakes... We admitted our wrongs honestly...** Column (4)
Where had (I) been selfish, self-centred or self-seeking?**	
Where had (I) been dishonest?**	
Where had (I) been frightened?**	
Where had (I) been (responsible) to blame?**	
What decisions did I make based on self that later placed me in a position to be hurt?*	
When in the past can I remember making this decision?* (Early memory.)	
Where was I wrong?** **What was my part?**	

I'm Resentful at or Fear: (1)	The Cause (2)	Affects my: (3) (Check below)
		☐ Self-Esteem ☐ Security ☐ Ambitions ☐ Personal Relations ☐ Sex Relations ☐ Pride/Shame ☐ Fear

List Major "Character Defects" in preparation for STEPS 6 & 7					

AMENDS		STEP 8
		☐ Now ☐ Later ☐ Never

I'm Resentful at or Fear: (1)	The Cause (2)	Affects my: (3) (Check below)
		☐ Self-Esteem ☐ Security ☐ Ambitions ☐ Personal Relations ☐ Sex Relations ☐ Pride/Shame ☐ Fear

List Major "Character Defects" in preparation for STEPS 6 & 7					

AMENDS		STEP 8
		☐ Now ☐ Later ☐ Never

I'm Resentful at or Fear: (1)	The Cause (2)	Affects my: (3) (Check below)
		☐ Self-Esteem ☐ Security ☐ Ambitions ☐ Personal Relations ☐ Sex Relations ☐ Pride/Shame ☐ Fear

List Major "Character Defects" in preparation for STEPS 6 & 7					

AMENDS		STEP 8
		☐ Now ☐ Later ☐ Never

Ask yourself: ** (AA 67.3) * (AA 62.2)	Putting out of our minds the wrongs others had done, we resolutely looked for our own mistakes... We admitted our wrongs honestly...** Column (4)
Where had (I) been selfish, self-centred or self-seeking?**	
Where had (I) been dishonest?**	
Where had (I) been frightened?**	
Where had (I) been (responsible) to blame?**	
What decisions did I make based on self that later placed me in a position to be hurt?*	
When in the past can I remember making this decision?* (Early memory.)	
Where was I wrong?** **What was my part?**	

Ask yourself: ** (AA 67.3) * (AA 62.2)	Putting out of our minds the wrongs others had done, we resolutely looked for our own mistakes... We admitted our wrongs honestly...** Column (4)
Where had (I) been selfish, self-centred or self-seeking?**	
Where had (I) been dishonest?**	
Where had (I) been frightened?**	
Where had (I) been (responsible) to blame?**	
What decisions did I make based on self that later placed me in a position to be hurt?*	
When in the past can I remember making this decision?* (Early memory.)	
Where was I wrong?** **What was my part?**	

Ask yourself: ** (AA 67.3) * (AA 62.2)	Putting out of our minds the wrongs others had done, we resolutely looked for our own mistakes... We admitted our wrongs honestly...** Column (4)
Where had (I) been selfish, self-centred or self-seeking?**	
Where had (I) been dishonest?**	
Where had (I) been frightened?**	
Where had (I) been (responsible) to blame?**	
What decisions did I make based on self that later placed me in a position to be hurt?*	
When in the past can I remember making this decision?* (Early memory.)	
Where was I wrong?** **What was my part?**	

I'm Resentful at or Fear: (1)	The Cause (2)	Affects my: (3) (Check below)
		❑ Self-Esteem ❑ Security ❑ Ambitions ❑ Personal Relations ❑ Sex Relations ❑ Pride/Shame ❑ Fear

List Major "Character Defects" in preparation for STEPS 6 & 7

AMENDS		STEP 8
		❑ Now ❑ Later ❑ Never

I'm Resentful at or Fear: (1)	The Cause (2)	Affects my: (3) (Check below)
		❑ Self-Esteem ❑ Security ❑ Ambitions ❑ Personal Relations ❑ Sex Relations ❑ Pride/Shame ❑ Fear

List Major "Character Defects" in preparation for STEPS 6 & 7

AMENDS		STEP 8
		❑ Now ❑ Later ❑ Never

I'm Resentful at or Fear: (1)	The Cause (2)	Affects my: (3) (Check below)
		❑ Self-Esteem ❑ Security ❑ Ambitions ❑ Personal Relations ❑ Sex Relations ❑ Pride/Shame ❑ Fear

List Major "Character Defects" in preparation for STEPS 6 & 7

AMENDS		STEP 8
		❑ Now ❑ Later ❑ Never

Ask yourself: ** (AA 67.3) * (AA 62.2)	Putting out of our minds the wrongs others had done, we resolutely looked for our own mistakes... We admitted our wrongs honestly...** Column (4)
Where had (I) been selfish, self-centred or self-seeking?**	
Where had (I) been dishonest?**	
Where had (I) been frightened?**	
Where had (I) been (responsible) to blame?**	
What decisions did I make based on self that later placed me in a position to be hurt?*	
When in the past can I remember making this decision?* (Early memory.)	
Where was I wrong?** **What was my part?**	

Ask yourself: ** (AA 67.3) * (AA 62.2)	Putting out of our minds the wrongs others had done, we resolutely looked for our own mistakes... We admitted our wrongs honestly...** Column (4)
Where had (I) been selfish, self-centred or self-seeking?**	
Where had (I) been dishonest?**	
Where had (I) been frightened?**	
Where had (I) been (responsible) to blame?**	
What decisions did I make based on self that later placed me in a position to be hurt?*	
When in the past can I remember making this decision?* (Early memory.)	
Where was I wrong?** **What was my part?**	

Ask yourself: ** (AA 67.3) * (AA 62.2)	Putting out of our minds the wrongs others had done, we resolutely looked for our own mistakes... We admitted our wrongs honestly...** Column (4)
Where had (I) been selfish, self-centred or self-seeking?**	
Where had (I) been dishonest?**	
Where had (I) been frightened?**	
Where had (I) been (responsible) to blame?**	
What decisions did I make based on self that later placed me in a position to be hurt?*	
When in the past can I remember making this decision?* (Early memory.)	
Where was I wrong?** **What was my part?**	

I'm Resentful at or Fear: (1)	The Cause (2)	Affects my: (3) (Check below)
		❑ Self-Esteem ❑ Security ❑ Ambitions ❑ Personal Relations ❑ Sex Relations ❑ Pride/Shame ❑ Fear

List Major "Character Defects" in preparation for STEPS 6 & 7

AMENDS		STEP 8
		❑ Now ❑ Later ❑ Never

I'm Resentful at or Fear: (1)	The Cause (2)	Affects my: (3) (Check below)
		❑ Self-Esteem ❑ Security ❑ Ambitions ❑ Personal Relations ❑ Sex Relations ❑ Pride/Shame ❑ Fear

List Major "Character Defects" in preparation for STEPS 6 & 7

AMENDS		STEP 8
		❑ Now ❑ Later ❑ Never

I'm Resentful at or Fear: (1)	The Cause (2)	Affects my: (3) (Check below)
		❑ Self-Esteem ❑ Security ❑ Ambitions ❑ Personal Relations ❑ Sex Relations ❑ Pride/Shame ❑ Fear

List Major "Character Defects" in preparation for STEPS 6 & 7

AMENDS		STEP 8
		❑ Now ❑ Later ❑ Never

Ask yourself: ** (AA 67.3) * (AA 62.2)	Putting out of our minds the wrongs others had done, we resolutely looked for our own mistakes... We admitted our wrongs honestly...** Column (4)
Where had (I) been selfish, self-centred or self-seeking?**	
Where had (I) been dishonest?**	
Where had (I) been frightened?**	
Where had (I) been (responsible) to blame?**	
What decisions did I make based on self that later placed me in a position to be hurt?*	
When in the past can I remember making this decision?* (Early memory.)	
Where was I wrong?** **What was my part?**	

Ask yourself: ** (AA 67.3) * (AA 62.2)	Putting out of our minds the wrongs others had done, we resolutely looked for our own mistakes... We admitted our wrongs honestly...** Column (4)
Where had (I) been selfish, self-centred or self-seeking?**	
Where had (I) been dishonest?**	
Where had (I) been frightened?**	
Where had (I) been (responsible) to blame?**	
What decisions did I make based on self that later placed me in a position to be hurt?*	
When in the past can I remember making this decision?* (Early memory.)	
Where was I wrong?** **What was my part?**	

Ask yourself: ** (AA 67.3) * (AA 62.2)	Putting out of our minds the wrongs others had done, we resolutely looked for our own mistakes... We admitted our wrongs honestly...** Column (4)
Where had (I) been selfish, self-centred or self-seeking?**	
Where had (I) been dishonest?**	
Where had (I) been frightened?**	
Where had (I) been (responsible) to blame?**	
What decisions did I make based on self that later placed me in a position to be hurt?*	
When in the past can I remember making this decision?* (Early memory.)	
Where was I wrong?** **What was my part?**	

I'm Resentful at or Fear: (1)	The Cause (2)	Affects my: (3) (Check below)
		☐ Self-Esteem ☐ Security ☐ Ambitions ☐ Personal Relations ☐ Sex Relations ☐ Pride/Shame ☐ Fear

List Major "Character Defects" in preparation for STEPS 6 & 7

AMENDS		STEP 8
		☐ Now ☐ Later ☐ Never

I'm Resentful at or Fear: (1)	The Cause (2)	Affects my: (3) (Check below)
		☐ Self-Esteem ☐ Security ☐ Ambitions ☐ Personal Relations ☐ Sex Relations ☐ Pride/Shame ☐ Fear

List Major "Character Defects" in preparation for STEPS 6 & 7

AMENDS		STEP 8
		☐ Now ☐ Later ☐ Never

I'm Resentful at or Fear: (1)	The Cause (2)	Affects my: (3) (Check below)
		☐ Self-Esteem ☐ Security ☐ Ambitions ☐ Personal Relations ☐ Sex Relations ☐ Pride/Shame ☐ Fear

List Major "Character Defects" in preparation for STEPS 6 & 7

AMENDS		STEP 8
		☐ Now ☐ Later ☐ Never

Ask yourself: ** (AA 67.3) * (AA 62.2)	Putting out of our minds the wrongs others had done, we resolutely looked for our own mistakes… We admitted our wrongs honestly…** Column (4)
Where had (I) been selfish, self-centred or self-seeking?**	
Where had (I) been dishonest?**	
Where had (I) been frightened?**	
Where had (I) been (responsible) to blame?**	
What decisions did I make based on self that later placed me in a position to be hurt?*	
When in the past can I remember making this decision?* (Early memory.)	
Where was I wrong?** **What was my part?**	

Ask yourself: ** (AA 67.3) * (AA 62.2)	Putting out of our minds the wrongs others had done, we resolutely looked for our own mistakes… We admitted our wrongs honestly…** Column (4)
Where had (I) been selfish, self-centred or self-seeking?**	
Where had (I) been dishonest?**	
Where had (I) been frightened?**	
Where had (I) been (responsible) to blame?**	
What decisions did I make based on self that later placed me in a position to be hurt?*	
When in the past can I remember making this decision?* (Early memory.)	
Where was I wrong?** **What was my part?**	

Ask yourself: ** (AA 67.3) * (AA 62.2)	Putting out of our minds the wrongs others had done, we resolutely looked for our own mistakes… We admitted our wrongs honestly…** Column (4)
Where had (I) been selfish, self-centred or self-seeking?**	
Where had (I) been dishonest?**	
Where had (I) been frightened?**	
Where had (I) been (responsible) to blame?**	
What decisions did I make based on self that later placed me in a position to be hurt?*	
When in the past can I remember making this decision?* (Early memory.)	
Where was I wrong?** **What was my part?**	

I'm Resentful at or Fear: (1)	The Cause (2)	Affects my: (3) (Check below)
		❑ Self-Esteem ❑ Security ❑ Ambitions ❑ Personal Relations ❑ Sex Relations ❑ Pride/Shame ❑ Fear

List Major "Character Defects" in preparation for STEPS 6 & 7

AMENDS		STEP 8
		❑ Now ❑ Later ❑ Never

I'm Resentful at or Fear: (1)	The Cause (2)	Affects my: (3) (Check below)
		❑ Self-Esteem ❑ Security ❑ Ambitions ❑ Personal Relations ❑ Sex Relations ❑ Pride/Shame ❑ Fear

List Major "Character Defects" in preparation for STEPS 6 & 7

AMENDS		STEP 8
		❑ Now ❑ Later ❑ Never

I'm Resentful at or Fear: (1)	The Cause (2)	Affects my: (3) (Check below)
		❑ Self-Esteem ❑ Security ❑ Ambitions ❑ Personal Relations ❑ Sex Relations ❑ Pride/Shame ❑ Fear

List Major "Character Defects" in preparation for STEPS 6 & 7

AMENDS		STEP 8
		❑ Now ❑ Later ❑ Never

Ask yourself: ** (AA 67.3) * (AA 62.2)	Putting out of our minds the wrongs others had done, we resolutely looked for our own mistakes... We admitted our wrongs honestly...** Column (4)
Where had (I) been selfish, self-centred or self-seeking?**	
Where had (I) been dishonest?**	
Where had (I) been frightened?**	
Where had (I) been (responsible) to blame?**	
What decisions did I make based on self that later placed me in a position to be hurt?*	
When in the past can I remember making this decision?* (Early memory.)	
Where was I wrong?** **What was my part?**	

Ask yourself: ** (AA 67.3) * (AA 62.2)	Putting out of our minds the wrongs others had done, we resolutely looked for our own mistakes... We admitted our wrongs honestly...** Column (4)
Where had (I) been selfish, self-centred or self-seeking?**	
Where had (I) been dishonest?**	
Where had (I) been frightened?**	
Where had (I) been (responsible) to blame?**	
What decisions did I make based on self that later placed me in a position to be hurt?*	
When in the past can I remember making this decision?* (Early memory.)	
Where was I wrong?** **What was my part?**	

Ask yourself: ** (AA 67.3) * (AA 62.2)	Putting out of our minds the wrongs others had done, we resolutely looked for our own mistakes... We admitted our wrongs honestly...** Column (4)
Where had (I) been selfish, self-centred or self-seeking?**	
Where had (I) been dishonest?**	
Where had (I) been frightened?**	
Where had (I) been (responsible) to blame?**	
What decisions did I make based on self that later placed me in a position to be hurt?*	
When in the past can I remember making this decision?* (Early memory.)	
Where was I wrong?** **What was my part?**	

I'm Resentful at or Fear: (1)	The Cause (2)	Affects my: (3) (Check below)
		☐ Self-Esteem ☐ Security ☐ Ambitions ☐ Personal Relations ☐ Sex Relations ☐ Pride/Shame ☐ Fear

List Major "Character Defects" in preparation for STEPS 6 & 7

AMENDS		STEP 8
		☐ Now ☐ Later ☐ Never

I'm Resentful at or Fear: (1)	The Cause (2)	Affects my: (3) (Check below)
		☐ Self-Esteem ☐ Security ☐ Ambitions ☐ Personal Relations ☐ Sex Relations ☐ Pride/Shame ☐ Fear

List Major "Character Defects" in preparation for STEPS 6 & 7

AMENDS		STEP 8
		☐ Now ☐ Later ☐ Never

I'm Resentful at or Fear: (1)	The Cause (2)	Affects my: (3) (Check below)
		☐ Self-Esteem ☐ Security ☐ Ambitions ☐ Personal Relations ☐ Sex Relations ☐ Pride/Shame ☐ Fear

List Major "Character Defects" in preparation for STEPS 6 & 7

AMENDS		STEP 8
		☐ Now ☐ Later ☐ Never

Ask yourself: ** (AA 67.3) * (AA 62.2)	Putting out of our minds the wrongs others had done, we resolutely looked for our own mistakes... We admitted our wrongs honestly...** Column (4)
Where had (I) been selfish, self-centred or self-seeking?**	
Where had (I) been dishonest?**	
Where had (I) been frightened?**	
Where had (I) been (responsible) to blame?**	
What decisions did I make based on self that later placed me in a position to be hurt?*	
When in the past can I remember making this decision?* (Early memory.)	
Where was I wrong?** **What was my part?**	

Ask yourself: ** (AA 67.3) * (AA 62.2)	Putting out of our minds the wrongs others had done, we resolutely looked for our own mistakes... We admitted our wrongs honestly...** Column (4)
Where had (I) been selfish, self-centred or self-seeking?**	
Where had (I) been dishonest?**	
Where had (I) been frightened?**	
Where had (I) been (responsible) to blame?**	
What decisions did I make based on self that later placed me in a position to be hurt?*	
When in the past can I remember making this decision?* (Early memory.)	
Where was I wrong?** **What was my part?**	

Ask yourself: ** (AA 67.3) * (AA 62.2)	Putting out of our minds the wrongs others had done, we resolutely looked for our own mistakes... We admitted our wrongs honestly...** Column (4)
Where had (I) been selfish, self-centred or self-seeking?**	
Where had (I) been dishonest?**	
Where had (I) been frightened?**	
Where had (I) been (responsible) to blame?**	
What decisions did I make based on self that later placed me in a position to be hurt?*	
When in the past can I remember making this decision?* (Early memory.)	
Where was I wrong?** **What was my part?**	

I'm Resentful at or Fear: (1)	The Cause (2)	Affects my: (3) (Check below)
		❑ Self-Esteem ❑ Security ❑ Ambitions ❑ Personal Relations ❑ Sex Relations ❑ Pride/Shame ❑ Fear

List Major "Character Defects" in preparation for STEPS 6 & 7				

AMENDS		STEP 8
		❑ Now ❑ Later ❑ Never

I'm Resentful at or Fear: (1)	The Cause (2)	Affects my: (3) (Check below)
		❑ Self-Esteem ❑ Security ❑ Ambitions ❑ Personal Relations ❑ Sex Relations ❑ Pride/Shame ❑ Fear

List Major "Character Defects" in preparation for STEPS 6 & 7				

AMENDS		STEP 8
		❑ Now ❑ Later ❑ Never

I'm Resentful at or Fear: (1)	The Cause (2)	Affects my: (3) (Check below)
		❑ Self-Esteem ❑ Security ❑ Ambitions ❑ Personal Relations ❑ Sex Relations ❑ Pride/Shame ❑ Fear

List Major "Character Defects" in preparation for STEPS 6 & 7				

AMENDS		STEP 8
		❑ Now ❑ Later ❑ Never

12 STEP WORKBOOK

Ask yourself: ** (AA 67.3) * (AA 62.2)	Putting out of our minds the wrongs others had done, we resolutely looked for our own mistakes... We admitted our wrongs honestly...** Column (4)
Where had (I) been selfish, self-centred or self-seeking?**	
Where had (I) been dishonest?**	
Where had (I) been frightened?**	
Where had (I) been (responsible) to blame?**	
What decisions did I make based on self that later placed me in a position to be hurt?*	
When in the past can I remember making this decision?* (Early memory.)	
Where was I wrong?** What was my part?	

Ask yourself: ** (AA 67.3) * (AA 62.2)	Putting out of our minds the wrongs others had done, we resolutely looked for our own mistakes... We admitted our wrongs honestly...** Column (4)
Where had (I) been selfish, self-centred or self-seeking?**	
Where had (I) been dishonest?**	
Where had (I) been frightened?**	
Where had (I) been (responsible) to blame?**	
What decisions did I make based on self that later placed me in a position to be hurt?*	
When in the past can I remember making this decision?* (Early memory.)	
Where was I wrong?** What was my part?	

Ask yourself: ** (AA 67.3) * (AA 62.2)	Putting out of our minds the wrongs others had done, we resolutely looked for our own mistakes... We admitted our wrongs honestly...** Column (4)
Where had (I) been selfish, self-centred or self-seeking?**	
Where had (I) been dishonest?**	
Where had (I) been frightened?**	
Where had (I) been (responsible) to blame?**	
What decisions did I make based on self that later placed me in a position to be hurt?*	
When in the past can I remember making this decision?* (Early memory.)	
Where was I wrong?** What was my part?	

I'm Resentful at or Fear: (1)	The Cause (2)	Affects my: (3) (Check below)
		☐ Self-Esteem ☐ Security ☐ Ambitions ☐ Personal Relations ☐ Sex Relations ☐ Pride/Shame ☐ Fear

List Major "Character Defects" in preparation for STEPS 6 & 7

AMENDS		STEP 8
		☐ Now ☐ Later ☐ Never

I'm Resentful at or Fear: (1)	The Cause (2)	Affects my: (3) (Check below)
		☐ Self-Esteem ☐ Security ☐ Ambitions ☐ Personal Relations ☐ Sex Relations ☐ Pride/Shame ☐ Fear

List Major "Character Defects" in preparation for STEPS 6 & 7

AMENDS		STEP 8
		☐ Now ☐ Later ☐ Never

I'm Resentful at or Fear: (1)	The Cause (2)	Affects my: (3) (Check below)
		☐ Self-Esteem ☐ Security ☐ Ambitions ☐ Personal Relations ☐ Sex Relations ☐ Pride/Shame ☐ Fear

List Major "Character Defects" in preparation for STEPS 6 & 7

AMENDS		STEP 8
		☐ Now ☐ Later ☐ Never

Ask yourself: ** (AA 67.3) * (AA 62.2)	Putting out of our minds the wrongs others had done, we resolutely looked for our own mistakes... We admitted our wrongs honestly... ** Column (4)
Where had (I) been selfish, self-centred or self-seeking?**	
Where had (I) been dishonest?**	
Where had (I) been frightened?**	
Where had (I) been (responsible) to blame?**	
What decisions did I make based on self that later placed me in a position to be hurt?*	
When in the past can I remember making this decision?* (Early memory.)	
Where was I wrong?** What was my part?	

Ask yourself: ** (AA 67.3) * (AA 62.2)	Putting out of our minds the wrongs others had done, we resolutely looked for our own mistakes... We admitted our wrongs honestly... ** Column (4)
Where had (I) been selfish, self-centred or self-seeking?**	
Where had (I) been dishonest?**	
Where had (I) been frightened?**	
Where had (I) been (responsible) to blame?**	
What decisions did I make based on self that later placed me in a position to be hurt?*	
When in the past can I remember making this decision?* (Early memory.)	
Where was I wrong?** What was my part?	

Ask yourself: ** (AA 67.3) * (AA 62.2)	Putting out of our minds the wrongs others had done, we resolutely looked for our own mistakes... We admitted our wrongs honestly... ** Column (4)
Where had (I) been selfish, self-centred or self-seeking?**	
Where had (I) been dishonest?**	
Where had (I) been frightened?**	
Where had (I) been (responsible) to blame?**	
What decisions did I make based on self that later placed me in a position to be hurt?*	
When in the past can I remember making this decision?* (Early memory.)	
Where was I wrong?** What was my part?	

I'm Resentful at or Fear: (1)	The Cause (2)	Affects my: (3) (Check below)
		❑ Self-Esteem ❑ Security ❑ Ambitions ❑ Personal Relations ❑ Sex Relations ❑ Pride/Shame ❑ Fear

List Major "Character Defects" in preparation for STEPS 6 & 7

AMENDS		STEP 8
		❑ Now ❑ Later ❑ Never

I'm Resentful at or Fear: (1)	The Cause (2)	Affects my: (3) (Check below)
		❑ Self-Esteem ❑ Security ❑ Ambitions ❑ Personal Relations ❑ Sex Relations ❑ Pride/Shame ❑ Fear

List Major "Character Defects" in preparation for STEPS 6 & 7

AMENDS		STEP 8
		❑ Now ❑ Later ❑ Never

I'm Resentful at or Fear: (1)	The Cause (2)	Affects my: (3) (Check below)
		❑ Self-Esteem ❑ Security ❑ Ambitions ❑ Personal Relations ❑ Sex Relations ❑ Pride/Shame ❑ Fear

List Major "Character Defects" in preparation for STEPS 6 & 7

AMENDS		STEP 8
		❑ Now ❑ Later ❑ Never

Ask yourself: ** (AA 67.3) * (AA 62.2)	Putting out of our minds the wrongs others had done, we resolutely looked for our own mistakes... We admitted our wrongs honestly...** Column (4)
Where had (I) been selfish, self-centred or self-seeking?**	
Where had (I) been dishonest?**	
Where had (I) been frightened?**	
Where had (I) been (responsible) to blame?**	
What decisions did I make based on self that later placed me in a position to be hurt?*	
When in the past can I remember making this decision?* (Early memory.)	
Where was I wrong?** **What was my part?**	

Ask yourself: ** (AA 67.3) * (AA 62.2)	Putting out of our minds the wrongs others had done, we resolutely looked for our own mistakes... We admitted our wrongs honestly...** Column (4)
Where had (I) been selfish, self-centred or self-seeking?**	
Where had (I) been dishonest?**	
Where had (I) been frightened?**	
Where had (I) been (responsible) to blame?**	
What decisions did I make based on self that later placed me in a position to be hurt?*	
When in the past can I remember making this decision?* (Early memory.)	
Where was I wrong?** **What was my part?**	

Ask yourself: ** (AA 67.3) * (AA 62.2)	Putting out of our minds the wrongs others had done, we resolutely looked for our own mistakes... We admitted our wrongs honestly...** Column (4)
Where had (I) been selfish, self-centred or self-seeking?**	
Where had (I) been dishonest?**	
Where had (I) been frightened?**	
Where had (I) been (responsible) to blame?**	
What decisions did I make based on self that later placed me in a position to be hurt?*	
When in the past can I remember making this decision?* (Early memory.)	
Where was I wrong?** **What was my part?**	

I'm Resentful at or Fear: (1)	The Cause (2)	Affects my: (3) (Check below)
		❑ Self-Esteem ❑ Security ❑ Ambitions ❑ Personal Relations ❑ Sex Relations ❑ Pride/Shame ❑ Fear

List Major "Character Defects" in preparation for STEPS 6 & 7

AMENDS		STEP 8
		❑ Now ❑ Later ❑ Never

I'm Resentful at or Fear: (1)	The Cause (2)	Affects my: (3) (Check below)
		❑ Self-Esteem ❑ Security ❑ Ambitions ❑ Personal Relations ❑ Sex Relations ❑ Pride/Shame ❑ Fear

List Major "Character Defects" in preparation for STEPS 6 & 7

AMENDS		STEP 8
		❑ Now ❑ Later ❑ Never

I'm Resentful at or Fear: (1)	The Cause (2)	Affects my: (3) (Check below)
		❑ Self-Esteem ❑ Security ❑ Ambitions ❑ Personal Relations ❑ Sex Relations ❑ Pride/Shame ❑ Fear

List Major "Character Defects" in preparation for STEPS 6 & 7

AMENDS		STEP 8
		❑ Now ❑ Later ❑ Never

Ask yourself: ** (AA 67.3) * (AA 62.2)	Putting out of our minds the wrongs others had done, we resolutely looked for our own mistakes... We admitted our wrongs honestly...** Column (4)
Where had (I) been selfish, self-centred or self-seeking?**	
Where had (I) been dishonest?**	
Where had (I) been frightened?**	
Where had (I) been (responsible) to blame?**	
What decisions did I make based on self that later placed me in a position to be hurt?*	
When in the past can I remember making this decision?* (Early memory.)	
Where was I wrong?** **What was my part?**	

Ask yourself: ** (AA 67.3) * (AA 62.2)	Putting out of our minds the wrongs others had done, we resolutely looked for our own mistakes... We admitted our wrongs honestly...** Column (4)
Where had (I) been selfish, self-centred or self-seeking?**	
Where had (I) been dishonest?**	
Where had (I) been frightened?**	
Where had (I) been (responsible) to blame?**	
What decisions did I make based on self that later placed me in a position to be hurt?*	
When in the past can I remember making this decision?* (Early memory.)	
Where was I wrong?** **What was my part?**	

Ask yourself: ** (AA 67.3) * (AA 62.2)	Putting out of our minds the wrongs others had done, we resolutely looked for our own mistakes... We admitted our wrongs honestly...** Column (4)
Where had (I) been selfish, self-centred or self-seeking?**	
Where had (I) been dishonest?**	
Where had (I) been frightened?**	
Where had (I) been (responsible) to blame?**	
What decisions did I make based on self that later placed me in a position to be hurt?*	
When in the past can I remember making this decision?* (Early memory.)	
Where was I wrong?** **What was my part?**	

I'm Resentful at or Fear: (1)	The Cause (2)	Affects my: (3) (Check below)
		❑ Self-Esteem ❑ Security ❑ Ambitions ❑ Personal Relations ❑ Sex Relations ❑ Pride/Shame ❑ Fear

List Major "Character Defects" in preparation for STEPS 6 & 7				

AMENDS		STEP 8
		❑ Now ❑ Later ❑ Never

I'm Resentful at or Fear: (1)	The Cause (2)	Affects my: (3) (Check below)
		❑ Self-Esteem ❑ Security ❑ Ambitions ❑ Personal Relations ❑ Sex Relations ❑ Pride/Shame ❑ Fear

List Major "Character Defects" in preparation for STEPS 6 & 7				

AMENDS		STEP 8
		❑ Now ❑ Later ❑ Never

I'm Resentful at or Fear: (1)	The Cause (2)	Affects my: (3) (Check below)
		❑ Self-Esteem ❑ Security ❑ Ambitions ❑ Personal Relations ❑ Sex Relations ❑ Pride/Shame ❑ Fear

List Major "Character Defects" in preparation for STEPS 6 & 7				

AMENDS		STEP 8
		❑ Now ❑ Later ❑ Never

12 STEP WORKBOOK

Ask yourself: ** (AA 67.3) * (AA 62.2)	Putting out of our minds the wrongs others had done, we resolutely looked for our own mistakes... We admitted our wrongs honestly...** Column (4)
Where had (I) been selfish, self-centred or self-seeking?**	
Where had (I) been dishonest?**	
Where had (I) been frightened?**	
Where had (I) been (responsible) to blame?**	
What decisions did I make based on self that later placed me in a position to be hurt?*	
When in the past can I remember making this decision?* (Early memory.)	
Where was I wrong?** **What was my part?**	

Ask yourself: ** (AA 67.3) * (AA 62.2)	Putting out of our minds the wrongs others had done, we resolutely looked for our own mistakes... We admitted our wrongs honestly...** Column (4)
Where had (I) been selfish, self-centred or self-seeking?**	
Where had (I) been dishonest?**	
Where had (I) been frightened?**	
Where had (I) been (responsible) to blame?**	
What decisions did I make based on self that later placed me in a position to be hurt?*	
When in the past can I remember making this decision?* (Early memory.)	
Where was I wrong?** **What was my part?**	

Ask yourself: ** (AA 67.3) * (AA 62.2)	Putting out of our minds the wrongs others had done, we resolutely looked for our own mistakes... We admitted our wrongs honestly...** Column (4)
Where had (I) been selfish, self-centred or self-seeking?**	
Where had (I) been dishonest?**	
Where had (I) been frightened?**	
Where had (I) been (responsible) to blame?**	
What decisions did I make based on self that later placed me in a position to be hurt?*	
When in the past can I remember making this decision?* (Early memory.)	
Where was I wrong?** **What was my part?**	

I'm Resentful at or Fear: (1)	The Cause (2)	Affects my: (3) (Check below)
		☐ Self-Esteem ☐ Security ☐ Ambitions ☐ Personal Relations ☐ Sex Relations ☐ Pride/Shame ☐ Fear

List Major "Character Defects" in preparation for STEPS 6 & 7					

AMENDS		STEP 8
		☐ Now ☐ Later ☐ Never

I'm Resentful at or Fear: (1)	The Cause (2)	Affects my: (3) (Check below)
		☐ Self-Esteem ☐ Security ☐ Ambitions ☐ Personal Relations ☐ Sex Relations ☐ Pride/Shame ☐ Fear

List Major "Character Defects" in preparation for STEPS 6 & 7					

AMENDS		STEP 8
		☐ Now ☐ Later ☐ Never

I'm Resentful at or Fear: (1)	The Cause (2)	Affects my: (3) (Check below)
		☐ Self-Esteem ☐ Security ☐ Ambitions ☐ Personal Relations ☐ Sex Relations ☐ Pride/Shame ☐ Fear

List Major "Character Defects" in preparation for STEPS 6 & 7					

AMENDS		STEP 8
		☐ Now ☐ Later ☐ Never

Ask yourself: ** (AA 67.3) * (AA 62.2)	Putting out of our minds the wrongs others had done, we resolutely looked for our own mistakes... We admitted our wrongs honestly...** Column (4)
Where had (I) been selfish, self-centred or self-seeking?**	
Where had (I) been dishonest?**	
Where had (I) been frightened?**	
Where had (I) been (responsible) to blame?**	
What decisions did I make based on self that later placed me in a position to be hurt?*	
When in the past can I remember making this decision?* (Early memory.)	
Where was I wrong?** **What was my part?**	

Ask yourself: ** (AA 67.3) * (AA 62.2)	Putting out of our minds the wrongs others had done, we resolutely looked for our own mistakes... We admitted our wrongs honestly...** Column (4)
Where had (I) been selfish, self-centred or self-seeking?**	
Where had (I) been dishonest?**	
Where had (I) been frightened?**	
Where had (I) been (responsible) to blame?**	
What decisions did I make based on self that later placed me in a position to be hurt?*	
When in the past can I remember making this decision?* (Early memory.)	
Where was I wrong?** **What was my part?**	

Ask yourself: ** (AA 67.3) * (AA 62.2)	Putting out of our minds the wrongs others had done, we resolutely looked for our own mistakes... We admitted our wrongs honestly...** Column (4)
Where had (I) been selfish, self-centred or self-seeking?**	
Where had (I) been dishonest?**	
Where had (I) been frightened?**	
Where had (I) been (responsible) to blame?**	
What decisions did I make based on self that later placed me in a position to be hurt?*	
When in the past can I remember making this decision?* (Early memory.)	
Where was I wrong?** **What was my part?**	

I'm Resentful at or Fear: (1)	The Cause (2)	Affects my: (3) (Check below)
		❑ Self-Esteem ❑ Security ❑ Ambitions ❑ Personal Relations ❑ Sex Relations ❑ Pride/Shame ❑ Fear

List Major "Character Defects" in preparation for STEPS 6 & 7

AMENDS		STEP 8
		❑ Now ❑ Later ❑ Never

I'm Resentful at or Fear: (1)	The Cause (2)	Affects my: (3) (Check below)
		❑ Self-Esteem ❑ Security ❑ Ambitions ❑ Personal Relations ❑ Sex Relations ❑ Pride/Shame ❑ Fear

List Major "Character Defects" in preparation for STEPS 6 & 7

AMENDS		STEP 8
		❑ Now ❑ Later ❑ Never

I'm Resentful at or Fear: (1)	The Cause (2)	Affects my: (3) (Check below)
		❑ Self-Esteem ❑ Security ❑ Ambitions ❑ Personal Relations ❑ Sex Relations ❑ Pride/Shame ❑ Fear

List Major "Character Defects" in preparation for STEPS 6 & 7

AMENDS		STEP 8
		❑ Now ❑ Later ❑ Never

12 STEP WORKBOOK

Ask yourself: ** (AA 67.3) * (AA 62.2)	Putting out of our minds the wrongs others had done, we resolutely looked for our own mistakes... We admitted our wrongs honestly...** Column (4)
Where had (I) been selfish, self-centred or self-seeking?**	
Where had (I) been dishonest?**	
Where had (I) been frightened?**	
Where had (I) been (responsible) to blame?**	
What decisions did I make based on self that later placed me in a position to be hurt?*	
When in the past can I remember making this decision?* (Early memory.)	
Where was I wrong?** **What was my part?**	

Ask yourself: ** (AA 67.3) * (AA 62.2)	Putting out of our minds the wrongs others had done, we resolutely looked for our own mistakes... We admitted our wrongs honestly...** Column (4)
Where had (I) been selfish, self-centred or self-seeking?**	
Where had (I) been dishonest?**	
Where had (I) been frightened?**	
Where had (I) been (responsible) to blame?**	
What decisions did I make based on self that later placed me in a position to be hurt?*	
When in the past can I remember making this decision?* (Early memory.)	
Where was I wrong?** **What was my part?**	

Ask yourself: ** (AA 67.3) * (AA 62.2)	Putting out of our minds the wrongs others had done, we resolutely looked for our own mistakes... We admitted our wrongs honestly...** Column (4)
Where had (I) been selfish, self-centred or self-seeking?**	
Where had (I) been dishonest?**	
Where had (I) been frightened?**	
Where had (I) been (responsible) to blame?**	
What decisions did I make based on self that later placed me in a position to be hurt?*	
When in the past can I remember making this decision?* (Early memory.)	
Where was I wrong?** **What was my part?**	

I'm Resentful at or Fear: (1)	The Cause (2)	Affects my: (3) (Check below)
		❏ Self-Esteem ❏ Security ❏ Ambitions ❏ Personal Relations ❏ Sex Relations ❏ Pride/Shame ❏ Fear

List Major "Character Defects" in preparation for STEPS 6 & 7

AMENDS		STEP 8
		❏ Now ❏ Later ❏ Never

I'm Resentful at or Fear: (1)	The Cause (2)	Affects my: (3) (Check below)
		❏ Self-Esteem ❏ Security ❏ Ambitions ❏ Personal Relations ❏ Sex Relations ❏ Pride/Shame ❏ Fear

List Major "Character Defects" in preparation for STEPS 6 & 7

AMENDS		STEP 8
		❏ Now ❏ Later ❏ Never

I'm Resentful at or Fear: (1)	The Cause (2)	Affects my: (3) (Check below)
		❏ Self-Esteem ❏ Security ❏ Ambitions ❏ Personal Relations ❏ Sex Relations ❏ Pride/Shame ❏ Fear

List Major "Character Defects" in preparation for STEPS 6 & 7

AMENDS		STEP 8
		❏ Now ❏ Later ❏ Never

Ask yourself: ** (AA 67.3) * (AA 62.2)	Putting out of our minds the wrongs others had done, we resolutely looked for our own mistakes... We admitted our wrongs honestly...** Column (4)
Where had (I) been selfish, self-centred or self-seeking?**	
Where had (I) been dishonest?**	
Where had (I) been frightened?**	
Where had (I) been (responsible) to blame?**	
What decisions did I make based on self that later placed me in a position to be hurt?*	
When in the past can I remember making this decision?* (Early memory.)	
Where was I wrong?** **What was my part?**	

Ask yourself: ** (AA 67.3) * (AA 62.2)	Putting out of our minds the wrongs others had done, we resolutely looked for our own mistakes... We admitted our wrongs honestly...** Column (4)
Where had (I) been selfish, self-centred or self-seeking?**	
Where had (I) been dishonest?**	
Where had (I) been frightened?**	
Where had (I) been (responsible) to blame?**	
What decisions did I make based on self that later placed me in a position to be hurt?*	
When in the past can I remember making this decision?* (Early memory.)	
Where was I wrong?** **What was my part?**	

Ask yourself: ** (AA 67.3) * (AA 62.2)	Putting out of our minds the wrongs others had done, we resolutely looked for our own mistakes... We admitted our wrongs honestly...** Column (4)
Where had (I) been selfish, self-centred or self-seeking?**	
Where had (I) been dishonest?**	
Where had (I) been frightened?**	
Where had (I) been (responsible) to blame?**	
What decisions did I make based on self that later placed me in a position to be hurt?*	
When in the past can I remember making this decision?* (Early memory.)	
Where was I wrong?** **What was my part?**	

I'm Resentful at or Fear: (1)	The Cause (2)	Affects my: (3) (Check below)
		☐ Self-Esteem ☐ Security ☐ Ambitions ☐ Personal Relations ☐ Sex Relations ☐ Pride/Shame ☐ Fear

List Major "Character Defects" in preparation for STEPS 6 & 7

AMENDS		STEP 8
		☐ Now ☐ Later ☐ Never

I'm Resentful at or Fear: (1)	The Cause (2)	Affects my: (3) (Check below)
		☐ Self-Esteem ☐ Security ☐ Ambitions ☐ Personal Relations ☐ Sex Relations ☐ Pride/Shame ☐ Fear

List Major "Character Defects" in preparation for STEPS 6 & 7

AMENDS		STEP 8
		☐ Now ☐ Later ☐ Never

I'm Resentful at or Fear: (1)	The Cause (2)	Affects my: (3) (Check below)
		☐ Self-Esteem ☐ Security ☐ Ambitions ☐ Personal Relations ☐ Sex Relations ☐ Pride/Shame ☐ Fear

List Major "Character Defects" in preparation for STEPS 6 & 7

AMENDS		STEP 8
		☐ Now ☐ Later ☐ Never

Ask yourself: ** (AA 67.3) * (AA 62.2)	Putting out of our minds the wrongs others had done, we resolutely looked for our own mistakes... We admitted our wrongs honestly...** Column (4)
Where had (I) been selfish, self-centred or self-seeking?**	
Where had (I) been dishonest?**	
Where had (I) been frightened?**	
Where had (I) been (responsible) to blame?**	
What decisions did I make based on self that later placed me in a position to be hurt?*	
When in the past can I remember making this decision?* (Early memory.)	
Where was I wrong?** **What was my part?**	

Ask yourself: ** (AA 67.3) * (AA 62.2)	Putting out of our minds the wrongs others had done, we resolutely looked for our own mistakes... We admitted our wrongs honestly...** Column (4)
Where had (I) been selfish, self-centred or self-seeking?**	
Where had (I) been dishonest?**	
Where had (I) been frightened?**	
Where had (I) been (responsible) to blame?**	
What decisions did I make based on self that later placed me in a position to be hurt?*	
When in the past can I remember making this decision?* (Early memory.)	
Where was I wrong?** **What was my part?**	

Ask yourself: ** (AA 67.3) * (AA 62.2)	Putting out of our minds the wrongs others had done, we resolutely looked for our own mistakes... We admitted our wrongs honestly...** Column (4)
Where had (I) been selfish, self-centred or self-seeking?**	
Where had (I) been dishonest?**	
Where had (I) been frightened?**	
Where had (I) been (responsible) to blame?**	
What decisions did I make based on self that later placed me in a position to be hurt?*	
When in the past can I remember making this decision?* (Early memory.)	
Where was I wrong?** **What was my part?**	

I'm Resentful at or Fear: (1)	The Cause (2)	Affects my: (3) (Check below)

Affects my: (3) (Check below)
- ❏ Self-Esteem
- ❏ Security
- ❏ Ambitions
- ❏ Personal Relations
- ❏ Sex Relations
- ❏ Pride/Shame
- ❏ Fear

List Major "Character Defects" in preparation for STEPS 6 & 7

AMENDS

STEP 8
- ❏ Now
- ❏ Later
- ❏ Never

I'm Resentful at or Fear: (1)	The Cause (2)	Affects my: (3) (Check below)

Affects my: (3) (Check below)
- ❏ Self-Esteem
- ❏ Security
- ❏ Ambitions
- ❏ Personal Relations
- ❏ Sex Relations
- ❏ Pride/Shame
- ❏ Fear

List Major "Character Defects" in preparation for STEPS 6 & 7

AMENDS

STEP 8
- ❏ Now
- ❏ Later
- ❏ Never

I'm Resentful at or Fear: (1)	The Cause (2)	Affects my: (3) (Check below)

Affects my: (3) (Check below)
- ❏ Self-Esteem
- ❏ Security
- ❏ Ambitions
- ❏ Personal Relations
- ❏ Sex Relations
- ❏ Pride/Shame
- ❏ Fear

List Major "Character Defects" in preparation for STEPS 6 & 7

AMENDS

STEP 8
- ❏ Now
- ❏ Later
- ❏ Never

Ask yourself: ** (AA 67.3) * (AA 62.2)	Putting out of our minds the wrongs others had done, we resolutely looked for our own mistakes... We admitted our wrongs honestly...** Column (4)
Where had (I) been selfish, self-centred or self-seeking?**	
Where had (I) been dishonest?**	
Where had (I) been frightened?**	
Where had (I) been (responsible) to blame?**	
What decisions did I make based on self that later placed me in a position to be hurt?*	
When in the past can I remember making this decision?* (Early memory.)	
Where was I wrong?** **What was my part?**	

Ask yourself: ** (AA 67.3) * (AA 62.2)	Putting out of our minds the wrongs others had done, we resolutely looked for our own mistakes... We admitted our wrongs honestly...** Column (4)
Where had (I) been selfish, self-centred or self-seeking?**	
Where had (I) been dishonest?**	
Where had (I) been frightened?**	
Where had (I) been (responsible) to blame?**	
What decisions did I make based on self that later placed me in a position to be hurt?*	
When in the past can I remember making this decision?* (Early memory.)	
Where was I wrong?** **What was my part?**	

Ask yourself: ** (AA 67.3) * (AA 62.2)	Putting out of our minds the wrongs others had done, we resolutely looked for our own mistakes... We admitted our wrongs honestly...** Column (4)
Where had (I) been selfish, self-centred or self-seeking?**	
Where had (I) been dishonest?**	
Where had (I) been frightened?**	
Where had (I) been (responsible) to blame?**	
What decisions did I make based on self that later placed me in a position to be hurt?*	
When in the past can I remember making this decision?* (Early memory.)	
Where was I wrong?** **What was my part?**	

I'm Resentful at or Fear: (1)	The Cause (2)	Affects my: (3) (Check below)
		☐ Self-Esteem ☐ Security ☐ Ambitions ☐ Personal Relations ☐ Sex Relations ☐ Pride/Shame ☐ Fear

List Major "Character Defects" in preparation for STEPS 6 & 7

AMENDS		STEP 8
		☐ Now ☐ Later ☐ Never

I'm Resentful at or Fear: (1)	The Cause (2)	Affects my: (3) (Check below)
		☐ Self-Esteem ☐ Security ☐ Ambitions ☐ Personal Relations ☐ Sex Relations ☐ Pride/Shame ☐ Fear

List Major "Character Defects" in preparation for STEPS 6 & 7

AMENDS		STEP 8
		☐ Now ☐ Later ☐ Never

I'm Resentful at or Fear: (1)	The Cause (2)	Affects my: (3) (Check below)
		☐ Self-Esteem ☐ Security ☐ Ambitions ☐ Personal Relations ☐ Sex Relations ☐ Pride/Shame ☐ Fear

List Major "Character Defects" in preparation for STEPS 6 & 7

AMENDS		STEP 8
		☐ Now ☐ Later ☐ Never

Ask yourself: ** (AA 67.3) * (AA 62.2)	Putting out of our minds the wrongs others had done, we resolutely looked for our own mistakes... We admitted our wrongs honestly...** Column (4)
Where had (I) been selfish, self-centred or self-seeking?**	
Where had (I) been dishonest?**	
Where had (I) been frightened?**	
Where had (I) been (responsible) to blame?**	
What decisions did I make based on self that later placed me in a position to be hurt?*	
When in the past can I remember making this decision?* (Early memory.)	
Where was I wrong?** **What was my part?**	

Ask yourself: ** (AA 67.3) * (AA 62.2)	Putting out of our minds the wrongs others had done, we resolutely looked for our own mistakes... We admitted our wrongs honestly...** Column (4)
Where had (I) been selfish, self-centred or self-seeking?**	
Where had (I) been dishonest?**	
Where had (I) been frightened?**	
Where had (I) been (responsible) to blame?**	
What decisions did I make based on self that later placed me in a position to be hurt?*	
When in the past can I remember making this decision?* (Early memory.)	
Where was I wrong?** **What was my part?**	

Ask yourself: ** (AA 67.3) * (AA 62.2)	Putting out of our minds the wrongs others had done, we resolutely looked for our own mistakes... We admitted our wrongs honestly...** Column (4)
Where had (I) been selfish, self-centred or self-seeking?**	
Where had (I) been dishonest?**	
Where had (I) been frightened?**	
Where had (I) been (responsible) to blame?**	
What decisions did I make based on self that later placed me in a position to be hurt?*	
When in the past can I remember making this decision?* (Early memory.)	
Where was I wrong?** **What was my part?**	

I'm Resentful at or Fear: (1)	The Cause (2)	Affects my: (3) (Check below)
		☐ Self-Esteem ☐ Security ☐ Ambitions ☐ Personal Relations ☐ Sex Relations ☐ Pride/Shame ☐ Fear

List Major "Character Defects" in preparation for STEPS 6 & 7

AMENDS		STEP 8
		☐ Now ☐ Later ☐ Never

I'm Resentful at or Fear: (1)	The Cause (2)	Affects my: (3) (Check below)
		☐ Self-Esteem ☐ Security ☐ Ambitions ☐ Personal Relations ☐ Sex Relations ☐ Pride/Shame ☐ Fear

List Major "Character Defects" in preparation for STEPS 6 & 7

AMENDS		STEP 8
		☐ Now ☐ Later ☐ Never

I'm Resentful at or Fear: (1)	The Cause (2)	Affects my: (3) (Check below)
		☐ Self-Esteem ☐ Security ☐ Ambitions ☐ Personal Relations ☐ Sex Relations ☐ Pride/Shame ☐ Fear

List Major "Character Defects" in preparation for STEPS 6 & 7

AMENDS		STEP 8
		☐ Now ☐ Later ☐ Never

Ask yourself: ** (AA 67.3) * (AA 62.2)	Putting out of our minds the wrongs others had done, we resolutely looked for our own mistakes... We admitted our wrongs honestly...** Column (4)
Where had (I) been selfish, self-centred or self-seeking?**	
Where had (I) been dishonest?**	
Where had (I) been frightened?**	
Where had (I) been (responsible) to blame?**	
What decisions did I make based on self that later placed me in a position to be hurt?*	
When in the past can I remember making this decision?* (Early memory.)	
Where was I wrong?** **What was my part?**	

Ask yourself: ** (AA 67.3) * (AA 62.2)	Putting out of our minds the wrongs others had done, we resolutely looked for our own mistakes... We admitted our wrongs honestly...** Column (4)
Where had (I) been selfish, self-centred or self-seeking?**	
Where had (I) been dishonest?**	
Where had (I) been frightened?**	
Where had (I) been (responsible) to blame?**	
What decisions did I make based on self that later placed me in a position to be hurt?*	
When in the past can I remember making this decision?* (Early memory.)	
Where was I wrong?** **What was my part?**	

Ask yourself: ** (AA 67.3) * (AA 62.2)	Putting out of our minds the wrongs others had done, we resolutely looked for our own mistakes... We admitted our wrongs honestly...** Column (4)
Where had (I) been selfish, self-centred or self-seeking?**	
Where had (I) been dishonest?**	
Where had (I) been frightened?**	
Where had (I) been (responsible) to blame?**	
What decisions did I make based on self that later placed me in a position to be hurt?*	
When in the past can I remember making this decision?* (Early memory.)	
Where was I wrong?** **What was my part?**	

I'm Resentful at or Fear: (1)	The Cause (2)	Affects my: (3) (Check below)
		❑ Self-Esteem ❑ Security ❑ Ambitions ❑ Personal Relations ❑ Sex Relations ❑ Pride/Shame ❑ Fear

List Major "Character Defects" in preparation for STEPS 6 & 7

AMENDS		STEP 8
		❑ Now ❑ Later ❑ Never

I'm Resentful at or Fear: (1)	The Cause (2)	Affects my: (3) (Check below)
		❑ Self-Esteem ❑ Security ❑ Ambitions ❑ Personal Relations ❑ Sex Relations ❑ Pride/Shame ❑ Fear

List Major "Character Defects" in preparation for STEPS 6 & 7

AMENDS		STEP 8
		❑ Now ❑ Later ❑ Never

I'm Resentful at or Fear: (1)	The Cause (2)	Affects my: (3) (Check below)
		❑ Self-Esteem ❑ Security ❑ Ambitions ❑ Personal Relations ❑ Sex Relations ❑ Pride/Shame ❑ Fear

List Major "Character Defects" in preparation for STEPS 6 & 7

AMENDS		STEP 8
		❑ Now ❑ Later ❑ Never

12 STEP WORKBOOK

Ask yourself: ** (AA 67.3) * (AA 62.2)	Putting out of our minds the wrongs others had done, we resolutely looked for our own mistakes... We admitted our wrongs honestly...** Column (4)
Where had (I) been selfish, self-centred or self-seeking?**	
Where had (I) been dishonest?**	
Where had (I) been frightened?**	
Where had (I) been (responsible) to blame?**	
What decisions did I make based on self that later placed me in a position to be hurt?*	
When in the past can I remember making this decision?* (Early memory.)	
Where was I wrong?** **What was my part?**	

Ask yourself: ** (AA 67.3) * (AA 62.2)	Putting out of our minds the wrongs others had done, we resolutely looked for our own mistakes... We admitted our wrongs honestly...** Column (4)
Where had (I) been selfish, self-centred or self-seeking?**	
Where had (I) been dishonest?**	
Where had (I) been frightened?**	
Where had (I) been (responsible) to blame?**	
What decisions did I make based on self that later placed me in a position to be hurt?*	
When in the past can I remember making this decision?* (Early memory.)	
Where was I wrong?** **What was my part?**	

Ask yourself: ** (AA 67.3) * (AA 62.2)	Putting out of our minds the wrongs others had done, we resolutely looked for our own mistakes... We admitted our wrongs honestly...** Column (4)
Where had (I) been selfish, self-centred or self-seeking?**	
Where had (I) been dishonest?**	
Where had (I) been frightened?**	
Where had (I) been (responsible) to blame?**	
What decisions did I make based on self that later placed me in a position to be hurt?*	
When in the past can I remember making this decision?* (Early memory.)	
Where was I wrong?** **What was my part?**	

I'm Resentful at or Fear: (1)	The Cause (2)	Affects my: (3) (Check below)
		❑ Self-Esteem ❑ Security ❑ Ambitions ❑ Personal Relations ❑ Sex Relations ❑ Pride/Shame ❑ Fear

List Major "Character Defects" in preparation for STEPS 6 & 7

AMENDS		STEP 8
		❑ Now ❑ Later ❑ Never

I'm Resentful at or Fear: (1)	The Cause (2)	Affects my: (3) (Check below)
		❑ Self-Esteem ❑ Security ❑ Ambitions ❑ Personal Relations ❑ Sex Relations ❑ Pride/Shame ❑ Fear

List Major "Character Defects" in preparation for STEPS 6 & 7

AMENDS		STEP 8
		❑ Now ❑ Later ❑ Never

I'm Resentful at or Fear: (1)	The Cause (2)	Affects my: (3) (Check below)
		❑ Self-Esteem ❑ Security ❑ Ambitions ❑ Personal Relations ❑ Sex Relations ❑ Pride/Shame ❑ Fear

List Major "Character Defects" in preparation for STEPS 6 & 7

AMENDS		STEP 8
		❑ Now ❑ Later ❑ Never

Ask yourself: ** (AA 67.3) * (AA 62.2)	Putting out of our minds the wrongs others had done, we resolutely looked for our own mistakes... We admitted our wrongs honestly...** Column (4)
Where had (I) been selfish, self-centred or self-seeking?**	
Where had (I) been dishonest?**	
Where had (I) been frightened?**	
Where had (I) been (responsible) to blame?**	
What decisions did I make based on self that later placed me in a position to be hurt?*	
When in the past can I remember making this decision?* (Early memory.)	
Where was I wrong?** **What was my part?**	

Ask yourself: ** (AA 67.3) * (AA 62.2)	Putting out of our minds the wrongs others had done, we resolutely looked for our own mistakes... We admitted our wrongs honestly...** Column (4)
Where had (I) been selfish, self-centred or self-seeking?**	
Where had (I) been dishonest?**	
Where had (I) been frightened?**	
Where had (I) been (responsible) to blame?**	
What decisions did I make based on self that later placed me in a position to be hurt?*	
When in the past can I remember making this decision?* (Early memory.)	
Where was I wrong?** **What was my part?**	

Ask yourself: ** (AA 67.3) * (AA 62.2)	Putting out of our minds the wrongs others had done, we resolutely looked for our own mistakes... We admitted our wrongs honestly...** Column (4)
Where had (I) been selfish, self-centred or self-seeking?**	
Where had (I) been dishonest?**	
Where had (I) been frightened?**	
Where had (I) been (responsible) to blame?**	
What decisions did I make based on self that later placed me in a position to be hurt?*	
When in the past can I remember making this decision?* (Early memory.)	
Where was I wrong?** **What was my part?**	

I'm Resentful at or Fear: (1)	The Cause (2)	Affects my: (3) (Check below)
		❑ Self-Esteem ❑ Security ❑ Ambitions ❑ Personal Relations ❑ Sex Relations ❑ Pride/Shame ❑ Fear

List Major "Character Defects" in preparation for STEPS 6 & 7

AMENDS		STEP 8
		❑ Now ❑ Later ❑ Never

I'm Resentful at or Fear: (1)	The Cause (2)	Affects my: (3) (Check below)
		❑ Self-Esteem ❑ Security ❑ Ambitions ❑ Personal Relations ❑ Sex Relations ❑ Pride/Shame ❑ Fear

List Major "Character Defects" in preparation for STEPS 6 & 7

AMENDS		STEP 8
		❑ Now ❑ Later ❑ Never

I'm Resentful at or Fear: (1)	The Cause (2)	Affects my: (3) (Check below)
		❑ Self-Esteem ❑ Security ❑ Ambitions ❑ Personal Relations ❑ Sex Relations ❑ Pride/Shame ❑ Fear

List Major "Character Defects" in preparation for STEPS 6 & 7

AMENDS		STEP 8
		❑ Now ❑ Later ❑ Never

12 STEP WORKBOOK

Ask yourself: ** (AA 67.3) * (AA 62.2)	Putting out of our minds the wrongs others had done, we resolutely looked for our own mistakes... We admitted our wrongs honestly...** Column (4)
Where had (I) been selfish, self-centred or self-seeking?**	
Where had (I) been dishonest?**	
Where had (I) been frightened?**	
Where had (I) been (responsible) to blame?**	
What decisions did I make based on self that later placed me in a position to be hurt?*	
When in the past can I remember making this decision?* (Early memory.)	
Where was I wrong?** **What was my part?**	

Ask yourself: ** (AA 67.3) * (AA 62.2)	Putting out of our minds the wrongs others had done, we resolutely looked for our own mistakes... We admitted our wrongs honestly...** Column (4)
Where had (I) been selfish, self-centred or self-seeking?**	
Where had (I) been dishonest?**	
Where had (I) been frightened?**	
Where had (I) been (responsible) to blame?**	
What decisions did I make based on self that later placed me in a position to be hurt?*	
When in the past can I remember making this decision?* (Early memory.)	
Where was I wrong?** **What was my part?**	

Ask yourself: ** (AA 67.3) * (AA 62.2)	Putting out of our minds the wrongs others had done, we resolutely looked for our own mistakes... We admitted our wrongs honestly...** Column (4)
Where had (I) been selfish, self-centred or self-seeking?**	
Where had (I) been dishonest?**	
Where had (I) been frightened?**	
Where had (I) been (responsible) to blame?**	
What decisions did I make based on self that later placed me in a position to be hurt?*	
When in the past can I remember making this decision?* (Early memory.)	
Where was I wrong?** **What was my part?**	

I'm Resentful at or Fear: (1)	The Cause (2)	Affects my: (3) (Check below)
		❑ Self-Esteem ❑ Security ❑ Ambitions ❑ Personal Relations ❑ Sex Relations ❑ Pride/Shame ❑ Fear

List Major "Character Defects" in preparation for STEPS 6 & 7

AMENDS		STEP 8
		❑ Now ❑ Later ❑ Never

I'm Resentful at or Fear: (1)	The Cause (2)	Affects my: (3) (Check below)
		❑ Self-Esteem ❑ Security ❑ Ambitions ❑ Personal Relations ❑ Sex Relations ❑ Pride/Shame ❑ Fear

List Major "Character Defects" in preparation for STEPS 6 & 7

AMENDS		STEP 8
		❑ Now ❑ Later ❑ Never

I'm Resentful at or Fear: (1)	The Cause (2)	Affects my: (3) (Check below)
		❑ Self-Esteem ❑ Security ❑ Ambitions ❑ Personal Relations ❑ Sex Relations ❑ Pride/Shame ❑ Fear

List Major "Character Defects" in preparation for STEPS 6 & 7

AMENDS		STEP 8
		❑ Now ❑ Later ❑ Never

Ask yourself: ** (AA 67.3) * (AA 62.2)	*Putting out of our minds the wrongs others had done, we resolutely looked for our own mistakes... We admitted our wrongs honestly...** Column (4)*
Where had (I) been selfish, self-centred or self-seeking?**	
Where had (I) been dishonest?**	
Where had (I) been frightened?**	
Where had (I) been (responsible) to blame?**	
What decisions did I make based on self that later placed me in a position to be hurt?*	
When in the past can I remember making this decision?* (Early memory.)	
Where was I wrong?** **What was my part?**	

Ask yourself: ** (AA 67.3) * (AA 62.2)	*Putting out of our minds the wrongs others had done, we resolutely looked for our own mistakes... We admitted our wrongs honestly...** Column (4)*
Where had (I) been selfish, self-centred or self-seeking?**	
Where had (I) been dishonest?**	
Where had (I) been frightened?**	
Where had (I) been (responsible) to blame?**	
What decisions did I make based on self that later placed me in a position to be hurt?*	
When in the past can I remember making this decision?* (Early memory.)	
Where was I wrong?** **What was my part?**	

Ask yourself: ** (AA 67.3) * (AA 62.2)	*Putting out of our minds the wrongs others had done, we resolutely looked for our own mistakes... We admitted our wrongs honestly...** Column (4)*
Where had (I) been selfish, self-centred or self-seeking?**	
Where had (I) been dishonest?**	
Where had (I) been frightened?**	
Where had (I) been (responsible) to blame?**	
What decisions did I make based on self that later placed me in a position to be hurt?*	
When in the past can I remember making this decision?* (Early memory.)	
Where was I wrong?** **What was my part?**	

I'm Resentful at or Fear: (1)	The Cause (2)	Affects my: (3) (Check below)
		❑ Self-Esteem ❑ Security ❑ Ambitions ❑ Personal Relations ❑ Sex Relations ❑ Pride/Shame ❑ Fear

List Major "Character Defects" in preparation for STEPS 6 & 7

AMENDS		STEP 8
		❑ Now ❑ Later ❑ Never

I'm Resentful at or Fear: (1)	The Cause (2)	Affects my: (3) (Check below)
		❑ Self-Esteem ❑ Security ❑ Ambitions ❑ Personal Relations ❑ Sex Relations ❑ Pride/Shame ❑ Fear

List Major "Character Defects" in preparation for STEPS 6 & 7

AMENDS		STEP 8
		❑ Now ❑ Later ❑ Never

I'm Resentful at or Fear: (1)	The Cause (2)	Affects my: (3) (Check below)
		❑ Self-Esteem ❑ Security ❑ Ambitions ❑ Personal Relations ❑ Sex Relations ❑ Pride/Shame ❑ Fear

List Major "Character Defects" in preparation for STEPS 6 & 7

AMENDS		STEP 8
		❑ Now ❑ Later ❑ Never

Ask yourself: ** (AA 67.3) * (AA 62.2)	Putting out of our minds the wrongs others had done, we resolutely looked for our own mistakes... We admitted our wrongs honestly...** Column (4)
Where had (I) been selfish, self-centred or self-seeking?**	
Where had (I) been dishonest?**	
Where had (I) been frightened?**	
Where had (I) been (responsible) to blame?**	
What decisions did I make based on self that later placed me in a position to be hurt?*	
When in the past can I remember making this decision?* (Early memory.)	
Where was I wrong?** **What was my part?**	

Ask yourself: ** (AA 67.3) * (AA 62.2)	Putting out of our minds the wrongs others had done, we resolutely looked for our own mistakes... We admitted our wrongs honestly...** Column (4)
Where had (I) been selfish, self-centred or self-seeking?**	
Where had (I) been dishonest?**	
Where had (I) been frightened?**	
Where had (I) been (responsible) to blame?**	
What decisions did I make based on self that later placed me in a position to be hurt?*	
When in the past can I remember making this decision?* (Early memory.)	
Where was I wrong?** **What was my part?**	

Ask yourself: ** (AA 67.3) * (AA 62.2)	Putting out of our minds the wrongs others had done, we resolutely looked for our own mistakes... We admitted our wrongs honestly...** Column (4)
Where had (I) been selfish, self-centred or self-seeking?**	
Where had (I) been dishonest?**	
Where had (I) been frightened?**	
Where had (I) been (responsible) to blame?**	
What decisions did I make based on self that later placed me in a position to be hurt?*	
When in the past can I remember making this decision?* (Early memory.)	
Where was I wrong?** **What was my part?**	

I'm Resentful at or Fear: (1)	The Cause (2)	Affects my: (3) (Check below)
		☐ Self-Esteem ☐ Security ☐ Ambitions ☐ Personal Relations ☐ Sex Relations ☐ Pride/Shame ☐ Fear

List Major "Character Defects" in preparation for STEPS 6 & 7

AMENDS		STEP 8
		☐ Now ☐ Later ☐ Never

I'm Resentful at or Fear: (1)	The Cause (2)	Affects my: (3) (Check below)
		☐ Self-Esteem ☐ Security ☐ Ambitions ☐ Personal Relations ☐ Sex Relations ☐ Pride/Shame ☐ Fear

List Major "Character Defects" in preparation for STEPS 6 & 7

AMENDS		STEP 8
		☐ Now ☐ Later ☐ Never

I'm Resentful at or Fear: (1)	The Cause (2)	Affects my: (3) (Check below)
		☐ Self-Esteem ☐ Security ☐ Ambitions ☐ Personal Relations ☐ Sex Relations ☐ Pride/Shame ☐ Fear

List Major "Character Defects" in preparation for STEPS 6 & 7

AMENDS		STEP 8
		☐ Now ☐ Later ☐ Never

Ask yourself: ** (AA 67.3) * (AA 62.2)	Putting out of our minds the wrongs others had done, we resolutely looked for our own mistakes... We admitted our wrongs honestly...** Column (4)
Where had (I) been selfish, self-centred or self-seeking?**	
Where had (I) been dishonest?**	
Where had (I) been frightened?**	
Where had (I) been (responsible) to blame?**	
What decisions did I make based on self that later placed me in a position to be hurt?*	
When in the past can I remember making this decision?* (Early memory.)	
Where was I wrong?** **What was my part?**	

Ask yourself: ** (AA 67.3) * (AA 62.2)	Putting out of our minds the wrongs others had done, we resolutely looked for our own mistakes... We admitted our wrongs honestly...** Column (4)
Where had (I) been selfish, self-centred or self-seeking?**	
Where had (I) been dishonest?**	
Where had (I) been frightened?**	
Where had (I) been (responsible) to blame?**	
What decisions did I make based on self that later placed me in a position to be hurt?*	
When in the past can I remember making this decision?* (Early memory.)	
Where was I wrong?** **What was my part?**	

Ask yourself: ** (AA 67.3) * (AA 62.2)	Putting out of our minds the wrongs others had done, we resolutely looked for our own mistakes... We admitted our wrongs honestly...** Column (4)
Where had (I) been selfish, self-centred or self-seeking?**	
Where had (I) been dishonest?**	
Where had (I) been frightened?**	
Where had (I) been (responsible) to blame?**	
What decisions did I make based on self that later placed me in a position to be hurt?*	
When in the past can I remember making this decision?* (Early memory.)	
Where was I wrong?** **What was my part?**	

I'm Resentful at or Fear: (1)	The Cause (2)	Affects my: (3) (Check below)
		❑ Self-Esteem ❑ Security ❑ Ambitions ❑ Personal Relations ❑ Sex Relations ❑ Pride/Shame ❑ Fear

List Major "Character Defects" in preparation for STEPS 6 & 7

AMENDS		STEP 8
		❑ Now ❑ Later ❑ Never

I'm Resentful at or Fear: (1)	The Cause (2)	Affects my: (3) (Check below)
		❑ Self-Esteem ❑ Security ❑ Ambitions ❑ Personal Relations ❑ Sex Relations ❑ Pride/Shame ❑ Fear

List Major "Character Defects" in preparation for STEPS 6 & 7

AMENDS		STEP 8
		❑ Now ❑ Later ❑ Never

I'm Resentful at or Fear: (1)	The Cause (2)	Affects my: (3) (Check below)
		❑ Self-Esteem ❑ Security ❑ Ambitions ❑ Personal Relations ❑ Sex Relations ❑ Pride/Shame ❑ Fear

List Major "Character Defects" in preparation for STEPS 6 & 7

AMENDS		STEP 8
		❑ Now ❑ Later ❑ Never

Ask yourself: ** (AA 67.3) * (AA 62.2)	Putting out of our minds the wrongs others had done, we resolutely looked for our own mistakes... We admitted our wrongs honestly...** Column (4)
Where had (I) been selfish, self-centred or self-seeking?**	
Where had (I) been dishonest?**	
Where had (I) been frightened?**	
Where had (I) been (responsible) to blame?**	
What decisions did I make based on self that later placed me in a position to be hurt?*	
When in the past can I remember making this decision?* (Early memory.)	
Where was I wrong?** **What was my part?**	

Ask yourself: ** (AA 67.3) * (AA 62.2)	Putting out of our minds the wrongs others had done, we resolutely looked for our own mistakes... We admitted our wrongs honestly...** Column (4)
Where had (I) been selfish, self-centred or self-seeking?**	
Where had (I) been dishonest?**	
Where had (I) been frightened?**	
Where had (I) been (responsible) to blame?**	
What decisions did I make based on self that later placed me in a position to be hurt?*	
When in the past can I remember making this decision?* (Early memory.)	
Where was I wrong?** **What was my part?**	

Ask yourself: ** (AA 67.3) * (AA 62.2)	Putting out of our minds the wrongs others had done, we resolutely looked for our own mistakes... We admitted our wrongs honestly...** Column (4)
Where had (I) been selfish, self-centred or self-seeking?**	
Where had (I) been dishonest?**	
Where had (I) been frightened?**	
Where had (I) been (responsible) to blame?**	
What decisions did I make based on self that later placed me in a position to be hurt?*	
When in the past can I remember making this decision?* (Early memory.)	
Where was I wrong?** **What was my part?**	

I'm Resentful at or Fear: (1)	The Cause (2)	Affects my: (3) (Check below)
		☐ Self-Esteem ☐ Security ☐ Ambitions ☐ Personal Relations ☐ Sex Relations ☐ Pride/Shame ☐ Fear

List Major "Character Defects" in preparation for STEPS 6 & 7				

AMENDS		STEP 8
		☐ Now ☐ Later ☐ Never

I'm Resentful at or Fear: (1)	The Cause (2)	Affects my: (3) (Check below)
		☐ Self-Esteem ☐ Security ☐ Ambitions ☐ Personal Relations ☐ Sex Relations ☐ Pride/Shame ☐ Fear

List Major "Character Defects" in preparation for STEPS 6 & 7				

AMENDS		STEP 8
		☐ Now ☐ Later ☐ Never

I'm Resentful at or Fear: (1)	The Cause (2)	Affects my: (3) (Check below)
		☐ Self-Esteem ☐ Security ☐ Ambitions ☐ Personal Relations ☐ Sex Relations ☐ Pride/Shame ☐ Fear

List Major "Character Defects" in preparation for STEPS 6 & 7				

AMENDS		STEP 8
		☐ Now ☐ Later ☐ Never

Ask yourself: ** (AA 67.3) * (AA 62.2)	Putting out of our minds the wrongs others had done, we resolutely looked for our own mistakes... We admitted our wrongs honestly...** Column (4)
Where had (I) been selfish, self-centred or self-seeking?**	
Where had (I) been dishonest?**	
Where had (I) been frightened?**	
Where had (I) been (responsible) to blame?**	
What decisions did I make based on self that later placed me in a position to be hurt?*	
When in the past can I remember making this decision?* (Early memory.)	
Where was I wrong?** **What was my part?**	

Ask yourself: ** (AA 67.3) * (AA 62.2)	Putting out of our minds the wrongs others had done, we resolutely looked for our own mistakes... We admitted our wrongs honestly...** Column (4)
Where had (I) been selfish, self-centred or self-seeking?**	
Where had (I) been dishonest?**	
Where had (I) been frightened?**	
Where had (I) been (responsible) to blame?**	
What decisions did I make based on self that later placed me in a position to be hurt?*	
When in the past can I remember making this decision?* (Early memory.)	
Where was I wrong?** **What was my part?**	

Ask yourself: ** (AA 67.3) * (AA 62.2)	Putting out of our minds the wrongs others had done, we resolutely looked for our own mistakes... We admitted our wrongs honestly...** Column (4)
Where had (I) been selfish, self-centred or self-seeking?**	
Where had (I) been dishonest?**	
Where had (I) been frightened?**	
Where had (I) been (responsible) to blame?**	
What decisions did I make based on self that later placed me in a position to be hurt?*	
When in the past can I remember making this decision?* (Early memory.)	
Where was I wrong?** **What was my part?**	

I'm Resentful at or Fear: (1)	The Cause (2)	Affects my: (3) (Check below)
		❑ Self-Esteem ❑ Security ❑ Ambitions ❑ Personal Relations ❑ Sex Relations ❑ Pride/Shame ❑ Fear

List Major "Character Defects" in preparation for STEPS 6 & 7

AMENDS		STEP 8
		❑ Now ❑ Later ❑ Never

I'm Resentful at or Fear: (1)	The Cause (2)	Affects my: (3) (Check below)
		❑ Self-Esteem ❑ Security ❑ Ambitions ❑ Personal Relations ❑ Sex Relations ❑ Pride/Shame ❑ Fear

List Major "Character Defects" in preparation for STEPS 6 & 7

AMENDS		STEP 8
		❑ Now ❑ Later ❑ Never

I'm Resentful at or Fear: (1)	The Cause (2)	Affects my: (3) (Check below)
		❑ Self-Esteem ❑ Security ❑ Ambitions ❑ Personal Relations ❑ Sex Relations ❑ Pride/Shame ❑ Fear

List Major "Character Defects" in preparation for STEPS 6 & 7

AMENDS		STEP 8
		❑ Now ❑ Later ❑ Never

Ask yourself: ** (AA 67.3) * (AA 62.2)	Putting out of our minds the wrongs others had done, we resolutely looked for our own mistakes... We admitted our wrongs honestly...** Column (4)
Where had (I) been selfish, self-centred or self-seeking?**	
Where had (I) been dishonest?**	
Where had (I) been frightened?**	
Where had (I) been (responsible) to blame?**	
What decisions did I make based on self that later placed me in a position to be hurt?*	
When in the past can I remember making this decision?* (Early memory.)	
Where was I wrong?** **What was my part?**	

Ask yourself: ** (AA 67.3) * (AA 62.2)	Putting out of our minds the wrongs others had done, we resolutely looked for our own mistakes... We admitted our wrongs honestly...** Column (4)
Where had (I) been selfish, self-centred or self-seeking?**	
Where had (I) been dishonest?**	
Where had (I) been frightened?**	
Where had (I) been (responsible) to blame?**	
What decisions did I make based on self that later placed me in a position to be hurt?*	
When in the past can I remember making this decision?* (Early memory.)	
Where was I wrong?** **What was my part?**	

Ask yourself: ** (AA 67.3) * (AA 62.2)	Putting out of our minds the wrongs others had done, we resolutely looked for our own mistakes... We admitted our wrongs honestly...** Column (4)
Where had (I) been selfish, self-centred or self-seeking?**	
Where had (I) been dishonest?**	
Where had (I) been frightened?**	
Where had (I) been (responsible) to blame?**	
What decisions did I make based on self that later placed me in a position to be hurt?*	
When in the past can I remember making this decision?* (Early memory.)	
Where was I wrong?** **What was my part?**	

I'm Resentful at or Fear: (1)	The Cause (2)	Affects my: (3) (Check below)
		☐ Self-Esteem ☐ Security ☐ Ambitions ☐ Personal Relations ☐ Sex Relations ☐ Pride/Shame ☐ Fear

List Major "Character Defects" in preparation for STEPS 6 & 7

AMENDS		STEP 8
		☐ Now ☐ Later ☐ Never

I'm Resentful at or Fear: (1)	The Cause (2)	Affects my: (3) (Check below)
		☐ Self-Esteem ☐ Security ☐ Ambitions ☐ Personal Relations ☐ Sex Relations ☐ Pride/Shame ☐ Fear

List Major "Character Defects" in preparation for STEPS 6 & 7

AMENDS		STEP 8
		☐ Now ☐ Later ☐ Never

I'm Resentful at or Fear: (1)	The Cause (2)	Affects my: (3) (Check below)
		☐ Self-Esteem ☐ Security ☐ Ambitions ☐ Personal Relations ☐ Sex Relations ☐ Pride/Shame ☐ Fear

List Major "Character Defects" in preparation for STEPS 6 & 7

AMENDS		STEP 8
		☐ Now ☐ Later ☐ Never

Ask yourself: ** (AA 67.3) * (AA 62.2)	Putting out of our minds the wrongs others had done, we resolutely looked for our own mistakes... We admitted our wrongs honestly...** Column (4)
Where had (I) been selfish, self-centred or self-seeking?**	
Where had (I) been dishonest?**	
Where had (I) been frightened?**	
Where had (I) been (responsible) to blame?**	
What decisions did I make based on self that later placed me in a position to be hurt?*	
When in the past can I remember making this decision?* (Early memory.)	
Where was I wrong?** **What was my part?**	

Ask yourself: ** (AA 67.3) * (AA 62.2)	Putting out of our minds the wrongs others had done, we resolutely looked for our own mistakes... We admitted our wrongs honestly...** Column (4)
Where had (I) been selfish, self-centred or self-seeking?**	
Where had (I) been dishonest?**	
Where had (I) been frightened?**	
Where had (I) been (responsible) to blame?**	
What decisions did I make based on self that later placed me in a position to be hurt?*	
When in the past can I remember making this decision?* (Early memory.)	
Where was I wrong?** **What was my part?**	

Ask yourself: ** (AA 67.3) * (AA 62.2)	Putting out of our minds the wrongs others had done, we resolutely looked for our own mistakes... We admitted our wrongs honestly...** Column (4)
Where had (I) been selfish, self-centred or self-seeking?**	
Where had (I) been dishonest?**	
Where had (I) been frightened?**	
Where had (I) been (responsible) to blame?**	
What decisions did I make based on self that later placed me in a position to be hurt?*	
When in the past can I remember making this decision?* (Early memory.)	
Where was I wrong?** **What was my part?**	

I'm Resentful at or Fear: (1)	The Cause (2)	Affects my: (3) (Check below)
		☐ Self-Esteem ☐ Security ☐ Ambitions ☐ Personal Relations ☐ Sex Relations ☐ Pride/Shame ☐ Fear

List Major "Character Defects" in preparation for STEPS 6 & 7

AMENDS		STEP 8
		☐ Now ☐ Later ☐ Never

I'm Resentful at or Fear: (1)	The Cause (2)	Affects my: (3) (Check below)
		☐ Self-Esteem ☐ Security ☐ Ambitions ☐ Personal Relations ☐ Sex Relations ☐ Pride/Shame ☐ Fear

List Major "Character Defects" in preparation for STEPS 6 & 7

AMENDS		STEP 8
		☐ Now ☐ Later ☐ Never

I'm Resentful at or Fear: (1)	The Cause (2)	Affects my: (3) (Check below)
		☐ Self-Esteem ☐ Security ☐ Ambitions ☐ Personal Relations ☐ Sex Relations ☐ Pride/Shame ☐ Fear

List Major "Character Defects" in preparation for STEPS 6 & 7

AMENDS		STEP 8
		☐ Now ☐ Later ☐ Never

12 STEP WORKBOOK

Ask yourself: ** (AA 67.3) * (AA 62.2)	Putting out of our minds the wrongs others had done, we resolutely looked for our own mistakes... We admitted our wrongs honestly...** Column (4)
Where had (I) been selfish, self-centred or self-seeking?**	
Where had (I) been dishonest?**	
Where had (I) been frightened?**	
Where had (I) been (responsible) to blame?**	
What decisions did I make based on self that later placed me in a position to be hurt?*	
When in the past can I remember making this decision?* (Early memory.)	
Where was I wrong?** **What was my part?**	

Ask yourself: ** (AA 67.3) * (AA 62.2)	Putting out of our minds the wrongs others had done, we resolutely looked for our own mistakes... We admitted our wrongs honestly...** Column (4)
Where had (I) been selfish, self-centred or self-seeking?**	
Where had (I) been dishonest?**	
Where had (I) been frightened?**	
Where had (I) been (responsible) to blame?**	
What decisions did I make based on self that later placed me in a position to be hurt?*	
When in the past can I remember making this decision?* (Early memory.)	
Where was I wrong?** **What was my part?**	

Ask yourself: ** (AA 67.3) * (AA 62.2)	Putting out of our minds the wrongs others had done, we resolutely looked for our own mistakes... We admitted our wrongs honestly...** Column (4)
Where had (I) been selfish, self-centred or self-seeking?**	
Where had (I) been dishonest?**	
Where had (I) been frightened?**	
Where had (I) been (responsible) to blame?**	
What decisions did I make based on self that later placed me in a position to be hurt?*	
When in the past can I remember making this decision?* (Early memory.)	
Where was I wrong?** **What was my part?**	

I'm Resentful at or Fear: (1)	The Cause (2)	Affects my: (3) (Check below)
		☐ Self-Esteem ☐ Security ☐ Ambitions ☐ Personal Relations ☐ Sex Relations ☐ Pride/Shame ☐ Fear

List Major "Character Defects" in preparation for STEPS 6 & 7

AMENDS		STEP 8
		☐ Now ☐ Later ☐ Never

I'm Resentful at or Fear: (1)	The Cause (2)	Affects my: (3) (Check below)
		☐ Self-Esteem ☐ Security ☐ Ambitions ☐ Personal Relations ☐ Sex Relations ☐ Pride/Shame ☐ Fear

List Major "Character Defects" in preparation for STEPS 6 & 7

AMENDS		STEP 8
		☐ Now ☐ Later ☐ Never

I'm Resentful at or Fear: (1)	The Cause (2)	Affects my: (3) (Check below)
		☐ Self-Esteem ☐ Security ☐ Ambitions ☐ Personal Relations ☐ Sex Relations ☐ Pride/Shame ☐ Fear

List Major "Character Defects" in preparation for STEPS 6 & 7

AMENDS		STEP 8
		☐ Now ☐ Later ☐ Never

Ask yourself: ** (AA 67.3) * (AA 62.2)	Putting out of our minds the wrongs others had done, we resolutely looked for our own mistakes... We admitted our wrongs honestly... ** Column (4)
Where had (I) been selfish, self-centred or self-seeking?**	
Where had (I) been dishonest?**	
Where had (I) been frightened?**	
Where had (I) been (responsible) to blame?**	
What decisions did I make based on self that later placed me in a position to be hurt?*	
When in the past can I remember making this decision?* (Early memory.)	
Where was I wrong?** **What was my part?**	

Ask yourself: ** (AA 67.3) * (AA 62.2)	Putting out of our minds the wrongs others had done, we resolutely looked for our own mistakes... We admitted our wrongs honestly... ** Column (4)
Where had (I) been selfish, self-centred or self-seeking?**	
Where had (I) been dishonest?**	
Where had (I) been frightened?**	
Where had (I) been (responsible) to blame?**	
What decisions did I make based on self that later placed me in a position to be hurt?*	
When in the past can I remember making this decision?* (Early memory.)	
Where was I wrong?** **What was my part?**	

Ask yourself: ** (AA 67.3) * (AA 62.2)	Putting out of our minds the wrongs others had done, we resolutely looked for our own mistakes... We admitted our wrongs honestly... ** Column (4)
Where had (I) been selfish, self-centred or self-seeking?**	
Where had (I) been dishonest?**	
Where had (I) been frightened?**	
Where had (I) been (responsible) to blame?**	
What decisions did I make based on self that later placed me in a position to be hurt?*	
When in the past can I remember making this decision?* (Early memory.)	
Where was I wrong?** **What was my part?**	

I'm Resentful at or Fear: (1)	The Cause (2)	Affects my: (3) (Check below)
		☐ Self-Esteem ☐ Security ☐ Ambitions ☐ Personal Relations ☐ Sex Relations ☐ Pride/Shame ☐ Fear

List Major "Character Defects" in preparation for STEPS 6 & 7

AMENDS		STEP 8
		☐ Now ☐ Later ☐ Never

I'm Resentful at or Fear: (1)	The Cause (2)	Affects my: (3) (Check below)
		☐ Self-Esteem ☐ Security ☐ Ambitions ☐ Personal Relations ☐ Sex Relations ☐ Pride/Shame ☐ Fear

List Major "Character Defects" in preparation for STEPS 6 & 7

AMENDS		STEP 8
		☐ Now ☐ Later ☐ Never

I'm Resentful at or Fear: (1)	The Cause (2)	Affects my: (3) (Check below)
		☐ Self-Esteem ☐ Security ☐ Ambitions ☐ Personal Relations ☐ Sex Relations ☐ Pride/Shame ☐ Fear

List Major "Character Defects" in preparation for STEPS 6 & 7

AMENDS		STEP 8
		☐ Now ☐ Later ☐ Never

Ask yourself: ** (AA 67.3) * (AA 62.2)	Putting out of our minds the wrongs others had done, we resolutely looked for our own mistakes... We admitted our wrongs honestly...** Column (4)
Where had (I) been selfish, self-centred or self-seeking?**	
Where had (I) been dishonest?**	
Where had (I) been frightened?**	
Where had (I) been (responsible) to blame?**	
What decisions did I make based on self that later placed me in a position to be hurt?*	
When in the past can I remember making this decision?* (Early memory.)	
Where was I wrong?** **What was my part?**	

Ask yourself: ** (AA 67.3) * (AA 62.2)	Putting out of our minds the wrongs others had done, we resolutely looked for our own mistakes... We admitted our wrongs honestly...** Column (4)
Where had (I) been selfish, self-centred or self-seeking?**	
Where had (I) been dishonest?**	
Where had (I) been frightened?**	
Where had (I) been (responsible) to blame?**	
What decisions did I make based on self that later placed me in a position to be hurt?*	
When in the past can I remember making this decision?* (Early memory.)	
Where was I wrong?** **What was my part?**	

Ask yourself: ** (AA 67.3) * (AA 62.2)	Putting out of our minds the wrongs others had done, we resolutely looked for our own mistakes... We admitted our wrongs honestly...** Column (4)
Where had (I) been selfish, self-centred or self-seeking?**	
Where had (I) been dishonest?**	
Where had (I) been frightened?**	
Where had (I) been (responsible) to blame?**	
What decisions did I make based on self that later placed me in a position to be hurt?*	
When in the past can I remember making this decision?* (Early memory.)	
Where was I wrong?** **What was my part?**	

I'm Resentful at or Fear: (1)	The Cause (2)	Affects my: (3) (Check below)
		☐ Self-Esteem ☐ Security ☐ Ambitions ☐ Personal Relations ☐ Sex Relations ☐ Pride/Shame ☐ Fear

List Major "Character Defects" in preparation for STEPS 6 & 7

AMENDS		STEP 8
		☐ Now ☐ Later ☐ Never

I'm Resentful at or Fear: (1)	The Cause (2)	Affects my: (3) (Check below)
		☐ Self-Esteem ☐ Security ☐ Ambitions ☐ Personal Relations ☐ Sex Relations ☐ Pride/Shame ☐ Fear

List Major "Character Defects" in preparation for STEPS 6 & 7

AMENDS		STEP 8
		☐ Now ☐ Later ☐ Never

I'm Resentful at or Fear: (1)	The Cause (2)	Affects my: (3) (Check below)
		☐ Self-Esteem ☐ Security ☐ Ambitions ☐ Personal Relations ☐ Sex Relations ☐ Pride/Shame ☐ Fear

List Major "Character Defects" in preparation for STEPS 6 & 7

AMENDS		STEP 8
		☐ Now ☐ Later ☐ Never

Ask yourself: ** (AA 67.3) * (AA 62.2)	Putting out of our minds the wrongs others had done, we resolutely looked for our own mistakes… We admitted our wrongs honestly…** Column (4)
Where had (I) been selfish, self-centred or self-seeking?**	
Where had (I) been dishonest?**	
Where had (I) been frightened?**	
Where had (I) been (responsible) to blame?**	
What decisions did I make based on self that later placed me in a position to be hurt?*	
When in the past can I remember making this decision?* (Early memory.)	
Where was I wrong?** **What was my part?**	

Ask yourself: ** (AA 67.3) * (AA 62.2)	Putting out of our minds the wrongs others had done, we resolutely looked for our own mistakes… We admitted our wrongs honestly…** Column (4)
Where had (I) been selfish, self-centred or self-seeking?**	
Where had (I) been dishonest?**	
Where had (I) been frightened?**	
Where had (I) been (responsible) to blame?**	
What decisions did I make based on self that later placed me in a position to be hurt?*	
When in the past can I remember making this decision?* (Early memory.)	
Where was I wrong?** **What was my part?**	

Ask yourself: ** (AA 67.3) * (AA 62.2)	Putting out of our minds the wrongs others had done, we resolutely looked for our own mistakes… We admitted our wrongs honestly…** Column (4)
Where had (I) been selfish, self-centred or self-seeking?**	
Where had (I) been dishonest?**	
Where had (I) been frightened?**	
Where had (I) been (responsible) to blame?**	
What decisions did I make based on self that later placed me in a position to be hurt?*	
When in the past can I remember making this decision?* (Early memory.)	
Where was I wrong?** **What was my part?**	

I'm Resentful at or Fear: (1)	The Cause (2)	Affects my: (3) (Check below)
		☐ Self-Esteem ☐ Security ☐ Ambitions ☐ Personal Relations ☐ Sex Relations ☐ Pride/Shame ☐ Fear

List Major "Character Defects" in preparation for STEPS 6 & 7

AMENDS		STEP 8
		☐ Now ☐ Later ☐ Never

I'm Resentful at or Fear: (1)	The Cause (2)	Affects my: (3) (Check below)
		☐ Self-Esteem ☐ Security ☐ Ambitions ☐ Personal Relations ☐ Sex Relations ☐ Pride/Shame ☐ Fear

List Major "Character Defects" in preparation for STEPS 6 & 7

AMENDS		STEP 8
		☐ Now ☐ Later ☐ Never

I'm Resentful at or Fear: (1)	The Cause (2)	Affects my: (3) (Check below)
		☐ Self-Esteem ☐ Security ☐ Ambitions ☐ Personal Relations ☐ Sex Relations ☐ Pride/Shame ☐ Fear

List Major "Character Defects" in preparation for STEPS 6 & 7

AMENDS		STEP 8
		☐ Now ☐ Later ☐ Never

Ask yourself: ** (AA 67.3) * (AA 62.2)	Putting out of our minds the wrongs others had done, we resolutely looked for our own mistakes... We admitted our wrongs honestly...** Column (4)
Where had (I) been selfish, self-centred or self-seeking?**	
Where had (I) been dishonest?**	
Where had (I) been frightened?**	
Where had (I) been (responsible) to blame?**	
What decisions did I make based on self that later placed me in a position to be hurt?*	
When in the past can I remember making this decision?* (Early memory.)	
Where was I wrong?** **What was my part?**	

Ask yourself: ** (AA 67.3) * (AA 62.2)	Putting out of our minds the wrongs others had done, we resolutely looked for our own mistakes... We admitted our wrongs honestly...** Column (4)
Where had (I) been selfish, self-centred or self-seeking?**	
Where had (I) been dishonest?**	
Where had (I) been frightened?**	
Where had (I) been (responsible) to blame?**	
What decisions did I make based on self that later placed me in a position to be hurt?*	
When in the past can I remember making this decision?* (Early memory.)	
Where was I wrong?** **What was my part?**	

Ask yourself: ** (AA 67.3) * (AA 62.2)	Putting out of our minds the wrongs others had done, we resolutely looked for our own mistakes... We admitted our wrongs honestly...** Column (4)
Where had (I) been selfish, self-centred or self-seeking?**	
Where had (I) been dishonest?**	
Where had (I) been frightened?**	
Where had (I) been (responsible) to blame?**	
What decisions did I make based on self that later placed me in a position to be hurt?*	
When in the past can I remember making this decision?* (Early memory.)	
Where was I wrong?** **What was my part?**	

I'm Resentful at or Fear: (1)	The Cause (2)	Affects my: (3) (Check below)
		☐ Self-Esteem ☐ Security ☐ Ambitions ☐ Personal Relations ☐ Sex Relations ☐ Pride/Shame ☐ Fear

List Major "Character Defects" in preparation for STEPS 6 & 7

AMENDS		STEP 8
		☐ Now ☐ Later ☐ Never

I'm Resentful at or Fear: (1)	The Cause (2)	Affects my: (3) (Check below)
		☐ Self-Esteem ☐ Security ☐ Ambitions ☐ Personal Relations ☐ Sex Relations ☐ Pride/Shame ☐ Fear

List Major "Character Defects" in preparation for STEPS 6 & 7

AMENDS		STEP 8
		☐ Now ☐ Later ☐ Never

I'm Resentful at or Fear: (1)	The Cause (2)	Affects my: (3) (Check below)
		☐ Self-Esteem ☐ Security ☐ Ambitions ☐ Personal Relations ☐ Sex Relations ☐ Pride/Shame ☐ Fear

List Major "Character Defects" in preparation for STEPS 6 & 7

AMENDS		STEP 8
		☐ Now ☐ Later ☐ Never

Ask yourself: ** (AA 67.3) * (AA 62.2)	Putting out of our minds the wrongs others had done, we resolutely looked for our own mistakes... We admitted our wrongs honestly...** Column (4)
Where had (I) been selfish, self-centred or self-seeking?**	
Where had (I) been dishonest?**	
Where had (I) been frightened?**	
Where had (I) been (responsible) to blame?**	
What decisions did I make based on self that later placed me in a position to be hurt?*	
When in the past can I remember making this decision?* (Early memory.)	
Where was I wrong?** **What was my part?**	

Ask yourself: ** (AA 67.3) * (AA 62.2)	Putting out of our minds the wrongs others had done, we resolutely looked for our own mistakes... We admitted our wrongs honestly...** Column (4)
Where had (I) been selfish, self-centred or self-seeking?**	
Where had (I) been dishonest?**	
Where had (I) been frightened?**	
Where had (I) been (responsible) to blame?**	
What decisions did I make based on self that later placed me in a position to be hurt?*	
When in the past can I remember making this decision?* (Early memory.)	
Where was I wrong?** **What was my part?**	

Ask yourself: ** (AA 67.3) * (AA 62.2)	Putting out of our minds the wrongs others had done, we resolutely looked for our own mistakes... We admitted our wrongs honestly...** Column (4)
Where had (I) been selfish, self-centred or self-seeking?**	
Where had (I) been dishonest?**	
Where had (I) been frightened?**	
Where had (I) been (responsible) to blame?**	
What decisions did I make based on self that later placed me in a position to be hurt?*	
When in the past can I remember making this decision?* (Early memory.)	
Where was I wrong?** **What was my part?**	

I'm Resentful at or Fear: (1)	The Cause (2)				Affects my: (3) (Check below)
					❑ Self-Esteem ❑ Security ❑ Ambitions ❑ Personal Relations ❑ Sex Relations ❑ Pride/Shame ❑ Fear
List Major "Character Defects" in preparation for STEPS 6 & 7					
AMENDS				**STEP 8**	
				❑ Now ❑ Later ❑ Never	

I'm Resentful at or Fear: (1)	The Cause (2)				Affects my: (3) (Check below)
					❑ Self-Esteem ❑ Security ❑ Ambitions ❑ Personal Relations ❑ Sex Relations ❑ Pride/Shame ❑ Fear
List Major "Character Defects" in preparation for STEPS 6 & 7					
AMENDS				**STEP 8**	
				❑ Now ❑ Later ❑ Never	

I'm Resentful at or Fear: (1)	The Cause (2)				Affects my: (3) (Check below)
					❑ Self-Esteem ❑ Security ❑ Ambitions ❑ Personal Relations ❑ Sex Relations ❑ Pride/Shame ❑ Fear
List Major "Character Defects" in preparation for STEPS 6 & 7					
AMENDS				**STEP 8**	
				❑ Now ❑ Later ❑ Never	

Ask yourself: ** (AA 67.3) * (AA 62.2)	Putting out of our minds the wrongs others had done, we resolutely looked for our own mistakes... We admitted our wrongs honestly...** Column (4)
Where had (I) been selfish, self-centred or self-seeking?**	
Where had (I) been dishonest?**	
Where had (I) been frightened?**	
Where had (I) been (responsible) to blame?**	
What decisions did I make based on self that later placed me in a position to be hurt?*	
When in the past can I remember making this decision?* (Early memory.)	
Where was I wrong?** **What was my part?**	

Ask yourself: ** (AA 67.3) * (AA 62.2)	Putting out of our minds the wrongs others had done, we resolutely looked for our own mistakes... We admitted our wrongs honestly...** Column (4)
Where had (I) been selfish, self-centred or self-seeking?**	
Where had (I) been dishonest?**	
Where had (I) been frightened?**	
Where had (I) been (responsible) to blame?**	
What decisions did I make based on self that later placed me in a position to be hurt?*	
When in the past can I remember making this decision?* (Early memory.)	
Where was I wrong?** **What was my part?**	

Ask yourself: ** (AA 67.3) * (AA 62.2)	Putting out of our minds the wrongs others had done, we resolutely looked for our own mistakes... We admitted our wrongs honestly...** Column (4)
Where had (I) been selfish, self-centred or self-seeking?**	
Where had (I) been dishonest?**	
Where had (I) been frightened?**	
Where had (I) been (responsible) to blame?**	
What decisions did I make based on self that later placed me in a position to be hurt?*	
When in the past can I remember making this decision?* (Early memory.)	
Where was I wrong?** **What was my part?**	

I'm Resentful at or Fear: (1)	The Cause (2)	Affects my: (3) (Check below)
		❑ Self-Esteem ❑ Security ❑ Ambitions ❑ Personal Relations ❑ Sex Relations ❑ Pride/Shame ❑ Fear

List Major "Character Defects" in preparation for STEPS 6 & 7

AMENDS		STEP 8
		❑ Now ❑ Later ❑ Never

I'm Resentful at or Fear: (1)	The Cause (2)	Affects my: (3) (Check below)
		❑ Self-Esteem ❑ Security ❑ Ambitions ❑ Personal Relations ❑ Sex Relations ❑ Pride/Shame ❑ Fear

List Major "Character Defects" in preparation for STEPS 6 & 7

AMENDS		STEP 8
		❑ Now ❑ Later ❑ Never

I'm Resentful at or Fear: (1)	The Cause (2)	Affects my: (3) (Check below)
		❑ Self-Esteem ❑ Security ❑ Ambitions ❑ Personal Relations ❑ Sex Relations ❑ Pride/Shame ❑ Fear

List Major "Character Defects" in preparation for STEPS 6 & 7

AMENDS		STEP 8
		❑ Now ❑ Later ❑ Never

Ask yourself: ** (AA 67.3) * (AA 62.2)	Putting out of our minds the wrongs others had done, we resolutely looked for our own mistakes… We admitted our wrongs honestly…** Column (4)
Where had (I) been selfish, self-centred or self-seeking?**	
Where had (I) been dishonest?**	
Where had (I) been frightened?**	
Where had (I) been (responsible) to blame?**	
What decisions did I make based on self that later placed me in a position to be hurt?*	
When in the past can I remember making this decision?* (Early memory.)	
Where was I wrong?** **What was my part?**	

Ask yourself: ** (AA 67.3) * (AA 62.2)	Putting out of our minds the wrongs others had done, we resolutely looked for our own mistakes… We admitted our wrongs honestly…** Column (4)
Where had (I) been selfish, self-centred or self-seeking?**	
Where had (I) been dishonest?**	
Where had (I) been frightened?**	
Where had (I) been (responsible) to blame?**	
What decisions did I make based on self that later placed me in a position to be hurt?*	
When in the past can I remember making this decision?* (Early memory.)	
Where was I wrong?** **What was my part?**	

Ask yourself: ** (AA 67.3) * (AA 62.2)	Putting out of our minds the wrongs others had done, we resolutely looked for our own mistakes… We admitted our wrongs honestly…** Column (4)
Where had (I) been selfish, self-centred or self-seeking?**	
Where had (I) been dishonest?**	
Where had (I) been frightened?**	
Where had (I) been (responsible) to blame?**	
What decisions did I make based on self that later placed me in a position to be hurt?*	
When in the past can I remember making this decision?* (Early memory.)	
Where was I wrong?** **What was my part?**	

I'm Resentful at or Fear: (1)	The Cause (2)	Affects my: (3) (Check below)
		❑ Self-Esteem ❑ Security ❑ Ambitions ❑ Personal Relations ❑ Sex Relations ❑ Pride/Shame ❑ Fear

List Major "Character Defects" in preparation for STEPS 6 & 7

AMENDS		STEP 8
		❑ Now ❑ Later ❑ Never

I'm Resentful at or Fear: (1)	The Cause (2)	Affects my: (3) (Check below)
		❑ Self-Esteem ❑ Security ❑ Ambitions ❑ Personal Relations ❑ Sex Relations ❑ Pride/Shame ❑ Fear

List Major "Character Defects" in preparation for STEPS 6 & 7

AMENDS		STEP 8
		❑ Now ❑ Later ❑ Never

I'm Resentful at or Fear: (1)	The Cause (2)	Affects my: (3) (Check below)
		❑ Self-Esteem ❑ Security ❑ Ambitions ❑ Personal Relations ❑ Sex Relations ❑ Pride/Shame ❑ Fear

List Major "Character Defects" in preparation for STEPS 6 & 7

AMENDS		STEP 8
		❑ Now ❑ Later ❑ Never

Ask yourself: ** (AA 67.3) * (AA 62.2)	Putting out of our minds the wrongs others had done, we resolutely looked for our own mistakes... We admitted our wrongs honestly...** Column (4)
Where had (I) been selfish, self-centred or self-seeking?**	
Where had (I) been dishonest?**	
Where had (I) been frightened?**	
Where had (I) been (responsible) to blame?**	
What decisions did I make based on self that later placed me in a position to be hurt?*	
When in the past can I remember making this decision?* (Early memory.)	
Where was I wrong?** **What was my part?**	

Ask yourself: ** (AA 67.3) * (AA 62.2)	Putting out of our minds the wrongs others had done, we resolutely looked for our own mistakes... We admitted our wrongs honestly...** Column (4)
Where had (I) been selfish, self-centred or self-seeking?**	
Where had (I) been dishonest?**	
Where had (I) been frightened?**	
Where had (I) been (responsible) to blame?**	
What decisions did I make based on self that later placed me in a position to be hurt?*	
When in the past can I remember making this decision?* (Early memory.)	
Where was I wrong?** **What was my part?**	

Ask yourself: ** (AA 67.3) * (AA 62.2)	Putting out of our minds the wrongs others had done, we resolutely looked for our own mistakes... We admitted our wrongs honestly...** Column (4)
Where had (I) been selfish, self-centred or self-seeking?**	
Where had (I) been dishonest?**	
Where had (I) been frightened?**	
Where had (I) been (responsible) to blame?**	
What decisions did I make based on self that later placed me in a position to be hurt?*	
When in the past can I remember making this decision?* (Early memory.)	
Where was I wrong?** **What was my part?**	

I'm Resentful at or Fear: (1)	The Cause (2)	Affects my: (3) (Check below)
		☐ Self-Esteem ☐ Security ☐ Ambitions ☐ Personal Relations ☐ Sex Relations ☐ Pride/Shame ☐ Fear

List Major "Character Defects" in preparation for STEPS 6 & 7

AMENDS		STEP 8
		☐ Now ☐ Later ☐ Never

I'm Resentful at or Fear: (1)	The Cause (2)	Affects my: (3) (Check below)
		☐ Self-Esteem ☐ Security ☐ Ambitions ☐ Personal Relations ☐ Sex Relations ☐ Pride/Shame ☐ Fear

List Major "Character Defects" in preparation for STEPS 6 & 7

AMENDS		STEP 8
		☐ Now ☐ Later ☐ Never

I'm Resentful at or Fear: (1)	The Cause (2)	Affects my: (3) (Check below)
		☐ Self-Esteem ☐ Security ☐ Ambitions ☐ Personal Relations ☐ Sex Relations ☐ Pride/Shame ☐ Fear

List Major "Character Defects" in preparation for STEPS 6 & 7

AMENDS		STEP 8
		☐ Now ☐ Later ☐ Never

Ask yourself: ** (AA 67.3) * (AA 62.2)	Putting out of our minds the wrongs others had done, we resolutely looked for our own mistakes... We admitted our wrongs honestly... ** Column (4)
Where had (I) been selfish, self-centred or self-seeking?**	
Where had (I) been dishonest?**	
Where had (I) been frightened?**	
Where had (I) been (responsible) to blame?**	
What decisions did I make based on self that later placed me in a position to be hurt?*	
When in the past can I remember making this decision?* (Early memory.)	
Where was I wrong?** **What was my part?**	

Ask yourself: ** (AA 67.3) * (AA 62.2)	Putting out of our minds the wrongs others had done, we resolutely looked for our own mistakes... We admitted our wrongs honestly... ** Column (4)
Where had (I) been selfish, self-centred or self-seeking?**	
Where had (I) been dishonest?**	
Where had (I) been frightened?**	
Where had (I) been (responsible) to blame?**	
What decisions did I make based on self that later placed me in a position to be hurt?*	
When in the past can I remember making this decision?* (Early memory.)	
Where was I wrong?** **What was my part?**	

Ask yourself: ** (AA 67.3) * (AA 62.2)	Putting out of our minds the wrongs others had done, we resolutely looked for our own mistakes... We admitted our wrongs honestly... ** Column (4)
Where had (I) been selfish, self-centred or self-seeking?**	
Where had (I) been dishonest?**	
Where had (I) been frightened?**	
Where had (I) been (responsible) to blame?**	
What decisions did I make based on self that later placed me in a position to be hurt?*	
When in the past can I remember making this decision?* (Early memory.)	
Where was I wrong?** **What was my part?**	

I'm Resentful at or Fear: (1)	The Cause (2)	Affects my: (3) (Check below)
		❑ Self-Esteem ❑ Security ❑ Ambitions ❑ Personal Relations ❑ Sex Relations ❑ Pride/Shame ❑ Fear

List Major "Character Defects" in preparation for STEPS 6 & 7

AMENDS		STEP 8
		❑ Now ❑ Later ❑ Never

I'm Resentful at or Fear: (1)	The Cause (2)	Affects my: (3) (Check below)
		❑ Self-Esteem ❑ Security ❑ Ambitions ❑ Personal Relations ❑ Sex Relations ❑ Pride/Shame ❑ Fear

List Major "Character Defects" in preparation for STEPS 6 & 7

AMENDS		STEP 8
		❑ Now ❑ Later ❑ Never

I'm Resentful at or Fear: (1)	The Cause (2)	Affects my: (3) (Check below)
		❑ Self-Esteem ❑ Security ❑ Ambitions ❑ Personal Relations ❑ Sex Relations ❑ Pride/Shame ❑ Fear

List Major "Character Defects" in preparation for STEPS 6 & 7

AMENDS		STEP 8
		❑ Now ❑ Later ❑ Never

Ask yourself: ** (AA 67.3) * (AA 62.2)	*Putting out of our minds the wrongs others had done, we resolutely looked for our own mistakes... We admitted our wrongs honestly...** Column (4)*
Where had (I) been selfish, self-centred or self-seeking?**	
Where had (I) been dishonest?**	
Where had (I) been frightened?**	
Where had (I) been (responsible) to blame?**	
What decisions did I make based on self that later placed me in a position to be hurt?*	
When in the past can I remember making this decision?* (Early memory.)	
Where was I wrong?** **What was my part?**	

Ask yourself: ** (AA 67.3) * (AA 62.2)	*Putting out of our minds the wrongs others had done, we resolutely looked for our own mistakes... We admitted our wrongs honestly...** Column (4)*
Where had (I) been selfish, self-centred or self-seeking?**	
Where had (I) been dishonest?**	
Where had (I) been frightened?**	
Where had (I) been (responsible) to blame?**	
What decisions did I make based on self that later placed me in a position to be hurt?*	
When in the past can I remember making this decision?* (Early memory.)	
Where was I wrong?** **What was my part?**	

Ask yourself: ** (AA 67.3) * (AA 62.2)	*Putting out of our minds the wrongs others had done, we resolutely looked for our own mistakes... We admitted our wrongs honestly...** Column (4)*
Where had (I) been selfish, self-centred or self-seeking?**	
Where had (I) been dishonest?**	
Where had (I) been frightened?**	
Where had (I) been (responsible) to blame?**	
What decisions did I make based on self that later placed me in a position to be hurt?*	
When in the past can I remember making this decision?* (Early memory.)	
Where was I wrong?** **What was my part?**	

I'm Resentful at or Fear: (1)	The Cause (2)	Affects my: (3) (Check below)
		❑ Self-Esteem ❑ Security ❑ Ambitions ❑ Personal Relations ❑ Sex Relations ❑ Pride/Shame ❑ Fear

List Major "Character Defects" in preparation for STEPS 6 & 7

AMENDS		STEP 8
		❑ Now ❑ Later ❑ Never

I'm Resentful at or Fear: (1)	The Cause (2)	Affects my: (3) (Check below)
		❑ Self-Esteem ❑ Security ❑ Ambitions ❑ Personal Relations ❑ Sex Relations ❑ Pride/Shame ❑ Fear

List Major "Character Defects" in preparation for STEPS 6 & 7

AMENDS		STEP 8
		❑ Now ❑ Later ❑ Never

I'm Resentful at or Fear: (1)	The Cause (2)	Affects my: (3) (Check below)
		❑ Self-Esteem ❑ Security ❑ Ambitions ❑ Personal Relations ❑ Sex Relations ❑ Pride/Shame ❑ Fear

List Major "Character Defects" in preparation for STEPS 6 & 7

AMENDS		STEP 8
		❑ Now ❑ Later ❑ Never

Ask yourself: ** (AA 67.3) * (AA 62.2)	Putting out of our minds the wrongs others had done, we resolutely looked for our own mistakes... We admitted our wrongs honestly...** Column (4)
Where had (I) been selfish, self-centred or self-seeking?**	
Where had (I) been dishonest?**	
Where had (I) been frightened?**	
Where had (I) been (responsible) to blame?**	
What decisions did I make based on self that later placed me in a position to be hurt?*	
When in the past can I remember making this decision?* (Early memory.)	
Where was I wrong?** **What was my part?**	

Ask yourself: ** (AA 67.3) * (AA 62.2)	Putting out of our minds the wrongs others had done, we resolutely looked for our own mistakes... We admitted our wrongs honestly...** Column (4)
Where had (I) been selfish, self-centred or self-seeking?**	
Where had (I) been dishonest?**	
Where had (I) been frightened?**	
Where had (I) been (responsible) to blame?**	
What decisions did I make based on self that later placed me in a position to be hurt?*	
When in the past can I remember making this decision?* (Early memory.)	
Where was I wrong?** **What was my part?**	

Ask yourself: ** (AA 67.3) * (AA 62.2)	Putting out of our minds the wrongs others had done, we resolutely looked for our own mistakes... We admitted our wrongs honestly...** Column (4)
Where had (I) been selfish, self-centred or self-seeking?**	
Where had (I) been dishonest?**	
Where had (I) been frightened?**	
Where had (I) been (responsible) to blame?**	
What decisions did I make based on self that later placed me in a position to be hurt?*	
When in the past can I remember making this decision?* (Early memory.)	
Where was I wrong?** **What was my part?**	

I'm Resentful at or Fear: (1)	The Cause (2)	Affects my: (3) (Check below)
		☐ Self-Esteem ☐ Security ☐ Ambitions ☐ Personal Relations ☐ Sex Relations ☐ Pride/Shame ☐ Fear

List Major "Character Defects" in preparation for STEPS 6 & 7				

AMENDS		STEP 8
		☐ Now ☐ Later ☐ Never

I'm Resentful at or Fear: (1)	The Cause (2)	Affects my: (3) (Check below)
		☐ Self-Esteem ☐ Security ☐ Ambitions ☐ Personal Relations ☐ Sex Relations ☐ Pride/Shame ☐ Fear

List Major "Character Defects" in preparation for STEPS 6 & 7				

AMENDS		STEP 8
		☐ Now ☐ Later ☐ Never

I'm Resentful at or Fear: (1)	The Cause (2)	Affects my: (3) (Check below)
		☐ Self-Esteem ☐ Security ☐ Ambitions ☐ Personal Relations ☐ Sex Relations ☐ Pride/Shame ☐ Fear

List Major "Character Defects" in preparation for STEPS 6 & 7				

AMENDS		STEP 8
		☐ Now ☐ Later ☐ Never

Ask yourself: ** (AA 67.3) * (AA 62.2)	Putting out of our minds the wrongs others had done, we resolutely looked for our own mistakes... We admitted our wrongs honestly...** Column (4)
Where had (I) been selfish, self-centred or self-seeking?**	
Where had (I) been dishonest?**	
Where had (I) been frightened?**	
Where had (I) been (responsible) to blame?**	
What decisions did I make based on self that later placed me in a position to be hurt?*	
When in the past can I remember making this decision?* (Early memory.)	
Where was I wrong?** **What was my part?**	

Ask yourself: ** (AA 67.3) * (AA 62.2)	Putting out of our minds the wrongs others had done, we resolutely looked for our own mistakes... We admitted our wrongs honestly...** Column (4)
Where had (I) been selfish, self-centred or self-seeking?**	
Where had (I) been dishonest?**	
Where had (I) been frightened?**	
Where had (I) been (responsible) to blame?**	
What decisions did I make based on self that later placed me in a position to be hurt?*	
When in the past can I remember making this decision?* (Early memory.)	
Where was I wrong?** **What was my part?**	

Ask yourself: ** (AA 67.3) * (AA 62.2)	Putting out of our minds the wrongs others had done, we resolutely looked for our own mistakes... We admitted our wrongs honestly...** Column (4)
Where had (I) been selfish, self-centred or self-seeking?**	
Where had (I) been dishonest?**	
Where had (I) been frightened?**	
Where had (I) been (responsible) to blame?**	
What decisions did I make based on self that later placed me in a position to be hurt?*	
When in the past can I remember making this decision?* (Early memory.)	
Where was I wrong?** **What was my part?**	

I'm Resentful at or Fear: (1)	The Cause (2)	Affects my: (3) (Check below)
		☐ Self-Esteem ☐ Security ☐ Ambitions ☐ Personal Relations ☐ Sex Relations ☐ Pride/Shame ☐ Fear

List Major "Character Defects" in preparation for STEPS 6 & 7

AMENDS		STEP 8
		☐ Now ☐ Later ☐ Never

I'm Resentful at or Fear: (1)	The Cause (2)	Affects my: (3) (Check below)
		☐ Self-Esteem ☐ Security ☐ Ambitions ☐ Personal Relations ☐ Sex Relations ☐ Pride/Shame ☐ Fear

List Major "Character Defects" in preparation for STEPS 6 & 7

AMENDS		STEP 8
		☐ Now ☐ Later ☐ Never

I'm Resentful at or Fear: (1)	The Cause (2)	Affects my: (3) (Check below)
		☐ Self-Esteem ☐ Security ☐ Ambitions ☐ Personal Relations ☐ Sex Relations ☐ Pride/Shame ☐ Fear

List Major "Character Defects" in preparation for STEPS 6 & 7

AMENDS		STEP 8
		☐ Now ☐ Later ☐ Never

Ask yourself: ** (AA 67.3) * (AA 62.2)	Putting out of our minds the wrongs others had done, we resolutely looked for our own mistakes... We admitted our wrongs honestly...** Column (4)
Where had (I) been selfish, self-centred or self-seeking?**	
Where had (I) been dishonest?**	
Where had (I) been frightened?**	
Where had (I) been (responsible) to blame?**	
What decisions did I make based on self that later placed me in a position to be hurt?*	
When in the past can I remember making this decision?* (Early memory.)	
Where was I wrong?** **What was my part?**	

Ask yourself: ** (AA 67.3) * (AA 62.2)	Putting out of our minds the wrongs others had done, we resolutely looked for our own mistakes... We admitted our wrongs honestly...** Column (4)
Where had (I) been selfish, self-centred or self-seeking?**	
Where had (I) been dishonest?**	
Where had (I) been frightened?**	
Where had (I) been (responsible) to blame?**	
What decisions did I make based on self that later placed me in a position to be hurt?*	
When in the past can I remember making this decision?* (Early memory.)	
Where was I wrong?** **What was my part?**	

Ask yourself: ** (AA 67.3) * (AA 62.2)	Putting out of our minds the wrongs others had done, we resolutely looked for our own mistakes... We admitted our wrongs honestly...** Column (4)
Where had (I) been selfish, self-centred or self-seeking?**	
Where had (I) been dishonest?**	
Where had (I) been frightened?**	
Where had (I) been (responsible) to blame?**	
What decisions did I make based on self that later placed me in a position to be hurt?*	
When in the past can I remember making this decision?* (Early memory.)	
Where was I wrong?** **What was my part?**	

I'm Resentful at or Fear: (1)	The Cause (2)	Affects my: (3) (Check below)
		❑ Self-Esteem ❑ Security ❑ Ambitions ❑ Personal Relations ❑ Sex Relations ❑ Pride/Shame ❑ Fear

List Major "Character Defects" in preparation for STEPS 6 & 7

AMENDS		STEP 8
		❑ Now ❑ Later ❑ Never

I'm Resentful at or Fear: (1)	The Cause (2)	Affects my: (3) (Check below)
		❑ Self-Esteem ❑ Security ❑ Ambitions ❑ Personal Relations ❑ Sex Relations ❑ Pride/Shame ❑ Fear

List Major "Character Defects" in preparation for STEPS 6 & 7

AMENDS		STEP 8
		❑ Now ❑ Later ❑ Never

I'm Resentful at or Fear: (1)	The Cause (2)	Affects my: (3) (Check below)
		❑ Self-Esteem ❑ Security ❑ Ambitions ❑ Personal Relations ❑ Sex Relations ❑ Pride/Shame ❑ Fear

List Major "Character Defects" in preparation for STEPS 6 & 7

AMENDS		STEP 8
		❑ Now ❑ Later ❑ Never

Ask yourself: ** (AA 67.3) * (AA 62.2)	Putting out of our minds the wrongs others had done, we resolutely looked for our own mistakes... We admitted our wrongs honestly...** Column (4)
Where had (I) been selfish, self-centred or self-seeking?**	
Where had (I) been dishonest?**	
Where had (I) been frightened?**	
Where had (I) been (responsible) to blame?**	
What decisions did I make based on self that later placed me in a position to be hurt?*	
When in the past can I remember making this decision?* (Early memory.)	
Where was I wrong?** **What was my part?**	

Ask yourself: ** (AA 67.3) * (AA 62.2)	Putting out of our minds the wrongs others had done, we resolutely looked for our own mistakes... We admitted our wrongs honestly...** Column (4)
Where had (I) been selfish, self-centred or self-seeking?**	
Where had (I) been dishonest?**	
Where had (I) been frightened?**	
Where had (I) been (responsible) to blame?**	
What decisions did I make based on self that later placed me in a position to be hurt?*	
When in the past can I remember making this decision?* (Early memory.)	
Where was I wrong?** **What was my part?**	

Ask yourself: ** (AA 67.3) * (AA 62.2)	Putting out of our minds the wrongs others had done, we resolutely looked for our own mistakes... We admitted our wrongs honestly...** Column (4)
Where had (I) been selfish, self-centred or self-seeking?**	
Where had (I) been dishonest?**	
Where had (I) been frightened?**	
Where had (I) been (responsible) to blame?**	
What decisions did I make based on self that later placed me in a position to be hurt?*	
When in the past can I remember making this decision?* (Early memory.)	
Where was I wrong?** **What was my part?**	

I'm Resentful at or Fear: (1)	The Cause (2)	Affects my: (3) (Check below)
		☐ Self-Esteem ☐ Security ☐ Ambitions ☐ Personal Relations ☐ Sex Relations ☐ Pride/Shame ☐ Fear

List Major "Character Defects" in preparation for STEPS 6 & 7

AMENDS		STEP 8
		☐ Now ☐ Later ☐ Never

I'm Resentful at or Fear: (1)	The Cause (2)	Affects my: (3) (Check below)
		☐ Self-Esteem ☐ Security ☐ Ambitions ☐ Personal Relations ☐ Sex Relations ☐ Pride/Shame ☐ Fear

List Major "Character Defects" in preparation for STEPS 6 & 7

AMENDS		STEP 8
		☐ Now ☐ Later ☐ Never

I'm Resentful at or Fear: (1)	The Cause (2)	Affects my: (3) (Check below)
		☐ Self-Esteem ☐ Security ☐ Ambitions ☐ Personal Relations ☐ Sex Relations ☐ Pride/Shame ☐ Fear

List Major "Character Defects" in preparation for STEPS 6 & 7

AMENDS		STEP 8
		☐ Now ☐ Later ☐ Never

Ask yourself: ** (AA 67.3) * (AA 62.2)	Putting out of our minds the wrongs others had done, we resolutely looked for our own mistakes... We admitted our wrongs honestly...** Column (4)
Where had (I) been selfish, self-centred or self-seeking?**	
Where had (I) been dishonest?**	
Where had (I) been frightened?**	
Where had (I) been (responsible) to blame?**	
What decisions did I make based on self that later placed me in a position to be hurt?*	
When in the past can I remember making this decision?* (Early memory.)	
Where was I wrong?** **What was my part?**	

Ask yourself: ** (AA 67.3) * (AA 62.2)	Putting out of our minds the wrongs others had done, we resolutely looked for our own mistakes... We admitted our wrongs honestly...** Column (4)
Where had (I) been selfish, self-centred or self-seeking?**	
Where had (I) been dishonest?**	
Where had (I) been frightened?**	
Where had (I) been (responsible) to blame?**	
What decisions did I make based on self that later placed me in a position to be hurt?*	
When in the past can I remember making this decision?* (Early memory.)	
Where was I wrong?** **What was my part?**	

Ask yourself: ** (AA 67.3) * (AA 62.2)	Putting out of our minds the wrongs others had done, we resolutely looked for our own mistakes... We admitted our wrongs honestly...** Column (4)
Where had (I) been selfish, self-centred or self-seeking?**	
Where had (I) been dishonest?**	
Where had (I) been frightened?**	
Where had (I) been (responsible) to blame?**	
What decisions did I make based on self that later placed me in a position to be hurt?*	
When in the past can I remember making this decision?* (Early memory.)	
Where was I wrong?** **What was my part?**	

I'm Resentful at or Fear: (1)	The Cause (2)	Affects my: (3) (Check below)
		❑ Self-Esteem ❑ Security ❑ Ambitions ❑ Personal Relations ❑ Sex Relations ❑ Pride/Shame ❑ Fear

List Major "Character Defects" in preparation for STEPS 6 & 7					

AMENDS		STEP 8
		❑ Now ❑ Later ❑ Never

I'm Resentful at or Fear: (1)	The Cause (2)	Affects my: (3) (Check below)
		❑ Self-Esteem ❑ Security ❑ Ambitions ❑ Personal Relations ❑ Sex Relations ❑ Pride/Shame ❑ Fear

List Major "Character Defects" in preparation for STEPS 6 & 7					

AMENDS		STEP 8
		❑ Now ❑ Later ❑ Never

I'm Resentful at or Fear: (1)	The Cause (2)	Affects my: (3) (Check below)
		❑ Self-Esteem ❑ Security ❑ Ambitions ❑ Personal Relations ❑ Sex Relations ❑ Pride/Shame ❑ Fear

List Major "Character Defects" in preparation for STEPS 6 & 7					

AMENDS		STEP 8
		❑ Now ❑ Later ❑ Never

12 STEP WORKBOOK

Ask yourself: ** (AA 67.3) * (AA 62.2)	Putting out of our minds the wrongs others had done, we resolutely looked for our own mistakes... We admitted our wrongs honestly...** Column (4)
Where had (I) been selfish, self-centred or self-seeking?**	
Where had (I) been dishonest?**	
Where had (I) been frightened?**	
Where had (I) been (responsible) to blame?**	
What decisions did I make based on self that later placed me in a position to be hurt?*	
When in the past can I remember making this decision?* (Early memory.)	
Where was I wrong?** What was my part?	

Ask yourself: ** (AA 67.3) * (AA 62.2)	Putting out of our minds the wrongs others had done, we resolutely looked for our own mistakes... We admitted our wrongs honestly...** Column (4)
Where had (I) been selfish, self-centred or self-seeking?**	
Where had (I) been dishonest?**	
Where had (I) been frightened?**	
Where had (I) been (responsible) to blame?**	
What decisions did I make based on self that later placed me in a position to be hurt?*	
When in the past can I remember making this decision?* (Early memory.)	
Where was I wrong?** What was my part?	

Ask yourself: ** (AA 67.3) * (AA 62.2)	Putting out of our minds the wrongs others had done, we resolutely looked for our own mistakes... We admitted our wrongs honestly...** Column (4)
Where had (I) been selfish, self-centred or self-seeking?**	
Where had (I) been dishonest?**	
Where had (I) been frightened?**	
Where had (I) been (responsible) to blame?**	
What decisions did I make based on self that later placed me in a position to be hurt?*	
When in the past can I remember making this decision?* (Early memory.)	
Where was I wrong?** What was my part?	

I'm Resentful at or Fear: (1)	The Cause (2)	Affects my: (3) (Check below)
		☐ Self-Esteem ☐ Security ☐ Ambitions ☐ Personal Relations ☐ Sex Relations ☐ Pride/Shame ☐ Fear

List Major "Character Defects" in preparation for STEPS 6 & 7

AMENDS		STEP 8
		☐ Now ☐ Later ☐ Never

I'm Resentful at or Fear: (1)	The Cause (2)	Affects my: (3) (Check below)
		☐ Self-Esteem ☐ Security ☐ Ambitions ☐ Personal Relations ☐ Sex Relations ☐ Pride/Shame ☐ Fear

List Major "Character Defects" in preparation for STEPS 6 & 7

AMENDS		STEP 8
		☐ Now ☐ Later ☐ Never

I'm Resentful at or Fear: (1)	The Cause (2)	Affects my: (3) (Check below)
		☐ Self-Esteem ☐ Security ☐ Ambitions ☐ Personal Relations ☐ Sex Relations ☐ Pride/Shame ☐ Fear

List Major "Character Defects" in preparation for STEPS 6 & 7

AMENDS		STEP 8
		☐ Now ☐ Later ☐ Never

12 STEP WORKBOOK

Ask yourself: ** (AA 67.3) * (AA 62.2)	Putting out of our minds the wrongs others had done, we resolutely looked for our own mistakes... We admitted our wrongs honestly...** Column (4)
Where had (I) been selfish, self-centred or self-seeking?**	
Where had (I) been dishonest?**	
Where had (I) been frightened?**	
Where had (I) been (responsible) to blame?**	
What decisions did I make based on self that later placed me in a position to be hurt?*	
When in the past can I remember making this decision?* (Early memory.)	
Where was I wrong?** **What was my part?**	

Ask yourself: ** (AA 67.3) * (AA 62.2)	Putting out of our minds the wrongs others had done, we resolutely looked for our own mistakes... We admitted our wrongs honestly...** Column (4)
Where had (I) been selfish, self-centred or self-seeking?**	
Where had (I) been dishonest?**	
Where had (I) been frightened?**	
Where had (I) been (responsible) to blame?**	
What decisions did I make based on self that later placed me in a position to be hurt?*	
When in the past can I remember making this decision?* (Early memory.)	
Where was I wrong?** **What was my part?**	

Ask yourself: ** (AA 67.3) * (AA 62.2)	Putting out of our minds the wrongs others had done, we resolutely looked for our own mistakes... We admitted our wrongs honestly...** Column (4)
Where had (I) been selfish, self-centred or self-seeking?**	
Where had (I) been dishonest?**	
Where had (I) been frightened?**	
Where had (I) been (responsible) to blame?**	
What decisions did I make based on self that later placed me in a position to be hurt?*	
When in the past can I remember making this decision?* (Early memory.)	
Where was I wrong?** **What was my part?**	

I'm Resentful at or Fear: (1)	The Cause (2)	Affects my: (3) (Check below)
		❑ Self-Esteem ❑ Security ❑ Ambitions ❑ Personal Relations ❑ Sex Relations ❑ Pride/Shame ❑ Fear

List Major "Character Defects" in preparation for STEPS 6 & 7

AMENDS		STEP 8
		❑ Now ❑ Later ❑ Never

I'm Resentful at or Fear: (1)	The Cause (2)	Affects my: (3) (Check below)
		❑ Self-Esteem ❑ Security ❑ Ambitions ❑ Personal Relations ❑ Sex Relations ❑ Pride/Shame ❑ Fear

List Major "Character Defects" in preparation for STEPS 6 & 7

AMENDS		STEP 8
		❑ Now ❑ Later ❑ Never

I'm Resentful at or Fear: (1)	The Cause (2)	Affects my: (3) (Check below)
		❑ Self-Esteem ❑ Security ❑ Ambitions ❑ Personal Relations ❑ Sex Relations ❑ Pride/Shame ❑ Fear

List Major "Character Defects" in preparation for STEPS 6 & 7

AMENDS		STEP 8
		❑ Now ❑ Later ❑ Never

Ask yourself: ** (AA 67.3) * (AA 62.2)	Putting out of our minds the wrongs others had done, we resolutely looked for our own mistakes... We admitted our wrongs honestly...** Column (4)
Where had (I) been selfish, self-centred or self-seeking?**	
Where had (I) been dishonest?**	
Where had (I) been frightened?**	
Where had (I) been (responsible) to blame?**	
What decisions did I make based on self that later placed me in a position to be hurt?*	
When in the past can I remember making this decision?* (Early memory.)	
Where was I wrong?** **What was my part?**	

Ask yourself: ** (AA 67.3) * (AA 62.2)	Putting out of our minds the wrongs others had done, we resolutely looked for our own mistakes... We admitted our wrongs honestly...** Column (4)
Where had (I) been selfish, self-centred or self-seeking?**	
Where had (I) been dishonest?**	
Where had (I) been frightened?**	
Where had (I) been (responsible) to blame?**	
What decisions did I make based on self that later placed me in a position to be hurt?*	
When in the past can I remember making this decision?* (Early memory.)	
Where was I wrong?** **What was my part?**	

Ask yourself: ** (AA 67.3) * (AA 62.2)	Putting out of our minds the wrongs others had done, we resolutely looked for our own mistakes... We admitted our wrongs honestly...** Column (4)
Where had (I) been selfish, self-centred or self-seeking?**	
Where had (I) been dishonest?**	
Where had (I) been frightened?**	
Where had (I) been (responsible) to blame?**	
What decisions did I make based on self that later placed me in a position to be hurt?*	
When in the past can I remember making this decision?* (Early memory.)	
Where was I wrong?** **What was my part?**	

I'm Resentful at or Fear: (1)	The Cause (2)	Affects my: (3) (Check below)
		☐ Self-Esteem ☐ Security ☐ Ambitions ☐ Personal Relations ☐ Sex Relations ☐ Pride/Shame ☐ Fear

List Major "Character Defects" in preparation for STEPS 6 & 7				

AMENDS		STEP 8
		☐ Now ☐ Later ☐ Never

I'm Resentful at or Fear: (1)	The Cause (2)	Affects my: (3) (Check below)
		☐ Self-Esteem ☐ Security ☐ Ambitions ☐ Personal Relations ☐ Sex Relations ☐ Pride/Shame ☐ Fear

List Major "Character Defects" in preparation for STEPS 6 & 7				

AMENDS		STEP 8
		☐ Now ☐ Later ☐ Never

I'm Resentful at or Fear: (1)	The Cause (2)	Affects my: (3) (Check below)
		☐ Self-Esteem ☐ Security ☐ Ambitions ☐ Personal Relations ☐ Sex Relations ☐ Pride/Shame ☐ Fear

List Major "Character Defects" in preparation for STEPS 6 & 7				

AMENDS		STEP 8
		☐ Now ☐ Later ☐ Never

Ask yourself: ** (AA 67.3) * (AA 62.2)	Putting out of our minds the wrongs others had done, we resolutely looked for our own mistakes... We admitted our wrongs honestly...** Column (4)
Where had (I) been selfish, self-centred or self-seeking?**	
Where had (I) been dishonest?**	
Where had (I) been frightened?**	
Where had (I) been (responsible) to blame?**	
What decisions did I make based on self that later placed me in a position to be hurt?*	
When in the past can I remember making this decision?* (Early memory.)	
Where was I wrong?** **What was my part?**	

Ask yourself: ** (AA 67.3) * (AA 62.2)	Putting out of our minds the wrongs others had done, we resolutely looked for our own mistakes... We admitted our wrongs honestly...** Column (4)
Where had (I) been selfish, self-centred or self-seeking?**	
Where had (I) been dishonest?**	
Where had (I) been frightened?**	
Where had (I) been (responsible) to blame?**	
What decisions did I make based on self that later placed me in a position to be hurt?*	
When in the past can I remember making this decision?* (Early memory.)	
Where was I wrong?** **What was my part?**	

Ask yourself: ** (AA 67.3) * (AA 62.2)	Putting out of our minds the wrongs others had done, we resolutely looked for our own mistakes... We admitted our wrongs honestly...** Column (4)
Where had (I) been selfish, self-centred or self-seeking?**	
Where had (I) been dishonest?**	
Where had (I) been frightened?**	
Where had (I) been (responsible) to blame?**	
What decisions did I make based on self that later placed me in a position to be hurt?*	
When in the past can I remember making this decision?* (Early memory.)	
Where was I wrong?** **What was my part?**	

I'm Resentful at or Fear: (1)	The Cause (2)				Affects my: (3) (Check below)
					❑ Self-Esteem ❑ Security ❑ Ambitions ❑ Personal Relations ❑ Sex Relations ❑ Pride/Shame ❑ Fear

List Major "Character Defects" in preparation for STEPS 6 & 7

AMENDS		STEP 8
		❑ Now ❑ Later ❑ Never

I'm Resentful at or Fear: (1)	The Cause (2)				Affects my: (3) (Check below)
					❑ Self-Esteem ❑ Security ❑ Ambitions ❑ Personal Relations ❑ Sex Relations ❑ Pride/Shame ❑ Fear

List Major "Character Defects" in preparation for STEPS 6 & 7

AMENDS		STEP 8
		❑ Now ❑ Later ❑ Never

I'm Resentful at or Fear: (1)	The Cause (2)				Affects my: (3) (Check below)
					❑ Self-Esteem ❑ Security ❑ Ambitions ❑ Personal Relations ❑ Sex Relations ❑ Pride/Shame ❑ Fear

List Major "Character Defects" in preparation for STEPS 6 & 7

AMENDS		STEP 8
		❑ Now ❑ Later ❑ Never

Ask yourself: ** (AA 67.3) * (AA 62.2)	Putting out of our minds the wrongs others had done, we resolutely looked for our own mistakes... We admitted our wrongs honestly... ** Column (4)
Where had (I) been selfish, self-centred or self-seeking?**	
Where had (I) been dishonest?**	
Where had (I) been frightened?**	
Where had (I) been (responsible) to blame?**	
What decisions did I make based on self that later placed me in a position to be hurt?*	
When in the past can I remember making this decision?* (Early memory.)	
Where was I wrong?** **What was my part?**	

Ask yourself: ** (AA 67.3) * (AA 62.2)	Putting out of our minds the wrongs others had done, we resolutely looked for our own mistakes... We admitted our wrongs honestly... ** Column (4)
Where had (I) been selfish, self-centred or self-seeking?**	
Where had (I) been dishonest?**	
Where had (I) been frightened?**	
Where had (I) been (responsible) to blame?**	
What decisions did I make based on self that later placed me in a position to be hurt?*	
When in the past can I remember making this decision?* (Early memory.)	
Where was I wrong?** **What was my part?**	

Ask yourself: ** (AA 67.3) * (AA 62.2)	Putting out of our minds the wrongs others had done, we resolutely looked for our own mistakes... We admitted our wrongs honestly... ** Column (4)
Where had (I) been selfish, self-centred or self-seeking?**	
Where had (I) been dishonest?**	
Where had (I) been frightened?**	
Where had (I) been (responsible) to blame?**	
What decisions did I make based on self that later placed me in a position to be hurt?*	
When in the past can I remember making this decision?* (Early memory.)	
Where was I wrong?** **What was my part?**	

I'm Resentful at or Fear: (1)	The Cause (2)	Affects my: (3) (Check below)
		☐ Self-Esteem ☐ Security ☐ Ambitions ☐ Personal Relations ☐ Sex Relations ☐ Pride/Shame ☐ Fear

List Major "Character Defects" in preparation for STEPS 6 & 7

AMENDS		STEP 8
		☐ Now ☐ Later ☐ Never

I'm Resentful at or Fear: (1)	The Cause (2)	Affects my: (3) (Check below)
		☐ Self-Esteem ☐ Security ☐ Ambitions ☐ Personal Relations ☐ Sex Relations ☐ Pride/Shame ☐ Fear

List Major "Character Defects" in preparation for STEPS 6 & 7

AMENDS		STEP 8
		☐ Now ☐ Later ☐ Never

I'm Resentful at or Fear: (1)	The Cause (2)	Affects my: (3) (Check below)
		☐ Self-Esteem ☐ Security ☐ Ambitions ☐ Personal Relations ☐ Sex Relations ☐ Pride/Shame ☐ Fear

List Major "Character Defects" in preparation for STEPS 6 & 7

AMENDS		STEP 8
		☐ Now ☐ Later ☐ Never

Ask yourself: ** (AA 67.3) * (AA 62.2)	Putting out of our minds the wrongs others had done, we resolutely looked for our own mistakes... We admitted our wrongs honestly...** Column (4)
Where had (I) been selfish, self-centred or self-seeking?**	
Where had (I) been dishonest?**	
Where had (I) been frightened?**	
Where had (I) been (responsible) to blame?**	
What decisions did I make based on self that later placed me in a position to be hurt?*	
When in the past can I remember making this decision?* (Early memory.)	
Where was I wrong?** **What was my part?**	

Ask yourself: ** (AA 67.3) * (AA 62.2)	Putting out of our minds the wrongs others had done, we resolutely looked for our own mistakes... We admitted our wrongs honestly...** Column (4)
Where had (I) been selfish, self-centred or self-seeking?**	
Where had (I) been dishonest?**	
Where had (I) been frightened?**	
Where had (I) been (responsible) to blame?**	
What decisions did I make based on self that later placed me in a position to be hurt?*	
When in the past can I remember making this decision?* (Early memory.)	
Where was I wrong?** **What was my part?**	

Ask yourself: ** (AA 67.3) * (AA 62.2)	Putting out of our minds the wrongs others had done, we resolutely looked for our own mistakes... We admitted our wrongs honestly...** Column (4)
Where had (I) been selfish, self-centred or self-seeking?**	
Where had (I) been dishonest?**	
Where had (I) been frightened?**	
Where had (I) been (responsible) to blame?**	
What decisions did I make based on self that later placed me in a position to be hurt?*	
When in the past can I remember making this decision?* (Early memory.)	
Where was I wrong?** **What was my part?**	

I'm Resentful at or Fear: (1)	The Cause (2)		Affects my: (3) (Check below)
			❑ Self-Esteem ❑ Security ❑ Ambitions ❑ Personal Relations ❑ Sex Relations ❑ Pride/Shame ❑ Fear

List Major "Character Defects" in preparation for STEPS 6 & 7				

AMENDS		STEP 8
		❑ Now ❑ Later ❑ Never

I'm Resentful at or Fear: (1)	The Cause (2)		Affects my: (3) (Check below)
			❑ Self-Esteem ❑ Security ❑ Ambitions ❑ Personal Relations ❑ Sex Relations ❑ Pride/Shame ❑ Fear

List Major "Character Defects" in preparation for STEPS 6 & 7				

AMENDS		STEP 8
		❑ Now ❑ Later ❑ Never

I'm Resentful at or Fear: (1)	The Cause (2)		Affects my: (3) (Check below)
			❑ Self-Esteem ❑ Security ❑ Ambitions ❑ Personal Relations ❑ Sex Relations ❑ Pride/Shame ❑ Fear

List Major "Character Defects" in preparation for STEPS 6 & 7				

AMENDS		STEP 8
		❑ Now ❑ Later ❑ Never

12 STEP WORKBOOK

Ask yourself: ** (AA 67.3) * (AA 62.2)	Putting out of our minds the wrongs others had done, we resolutely looked for our own mistakes... We admitted our wrongs honestly...** Column (4)
Where had (I) been selfish, self-centred or self-seeking?**	
Where had (I) been dishonest?**	
Where had (I) been frightened?**	
Where had (I) been (responsible) to blame?**	
What decisions did I make based on self that later placed me in a position to be hurt?*	
When in the past can I remember making this decision?* (Early memory.)	
Where was I wrong?** What was my part?	

Ask yourself: ** (AA 67.3) * (AA 62.2)	Putting out of our minds the wrongs others had done, we resolutely looked for our own mistakes... We admitted our wrongs honestly...** Column (4)
Where had (I) been selfish, self-centred or self-seeking?**	
Where had (I) been dishonest?**	
Where had (I) been frightened?**	
Where had (I) been (responsible) to blame?**	
What decisions did I make based on self that later placed me in a position to be hurt?*	
When in the past can I remember making this decision?* (Early memory.)	
Where was I wrong?** What was my part?	

Ask yourself: ** (AA 67.3) * (AA 62.2)	Putting out of our minds the wrongs others had done, we resolutely looked for our own mistakes... We admitted our wrongs honestly...** Column (4)
Where had (I) been selfish, self-centred or self-seeking?**	
Where had (I) been dishonest?**	
Where had (I) been frightened?**	
Where had (I) been (responsible) to blame?**	
What decisions did I make based on self that later placed me in a position to be hurt?*	
When in the past can I remember making this decision?* (Early memory.)	
Where was I wrong?** What was my part?	

I'm Resentful at or Fear: (1)	The Cause (2)	Affects my: (3) (Check below)
		☐ Self-Esteem ☐ Security ☐ Ambitions ☐ Personal Relations ☐ Sex Relations ☐ Pride/Shame ☐ Fear

List Major "Character Defects" in preparation for STEPS 6 & 7

AMENDS		STEP 8
		☐ Now ☐ Later ☐ Never

I'm Resentful at or Fear: (1)	The Cause (2)	Affects my: (3) (Check below)
		☐ Self-Esteem ☐ Security ☐ Ambitions ☐ Personal Relations ☐ Sex Relations ☐ Pride/Shame ☐ Fear

List Major "Character Defects" in preparation for STEPS 6 & 7

AMENDS		STEP 8
		☐ Now ☐ Later ☐ Never

I'm Resentful at or Fear: (1)	The Cause (2)	Affects my: (3) (Check below)
		☐ Self-Esteem ☐ Security ☐ Ambitions ☐ Personal Relations ☐ Sex Relations ☐ Pride/Shame ☐ Fear

List Major "Character Defects" in preparation for STEPS 6 & 7

AMENDS		STEP 8
		☐ Now ☐ Later ☐ Never

Ask yourself: ** (AA 67.3) * (AA 62.2)	Putting out of our minds the wrongs others had done, we resolutely looked for our own mistakes... We admitted our wrongs honestly...** Column (4)
Where had (I) been selfish, self-centred or self-seeking?**	
Where had (I) been dishonest?**	
Where had (I) been frightened?**	
Where had (I) been (responsible) to blame?**	
What decisions did I make based on self that later placed me in a position to be hurt?*	
When in the past can I remember making this decision?* (Early memory.)	
Where was I wrong?** **What was my part?**	

Ask yourself: ** (AA 67.3) * (AA 62.2)	Putting out of our minds the wrongs others had done, we resolutely looked for our own mistakes... We admitted our wrongs honestly...** Column (4)
Where had (I) been selfish, self-centred or self-seeking?**	
Where had (I) been dishonest?**	
Where had (I) been frightened?**	
Where had (I) been (responsible) to blame?**	
What decisions did I make based on self that later placed me in a position to be hurt?*	
When in the past can I remember making this decision?* (Early memory.)	
Where was I wrong?** **What was my part?**	

Ask yourself: ** (AA 67.3) * (AA 62.2)	Putting out of our minds the wrongs others had done, we resolutely looked for our own mistakes... We admitted our wrongs honestly...** Column (4)
Where had (I) been selfish, self-centred or self-seeking?**	
Where had (I) been dishonest?**	
Where had (I) been frightened?**	
Where had (I) been (responsible) to blame?**	
What decisions did I make based on self that later placed me in a position to be hurt?*	
When in the past can I remember making this decision?* (Early memory.)	
Where was I wrong?** **What was my part?**	

I'm Resentful at or Fear: (1)	The Cause (2)	Affects my: (3) (Check below)
		☐ Self-Esteem ☐ Security ☐ Ambitions ☐ Personal Relations ☐ Sex Relations ☐ Pride/Shame ☐ Fear

List Major "Character Defects" in preparation for STEPS 6 & 7

AMENDS		STEP 8
		☐ Now ☐ Later ☐ Never

I'm Resentful at or Fear: (1)	The Cause (2)	Affects my: (3) (Check below)
		☐ Self-Esteem ☐ Security ☐ Ambitions ☐ Personal Relations ☐ Sex Relations ☐ Pride/Shame ☐ Fear

List Major "Character Defects" in preparation for STEPS 6 & 7

AMENDS		STEP 8
		☐ Now ☐ Later ☐ Never

I'm Resentful at or Fear: (1)	The Cause (2)	Affects my: (3) (Check below)
		☐ Self-Esteem ☐ Security ☐ Ambitions ☐ Personal Relations ☐ Sex Relations ☐ Pride/Shame ☐ Fear

List Major "Character Defects" in preparation for STEPS 6 & 7

AMENDS		STEP 8
		☐ Now ☐ Later ☐ Never

Ask yourself: ** (AA 67.3) * (AA 62.2)	Putting out of our minds the wrongs others had done, we resolutely looked for our own mistakes... We admitted our wrongs honestly...** Column (4)
Where had (I) been selfish, self-centred or self-seeking?**	
Where had (I) been dishonest?**	
Where had (I) been frightened?**	
Where had (I) been (responsible) to blame?**	
What decisions did I make based on self that later placed me in a position to be hurt?*	
When in the past can I remember making this decision?* (Early memory.)	
Where was I wrong?** What was my part?	

Ask yourself: ** (AA 67.3) * (AA 62.2)	Putting out of our minds the wrongs others had done, we resolutely looked for our own mistakes... We admitted our wrongs honestly...** Column (4)
Where had (I) been selfish, self-centred or self-seeking?**	
Where had (I) been dishonest?**	
Where had (I) been frightened?**	
Where had (I) been (responsible) to blame?**	
What decisions did I make based on self that later placed me in a position to be hurt?*	
When in the past can I remember making this decision?* (Early memory.)	
Where was I wrong?** What was my part?	

Ask yourself: ** (AA 67.3) * (AA 62.2)	Putting out of our minds the wrongs others had done, we resolutely looked for our own mistakes... We admitted our wrongs honestly...** Column (4)
Where had (I) been selfish, self-centred or self-seeking?**	
Where had (I) been dishonest?**	
Where had (I) been frightened?**	
Where had (I) been (responsible) to blame?**	
What decisions did I make based on self that later placed me in a position to be hurt?*	
When in the past can I remember making this decision?* (Early memory.)	
Where was I wrong?** What was my part?	

I'm Resentful at or Fear: (1)	The Cause (2)	Affects my: (3) (Check below)
		❑ Self-Esteem ❑ Security ❑ Ambitions ❑ Personal Relations ❑ Sex Relations ❑ Pride/Shame ❑ Fear

List Major "Character Defects" in preparation for STEPS 6 & 7

AMENDS		STEP 8
		❑ Now ❑ Later ❑ Never

I'm Resentful at or Fear: (1)	The Cause (2)	Affects my: (3) (Check below)
		❑ Self-Esteem ❑ Security ❑ Ambitions ❑ Personal Relations ❑ Sex Relations ❑ Pride/Shame ❑ Fear

List Major "Character Defects" in preparation for STEPS 6 & 7

AMENDS		STEP 8
		❑ Now ❑ Later ❑ Never

I'm Resentful at or Fear: (1)	The Cause (2)	Affects my: (3) (Check below)
		❑ Self-Esteem ❑ Security ❑ Ambitions ❑ Personal Relations ❑ Sex Relations ❑ Pride/Shame ❑ Fear

List Major "Character Defects" in preparation for STEPS 6 & 7

AMENDS		STEP 8
		❑ Now ❑ Later ❑ Never

Ask yourself: ** (AA 67.3) * (AA 62.2)	Putting out of our minds the wrongs others had done, we resolutely looked for our own mistakes... We admitted our wrongs honestly...** Column (4)
Where had (I) been selfish, self-centred or self-seeking?**	
Where had (I) been dishonest?**	
Where had (I) been frightened?**	
Where had (I) been (responsible) to blame?**	
What decisions did I make based on self that later placed me in a position to be hurt?*	
When in the past can I remember making this decision?* (Early memory.)	
Where was I wrong?** **What was my part?**	

Ask yourself: ** (AA 67.3) * (AA 62.2)	Putting out of our minds the wrongs others had done, we resolutely looked for our own mistakes... We admitted our wrongs honestly...** Column (4)
Where had (I) been selfish, self-centred or self-seeking?**	
Where had (I) been dishonest?**	
Where had (I) been frightened?**	
Where had (I) been (responsible) to blame?**	
What decisions did I make based on self that later placed me in a position to be hurt?*	
When in the past can I remember making this decision?* (Early memory.)	
Where was I wrong?** **What was my part?**	

Ask yourself: ** (AA 67.3) * (AA 62.2)	Putting out of our minds the wrongs others had done, we resolutely looked for our own mistakes... We admitted our wrongs honestly...** Column (4)
Where had (I) been selfish, self-centred or self-seeking?**	
Where had (I) been dishonest?**	
Where had (I) been frightened?**	
Where had (I) been (responsible) to blame?**	
What decisions did I make based on self that later placed me in a position to be hurt?*	
When in the past can I remember making this decision?* (Early memory.)	
Where was I wrong?** **What was my part?**	

I'm Resentful at or Fear: (1)	The Cause (2)	Affects my: (3) (Check below)
		☐ Self-Esteem ☐ Security ☐ Ambitions ☐ Personal Relations ☐ Sex Relations ☐ Pride/Shame ☐ Fear

List Major "Character Defects" in preparation for STEPS 6 & 7

AMENDS		STEP 8
		☐ Now ☐ Later ☐ Never

I'm Resentful at or Fear: (1)	The Cause (2)	Affects my: (3) (Check below)
		☐ Self-Esteem ☐ Security ☐ Ambitions ☐ Personal Relations ☐ Sex Relations ☐ Pride/Shame ☐ Fear

List Major "Character Defects" in preparation for STEPS 6 & 7

AMENDS		STEP 8
		☐ Now ☐ Later ☐ Never

I'm Resentful at or Fear: (1)	The Cause (2)	Affects my: (3) (Check below)
		☐ Self-Esteem ☐ Security ☐ Ambitions ☐ Personal Relations ☐ Sex Relations ☐ Pride/Shame ☐ Fear

List Major "Character Defects" in preparation for STEPS 6 & 7

AMENDS		STEP 8
		☐ Now ☐ Later ☐ Never

Ask yourself: ** (AA 67.3) * (AA 62.2)	Putting out of our minds the wrongs others had done, we resolutely looked for our own mistakes... We admitted our wrongs honestly...** Column (4)
Where had (I) been selfish, self-centred or self-seeking?**	
Where had (I) been dishonest?**	
Where had (I) been frightened?**	
Where had (I) been (responsible) to blame?**	
What decisions did I make based on self that later placed me in a position to be hurt?*	
When in the past can I remember making this decision?* (Early memory.)	
Where was I wrong?** **What was my part?**	

Ask yourself: ** (AA 67.3) * (AA 62.2)	Putting out of our minds the wrongs others had done, we resolutely looked for our own mistakes... We admitted our wrongs honestly...** Column (4)
Where had (I) been selfish, self-centred or self-seeking?**	
Where had (I) been dishonest?**	
Where had (I) been frightened?**	
Where had (I) been (responsible) to blame?**	
What decisions did I make based on self that later placed me in a position to be hurt?*	
When in the past can I remember making this decision?* (Early memory.)	
Where was I wrong?** **What was my part?**	

Ask yourself: ** (AA 67.3) * (AA 62.2)	Putting out of our minds the wrongs others had done, we resolutely looked for our own mistakes... We admitted our wrongs honestly...** Column (4)
Where had (I) been selfish, self-centred or self-seeking?**	
Where had (I) been dishonest?**	
Where had (I) been frightened?**	
Where had (I) been (responsible) to blame?**	
What decisions did I make based on self that later placed me in a position to be hurt?*	
When in the past can I remember making this decision?* (Early memory.)	
Where was I wrong?** **What was my part?**	

Block 1

I'm Resentful at or Fear: (1)	The Cause (2)	Affects my: (3) (Check below)
		☐ Self-Esteem ☐ Security ☐ Ambitions ☐ Personal Relations ☐ Sex Relations ☐ Pride/Shame ☐ Fear

List Major "Character Defects" in preparation for STEPS 6 & 7

AMENDS		STEP 8
		☐ Now ☐ Later ☐ Never

Block 2

I'm Resentful at or Fear: (1)	The Cause (2)	Affects my: (3) (Check below)
		☐ Self-Esteem ☐ Security ☐ Ambitions ☐ Personal Relations ☐ Sex Relations ☐ Pride/Shame ☐ Fear

List Major "Character Defects" in preparation for STEPS 6 & 7

AMENDS		STEP 8
		☐ Now ☐ Later ☐ Never

Block 3

I'm Resentful at or Fear: (1)	The Cause (2)	Affects my: (3) (Check below)
		☐ Self-Esteem ☐ Security ☐ Ambitions ☐ Personal Relations ☐ Sex Relations ☐ Pride/Shame ☐ Fear

List Major "Character Defects" in preparation for STEPS 6 & 7

AMENDS		STEP 8
		☐ Now ☐ Later ☐ Never

12 STEP WORKBOOK

Ask yourself: ** (AA 67.3) * (AA 62.2)	Putting out of our minds the wrongs others had done, we resolutely looked for our own mistakes... We admitted our wrongs honestly...** Column (4)
Where had (I) been selfish, self-centred or self-seeking?**	
Where had (I) been dishonest?**	
Where had (I) been frightened?**	
Where had (I) been (responsible) to blame?**	
What decisions did I make based on self that later placed me in a position to be hurt?*	
When in the past can I remember making this decision?* (Early memory.)	
Where was I wrong?** **What was my part?**	

Ask yourself: ** (AA 67.3) * (AA 62.2)	Putting out of our minds the wrongs others had done, we resolutely looked for our own mistakes... We admitted our wrongs honestly...** Column (4)
Where had (I) been selfish, self-centred or self-seeking?**	
Where had (I) been dishonest?**	
Where had (I) been frightened?**	
Where had (I) been (responsible) to blame?**	
What decisions did I make based on self that later placed me in a position to be hurt?*	
When in the past can I remember making this decision?* (Early memory.)	
Where was I wrong?** **What was my part?**	

Ask yourself: ** (AA 67.3) * (AA 62.2)	Putting out of our minds the wrongs others had done, we resolutely looked for our own mistakes... We admitted our wrongs honestly...** Column (4)
Where had (I) been selfish, self-centred or self-seeking?**	
Where had (I) been dishonest?**	
Where had (I) been frightened?**	
Where had (I) been (responsible) to blame?**	
What decisions did I make based on self that later placed me in a position to be hurt?*	
When in the past can I remember making this decision?* (Early memory.)	
Where was I wrong?** **What was my part?**	

I'm Resentful at or Fear: (1)	The Cause (2)	Affects my: (3) (Check below)

Affects my: (3) (Check below)
- ☐ Self-Esteem
- ☐ Security
- ☐ Ambitions
- ☐ Personal Relations
- ☐ Sex Relations
- ☐ Pride/Shame
- ☐ Fear

List Major "Character Defects" in preparation for STEPS 6 & 7

AMENDS

STEP 8
- ☐ Now
- ☐ Later
- ☐ Never

I'm Resentful at or Fear: (1)	The Cause (2)	Affects my: (3) (Check below)

Affects my: (3) (Check below)
- ☐ Self-Esteem
- ☐ Security
- ☐ Ambitions
- ☐ Personal Relations
- ☐ Sex Relations
- ☐ Pride/Shame
- ☐ Fear

List Major "Character Defects" in preparation for STEPS 6 & 7

AMENDS

STEP 8
- ☐ Now
- ☐ Later
- ☐ Never

I'm Resentful at or Fear: (1)	The Cause (2)	Affects my: (3) (Check below)

Affects my: (3) (Check below)
- ☐ Self-Esteem
- ☐ Security
- ☐ Ambitions
- ☐ Personal Relations
- ☐ Sex Relations
- ☐ Pride/Shame
- ☐ Fear

List Major "Character Defects" in preparation for STEPS 6 & 7

AMENDS

STEP 8
- ☐ Now
- ☐ Later
- ☐ Never

Ask yourself: ** (AA 67.3) * (AA 62.2)	Putting out of our minds the wrongs others had done, we resolutely looked for our own mistakes... We admitted our wrongs honestly...** Column (4)
Where had (I) been selfish, self-centred or self-seeking?**	
Where had (I) been dishonest?**	
Where had (I) been frightened?**	
Where had (I) been (responsible) to blame?**	
What decisions did I make based on self that later placed me in a position to be hurt?*	
When in the past can I remember making this decision?* (Early memory.)	
Where was I wrong?** **What was my part?**	

Ask yourself: ** (AA 67.3) * (AA 62.2)	Putting out of our minds the wrongs others had done, we resolutely looked for our own mistakes... We admitted our wrongs honestly...** Column (4)
Where had (I) been selfish, self-centred or self-seeking?**	
Where had (I) been dishonest?**	
Where had (I) been frightened?**	
Where had (I) been (responsible) to blame?**	
What decisions did I make based on self that later placed me in a position to be hurt?*	
When in the past can I remember making this decision?* (Early memory.)	
Where was I wrong?** **What was my part?**	

Ask yourself: ** (AA 67.3) * (AA 62.2)	Putting out of our minds the wrongs others had done, we resolutely looked for our own mistakes... We admitted our wrongs honestly...** Column (4)
Where had (I) been selfish, self-centred or self-seeking?**	
Where had (I) been dishonest?**	
Where had (I) been frightened?**	
Where had (I) been (responsible) to blame?**	
What decisions did I make based on self that later placed me in a position to be hurt?*	
When in the past can I remember making this decision?* (Early memory.)	
Where was I wrong?** **What was my part?**	

I'm Resentful at or Fear: (1)	The Cause (2)	Affects my: (3) (Check below)
		☐ Self-Esteem ☐ Security ☐ Ambitions ☐ Personal Relations ☐ Sex Relations ☐ Pride/Shame ☐ Fear

List Major "Character Defects" in preparation for STEPS 6 & 7

AMENDS		STEP 8
		☐ Now ☐ Later ☐ Never

I'm Resentful at or Fear: (1)	The Cause (2)	Affects my: (3) (Check below)
		☐ Self-Esteem ☐ Security ☐ Ambitions ☐ Personal Relations ☐ Sex Relations ☐ Pride/Shame ☐ Fear

List Major "Character Defects" in preparation for STEPS 6 & 7

AMENDS		STEP 8
		☐ Now ☐ Later ☐ Never

I'm Resentful at or Fear: (1)	The Cause (2)	Affects my: (3) (Check below)
		☐ Self-Esteem ☐ Security ☐ Ambitions ☐ Personal Relations ☐ Sex Relations ☐ Pride/Shame ☐ Fear

List Major "Character Defects" in preparation for STEPS 6 & 7

AMENDS		STEP 8
		☐ Now ☐ Later ☐ Never

12 STEP WORKBOOK

Ask yourself: ** (AA 67.3) * (AA 62.2)	Putting out of our minds the wrongs others had done, we resolutely looked for our own mistakes... We admitted our wrongs honestly...** Column (4)
Where had (I) been selfish, self-centred or self-seeking?**	
Where had (I) been dishonest?**	
Where had (I) been frightened?**	
Where had (I) been (responsible) to blame?**	
What decisions did I make based on self that later placed me in a position to be hurt?*	
When in the past can I remember making this decision?* (Early memory.)	
Where was I wrong?** **What was my part?**	

Ask yourself: ** (AA 67.3) * (AA 62.2)	Putting out of our minds the wrongs others had done, we resolutely looked for our own mistakes... We admitted our wrongs honestly...** Column (4)
Where had (I) been selfish, self-centred or self-seeking?**	
Where had (I) been dishonest?**	
Where had (I) been frightened?**	
Where had (I) been (responsible) to blame?**	
What decisions did I make based on self that later placed me in a position to be hurt?*	
When in the past can I remember making this decision?* (Early memory.)	
Where was I wrong?** **What was my part?**	

Ask yourself: ** (AA 67.3) * (AA 62.2)	Putting out of our minds the wrongs others had done, we resolutely looked for our own mistakes... We admitted our wrongs honestly...** Column (4)
Where had (I) been selfish, self-centred or self-seeking?**	
Where had (I) been dishonest?**	
Where had (I) been frightened?**	
Where had (I) been (responsible) to blame?**	
What decisions did I make based on self that later placed me in a position to be hurt?*	
When in the past can I remember making this decision?* (Early memory.)	
Where was I wrong?** **What was my part?**	

I'm Resentful at or Fear: (1)	The Cause (2)	Affects my: (3) (Check below)
		☐ Self-Esteem ☐ Security ☐ Ambitions ☐ Personal Relations ☐ Sex Relations ☐ Pride/Shame ☐ Fear

List Major "Character Defects" in preparation for STEPS 6 & 7

AMENDS		STEP 8
		☐ Now ☐ Later ☐ Never

I'm Resentful at or Fear: (1)	The Cause (2)	Affects my: (3) (Check below)
		☐ Self-Esteem ☐ Security ☐ Ambitions ☐ Personal Relations ☐ Sex Relations ☐ Pride/Shame ☐ Fear

List Major "Character Defects" in preparation for STEPS 6 & 7

AMENDS		STEP 8
		☐ Now ☐ Later ☐ Never

I'm Resentful at or Fear: (1)	The Cause (2)	Affects my: (3) (Check below)
		☐ Self-Esteem ☐ Security ☐ Ambitions ☐ Personal Relations ☐ Sex Relations ☐ Pride/Shame ☐ Fear

List Major "Character Defects" in preparation for STEPS 6 & 7

AMENDS		STEP 8
		☐ Now ☐ Later ☐ Never

Ask yourself: ** (AA 67.3) * (AA 62.2)	Putting out of our minds the wrongs others had done, we resolutely looked for our own mistakes... We admitted our wrongs honestly...** Column (4)
Where had (I) been selfish, self-centred or self-seeking?**	
Where had (I) been dishonest?**	
Where had (I) been frightened?**	
Where had (I) been (responsible) to blame?**	
What decisions did I make based on self that later placed me in a position to be hurt?*	
When in the past can I remember making this decision?* (Early memory.)	
Where was I wrong?** What was my part?	

Ask yourself: ** (AA 67.3) * (AA 62.2)	Putting out of our minds the wrongs others had done, we resolutely looked for our own mistakes... We admitted our wrongs honestly...** Column (4)
Where had (I) been selfish, self-centred or self-seeking?**	
Where had (I) been dishonest?**	
Where had (I) been frightened?**	
Where had (I) been (responsible) to blame?**	
What decisions did I make based on self that later placed me in a position to be hurt?*	
When in the past can I remember making this decision?* (Early memory.)	
Where was I wrong?** What was my part?	

Ask yourself: ** (AA 67.3) * (AA 62.2)	Putting out of our minds the wrongs others had done, we resolutely looked for our own mistakes... We admitted our wrongs honestly...** Column (4)
Where had (I) been selfish, self-centred or self-seeking?**	
Where had (I) been dishonest?**	
Where had (I) been frightened?**	
Where had (I) been (responsible) to blame?**	
What decisions did I make based on self that later placed me in a position to be hurt?*	
When in the past can I remember making this decision?* (Early memory.)	
Where was I wrong?** What was my part?	

I'm Resentful at or Fear: (1)	The Cause (2)	Affects my: (3) (Check below)
		☐ Self-Esteem ☐ Security ☐ Ambitions ☐ Personal Relations ☐ Sex Relations ☐ Pride/Shame ☐ Fear

List Major "Character Defects" in preparation for STEPS 6 & 7

AMENDS		STEP 8
		☐ Now ☐ Later ☐ Never

I'm Resentful at or Fear: (1)	The Cause (2)	Affects my: (3) (Check below)
		☐ Self-Esteem ☐ Security ☐ Ambitions ☐ Personal Relations ☐ Sex Relations ☐ Pride/Shame ☐ Fear

List Major "Character Defects" in preparation for STEPS 6 & 7

AMENDS		STEP 8
		☐ Now ☐ Later ☐ Never

I'm Resentful at or Fear: (1)	The Cause (2)	Affects my: (3) (Check below)
		☐ Self-Esteem ☐ Security ☐ Ambitions ☐ Personal Relations ☐ Sex Relations ☐ Pride/Shame ☐ Fear

List Major "Character Defects" in preparation for STEPS 6 & 7

AMENDS		STEP 8
		☐ Now ☐ Later ☐ Never

Ask yourself: ** (AA 67.3) * (AA 62.2)	Putting out of our minds the wrongs others had done, we resolutely looked for our own mistakes... We admitted our wrongs honestly...** Column (4)
Where had (I) been selfish, self-centred or self-seeking?**	
Where had (I) been dishonest?**	
Where had (I) been frightened?**	
Where had (I) been (responsible) to blame?**	
What decisions did I make based on self that later placed me in a position to be hurt?*	
When in the past can I remember making this decision?* (Early memory.)	
Where was I wrong?** **What was my part?**	

Ask yourself: ** (AA 67.3) * (AA 62.2)	Putting out of our minds the wrongs others had done, we resolutely looked for our own mistakes... We admitted our wrongs honestly...** Column (4)
Where had (I) been selfish, self-centred or self-seeking?**	
Where had (I) been dishonest?**	
Where had (I) been frightened?**	
Where had (I) been (responsible) to blame?**	
What decisions did I make based on self that later placed me in a position to be hurt?*	
When in the past can I remember making this decision?* (Early memory.)	
Where was I wrong?** **What was my part?**	

Ask yourself: ** (AA 67.3) * (AA 62.2)	Putting out of our minds the wrongs others had done, we resolutely looked for our own mistakes... We admitted our wrongs honestly...** Column (4)
Where had (I) been selfish, self-centred or self-seeking?**	
Where had (I) been dishonest?**	
Where had (I) been frightened?**	
Where had (I) been (responsible) to blame?**	
What decisions did I make based on self that later placed me in a position to be hurt?*	
When in the past can I remember making this decision?* (Early memory.)	
Where was I wrong?** **What was my part?**	

I'm Resentful at or Fear: (1)	The Cause (2)	Affects my: (3) (Check below)
		☐ Self-Esteem ☐ Security ☐ Ambitions ☐ Personal Relations ☐ Sex Relations ☐ Pride/Shame ☐ Fear

List Major "Character Defects" in preparation for STEPS 6 & 7

AMENDS		STEP 8
		☐ Now ☐ Later ☐ Never

I'm Resentful at or Fear: (1)	The Cause (2)	Affects my: (3) (Check below)
		☐ Self-Esteem ☐ Security ☐ Ambitions ☐ Personal Relations ☐ Sex Relations ☐ Pride/Shame ☐ Fear

List Major "Character Defects" in preparation for STEPS 6 & 7

AMENDS		STEP 8
		☐ Now ☐ Later ☐ Never

I'm Resentful at or Fear: (1)	The Cause (2)	Affects my: (3) (Check below)
		☐ Self-Esteem ☐ Security ☐ Ambitions ☐ Personal Relations ☐ Sex Relations ☐ Pride/Shame ☐ Fear

List Major "Character Defects" in preparation for STEPS 6 & 7

AMENDS		STEP 8
		☐ Now ☐ Later ☐ Never

12 STEP WORKBOOK

Ask yourself: ** (AA 67.3) * (AA 62.2)	Putting out of our minds the wrongs others had done, we resolutely looked for our own mistakes... We admitted our wrongs honestly...** Column (4)
Where had (I) been selfish, self-centred or self-seeking?**	
Where had (I) been dishonest?**	
Where had (I) been frightened?**	
Where had (I) been (responsible) to blame?**	
What decisions did I make based on self that later placed me in a position to be hurt?*	
When in the past can I remember making this decision?* (Early memory.)	
Where was I wrong?** What was my part?	

Ask yourself: ** (AA 67.3) * (AA 62.2)	Putting out of our minds the wrongs others had done, we resolutely looked for our own mistakes... We admitted our wrongs honestly...** Column (4)
Where had (I) been selfish, self-centred or self-seeking?**	
Where had (I) been dishonest?**	
Where had (I) been frightened?**	
Where had (I) been (responsible) to blame?**	
What decisions did I make based on self that later placed me in a position to be hurt?*	
When in the past can I remember making this decision?* (Early memory.)	
Where was I wrong?** What was my part?	

Ask yourself: ** (AA 67.3) * (AA 62.2)	Putting out of our minds the wrongs others had done, we resolutely looked for our own mistakes... We admitted our wrongs honestly...** Column (4)
Where had (I) been selfish, self-centred or self-seeking?**	
Where had (I) been dishonest?**	
Where had (I) been frightened?**	
Where had (I) been (responsible) to blame?**	
What decisions did I make based on self that later placed me in a position to be hurt?*	
When in the past can I remember making this decision?* (Early memory.)	
Where was I wrong?** What was my part?	

I'm Resentful at or Fear: (1)	The Cause (2)	Affects my: (3) (Check below)
		❑ Self-Esteem ❑ Security ❑ Ambitions ❑ Personal Relations ❑ Sex Relations ❑ Pride/Shame ❑ Fear

List Major "Character Defects" in preparation for STEPS 6 & 7

AMENDS		STEP 8
		❑ Now ❑ Later ❑ Never

I'm Resentful at or Fear: (1)	The Cause (2)	Affects my: (3) (Check below)
		❑ Self-Esteem ❑ Security ❑ Ambitions ❑ Personal Relations ❑ Sex Relations ❑ Pride/Shame ❑ Fear

List Major "Character Defects" in preparation for STEPS 6 & 7

AMENDS		STEP 8
		❑ Now ❑ Later ❑ Never

I'm Resentful at or Fear: (1)	The Cause (2)	Affects my: (3) (Check below)
		❑ Self-Esteem ❑ Security ❑ Ambitions ❑ Personal Relations ❑ Sex Relations ❑ Pride/Shame ❑ Fear

List Major "Character Defects" in preparation for STEPS 6 & 7

AMENDS		STEP 8
		❑ Now ❑ Later ❑ Never

Ask yourself: ** (AA 67.3) * (AA 62.2)	Putting out of our minds the wrongs others had done, we resolutely looked for our own mistakes... We admitted our wrongs honestly... ** Column (4)
Where had (I) been selfish, self-centred or self-seeking?**	
Where had (I) been dishonest?**	
Where had (I) been frightened?**	
Where had (I) been (responsible) to blame?**	
What decisions did I make based on self that later placed me in a position to be hurt?*	
When in the past can I remember making this decision?* (Early memory.)	
Where was I wrong?** What was my part?	

Ask yourself: ** (AA 67.3) * (AA 62.2)	Putting out of our minds the wrongs others had done, we resolutely looked for our own mistakes... We admitted our wrongs honestly... ** Column (4)
Where had (I) been selfish, self-centred or self-seeking?**	
Where had (I) been dishonest?**	
Where had (I) been frightened?**	
Where had (I) been (responsible) to blame?**	
What decisions did I make based on self that later placed me in a position to be hurt?*	
When in the past can I remember making this decision?* (Early memory.)	
Where was I wrong?** What was my part?	

Ask yourself: ** (AA 67.3) * (AA 62.2)	Putting out of our minds the wrongs others had done, we resolutely looked for our own mistakes... We admitted our wrongs honestly... ** Column (4)
Where had (I) been selfish, self-centred or self-seeking?**	
Where had (I) been dishonest?**	
Where had (I) been frightened?**	
Where had (I) been (responsible) to blame?**	
What decisions did I make based on self that later placed me in a position to be hurt?*	
When in the past can I remember making this decision?* (Early memory.)	
Where was I wrong?** What was my part?	

I'm Resentful at or Fear: (1)	The Cause (2)	Affects my: (3) (Check below)
		☐ Self-Esteem ☐ Security ☐ Ambitions ☐ Personal Relations ☐ Sex Relations ☐ Pride/Shame ☐ Fear

List Major "Character Defects" in preparation for STEPS 6 & 7

AMENDS		STEP 8
		☐ Now ☐ Later ☐ Never

I'm Resentful at or Fear: (1)	The Cause (2)	Affects my: (3) (Check below)
		☐ Self-Esteem ☐ Security ☐ Ambitions ☐ Personal Relations ☐ Sex Relations ☐ Pride/Shame ☐ Fear

List Major "Character Defects" in preparation for STEPS 6 & 7

AMENDS		STEP 8
		☐ Now ☐ Later ☐ Never

I'm Resentful at or Fear: (1)	The Cause (2)	Affects my: (3) (Check below)
		☐ Self-Esteem ☐ Security ☐ Ambitions ☐ Personal Relations ☐ Sex Relations ☐ Pride/Shame ☐ Fear

List Major "Character Defects" in preparation for STEPS 6 & 7

AMENDS		STEP 8
		☐ Now ☐ Later ☐ Never

Ask yourself: ** (AA 67.3) * (AA 62.2)	Putting out of our minds the wrongs others had done, we resolutely looked for our own mistakes... We admitted our wrongs honestly...** Column (4)
Where had (I) been selfish, self-centred or self-seeking?**	
Where had (I) been dishonest?**	
Where had (I) been frightened?**	
Where had (I) been (responsible) to blame?**	
What decisions did I make based on self that later placed me in a position to be hurt?*	
When in the past can I remember making this decision?* (Early memory.)	
Where was I wrong?** **What was my part?**	

Ask yourself: ** (AA 67.3) * (AA 62.2)	Putting out of our minds the wrongs others had done, we resolutely looked for our own mistakes... We admitted our wrongs honestly...** Column (4)
Where had (I) been selfish, self-centred or self-seeking?**	
Where had (I) been dishonest?**	
Where had (I) been frightened?**	
Where had (I) been (responsible) to blame?**	
What decisions did I make based on self that later placed me in a position to be hurt?*	
When in the past can I remember making this decision?* (Early memory.)	
Where was I wrong?** **What was my part?**	

Ask yourself: ** (AA 67.3) * (AA 62.2)	Putting out of our minds the wrongs others had done, we resolutely looked for our own mistakes... We admitted our wrongs honestly...** Column (4)
Where had (I) been selfish, self-centred or self-seeking?**	
Where had (I) been dishonest?**	
Where had (I) been frightened?**	
Where had (I) been (responsible) to blame?**	
What decisions did I make based on self that later placed me in a position to be hurt?*	
When in the past can I remember making this decision?* (Early memory.)	
Where was I wrong?** **What was my part?**	

I'm Resentful at or Fear: (1)	The Cause (2)	Affects my: (3) (Check below)
		☐ Self-Esteem ☐ Security ☐ Ambitions ☐ Personal Relations ☐ Sex Relations ☐ Pride/Shame ☐ Fear

List Major "Character Defects" in preparation for STEPS 6 & 7

AMENDS		STEP 8
		☐ Now ☐ Later ☐ Never

I'm Resentful at or Fear: (1)	The Cause (2)	Affects my: (3) (Check below)
		☐ Self-Esteem ☐ Security ☐ Ambitions ☐ Personal Relations ☐ Sex Relations ☐ Pride/Shame ☐ Fear

List Major "Character Defects" in preparation for STEPS 6 & 7

AMENDS		STEP 8
		☐ Now ☐ Later ☐ Never

I'm Resentful at or Fear: (1)	The Cause (2)	Affects my: (3) (Check below)
		☐ Self-Esteem ☐ Security ☐ Ambitions ☐ Personal Relations ☐ Sex Relations ☐ Pride/Shame ☐ Fear

List Major "Character Defects" in preparation for STEPS 6 & 7

AMENDS		STEP 8
		☐ Now ☐ Later ☐ Never

Ask yourself: ** (AA 67.3) * (AA 62.2)	Putting out of our minds the wrongs others had done, we resolutely looked for our own mistakes... We admitted our wrongs honestly...** Column (4)
Where had (I) been selfish, self-centred or self-seeking?**	
Where had (I) been dishonest?**	
Where had (I) been frightened?**	
Where had (I) been (responsible) to blame?**	
What decisions did I make based on self that later placed me in a position to be hurt?*	
When in the past can I remember making this decision?* (Early memory.)	
Where was I wrong?** **What was my part?**	

Ask yourself: ** (AA 67.3) * (AA 62.2)	Putting out of our minds the wrongs others had done, we resolutely looked for our own mistakes... We admitted our wrongs honestly...** Column (4)
Where had (I) been selfish, self-centred or self-seeking?**	
Where had (I) been dishonest?**	
Where had (I) been frightened?**	
Where had (I) been (responsible) to blame?**	
What decisions did I make based on self that later placed me in a position to be hurt?*	
When in the past can I remember making this decision?* (Early memory.)	
Where was I wrong?** **What was my part?**	

Ask yourself: ** (AA 67.3) * (AA 62.2)	Putting out of our minds the wrongs others had done, we resolutely looked for our own mistakes... We admitted our wrongs honestly...** Column (4)
Where had (I) been selfish, self-centred or self-seeking?**	
Where had (I) been dishonest?**	
Where had (I) been frightened?**	
Where had (I) been (responsible) to blame?**	
What decisions did I make based on self that later placed me in a position to be hurt?*	
When in the past can I remember making this decision?* (Early memory.)	
Where was I wrong?** **What was my part?**	

I'm Resentful at or Fear: (1)	The Cause (2)	Affects my: (3) (Check below)
		❑ Self-Esteem ❑ Security ❑ Ambitions ❑ Personal Relations ❑ Sex Relations ❑ Pride/Shame ❑ Fear

List Major "Character Defects" in preparation for STEPS 6 & 7

AMENDS		STEP 8
		❑ Now ❑ Later ❑ Never

I'm Resentful at or Fear: (1)	The Cause (2)	Affects my: (3) (Check below)
		❑ Self-Esteem ❑ Security ❑ Ambitions ❑ Personal Relations ❑ Sex Relations ❑ Pride/Shame ❑ Fear

List Major "Character Defects" in preparation for STEPS 6 & 7

AMENDS		STEP 8
		❑ Now ❑ Later ❑ Never

I'm Resentful at or Fear: (1)	The Cause (2)	Affects my: (3) (Check below)
		❑ Self-Esteem ❑ Security ❑ Ambitions ❑ Personal Relations ❑ Sex Relations ❑ Pride/Shame ❑ Fear

List Major "Character Defects" in preparation for STEPS 6 & 7

AMENDS		STEP 8
		❑ Now ❑ Later ❑ Never

Ask yourself: ** (AA 67.3) * (AA 62.2)	Putting out of our minds the wrongs others had done, we resolutely looked for our own mistakes... We admitted our wrongs honestly...** Column (4)
Where had (I) been selfish, self-centred or self-seeking?**	
Where had (I) been dishonest?**	
Where had (I) been frightened?**	
Where had (I) been (responsible) to blame?**	
What decisions did I make based on self that later placed me in a position to be hurt?*	
When in the past can I remember making this decision?* (Early memory.)	
Where was I wrong?** **What was my part?**	

Ask yourself: ** (AA 67.3) * (AA 62.2)	Putting out of our minds the wrongs others had done, we resolutely looked for our own mistakes... We admitted our wrongs honestly...** Column (4)
Where had (I) been selfish, self-centred or self-seeking?**	
Where had (I) been dishonest?**	
Where had (I) been frightened?**	
Where had (I) been (responsible) to blame?**	
What decisions did I make based on self that later placed me in a position to be hurt?*	
When in the past can I remember making this decision?* (Early memory.)	
Where was I wrong?** **What was my part?**	

Ask yourself: ** (AA 67.3) * (AA 62.2)	Putting out of our minds the wrongs others had done, we resolutely looked for our own mistakes... We admitted our wrongs honestly...** Column (4)
Where had (I) been selfish, self-centred or self-seeking?**	
Where had (I) been dishonest?**	
Where had (I) been frightened?**	
Where had (I) been (responsible) to blame?**	
What decisions did I make based on self that later placed me in a position to be hurt?*	
When in the past can I remember making this decision?* (Early memory.)	
Where was I wrong?** **What was my part?**	

I'm Resentful at or Fear: (1)	The Cause (2)	Affects my: (3) (Check below)
		☐ Self-Esteem ☐ Security ☐ Ambitions ☐ Personal Relations ☐ Sex Relations ☐ Pride/Shame ☐ Fear

List Major "Character Defects" in preparation for STEPS 6 & 7

AMENDS		STEP 8
		☐ Now ☐ Later ☐ Never

I'm Resentful at or Fear: (1)	The Cause (2)	Affects my: (3) (Check below)
		☐ Self-Esteem ☐ Security ☐ Ambitions ☐ Personal Relations ☐ Sex Relations ☐ Pride/Shame ☐ Fear

List Major "Character Defects" in preparation for STEPS 6 & 7

AMENDS		STEP 8
		☐ Now ☐ Later ☐ Never

I'm Resentful at or Fear: (1)	The Cause (2)	Affects my: (3) (Check below)
		☐ Self-Esteem ☐ Security ☐ Ambitions ☐ Personal Relations ☐ Sex Relations ☐ Pride/Shame ☐ Fear

List Major "Character Defects" in preparation for STEPS 6 & 7

AMENDS		STEP 8
		☐ Now ☐ Later ☐ Never

Ask yourself: ** (AA 67.3) * (AA 62.2)	Putting out of our minds the wrongs others had done, we resolutely looked for our own mistakes... We admitted our wrongs honestly...** Column (4)
Where had (I) been selfish, self-centred or self-seeking?**	
Where had (I) been dishonest?**	
Where had (I) been frightened?**	
Where had (I) been (responsible) to blame?**	
What decisions did I make based on self that later placed me in a position to be hurt?*	
When in the past can I remember making this decision?* (Early memory.)	
Where was I wrong?** **What was my part?**	

Ask yourself: ** (AA 67.3) * (AA 62.2)	Putting out of our minds the wrongs others had done, we resolutely looked for our own mistakes... We admitted our wrongs honestly...** Column (4)
Where had (I) been selfish, self-centred or self-seeking?**	
Where had (I) been dishonest?**	
Where had (I) been frightened?**	
Where had (I) been (responsible) to blame?**	
What decisions did I make based on self that later placed me in a position to be hurt?*	
When in the past can I remember making this decision?* (Early memory.)	
Where was I wrong?** **What was my part?**	

Ask yourself: ** (AA 67.3) * (AA 62.2)	Putting out of our minds the wrongs others had done, we resolutely looked for our own mistakes... We admitted our wrongs honestly...** Column (4)
Where had (I) been selfish, self-centred or self-seeking?**	
Where had (I) been dishonest?**	
Where had (I) been frightened?**	
Where had (I) been (responsible) to blame?**	
What decisions did I make based on self that later placed me in a position to be hurt?*	
When in the past can I remember making this decision?* (Early memory.)	
Where was I wrong?** **What was my part?**	

I'm Resentful at or Fear: (1)	The Cause (2)	Affects my: (3) (Check below)
		❑ Self-Esteem ❑ Security ❑ Ambitions ❑ Personal Relations ❑ Sex Relations ❑ Pride/Shame ❑ Fear

List Major "Character Defects" in preparation for STEPS 6 & 7

AMENDS		STEP 8
		❑ Now ❑ Later ❑ Never

I'm Resentful at or Fear: (1)	The Cause (2)	Affects my: (3) (Check below)
		❑ Self-Esteem ❑ Security ❑ Ambitions ❑ Personal Relations ❑ Sex Relations ❑ Pride/Shame ❑ Fear

List Major "Character Defects" in preparation for STEPS 6 & 7

AMENDS		STEP 8
		❑ Now ❑ Later ❑ Never

I'm Resentful at or Fear: (1)	The Cause (2)	Affects my: (3) (Check below)
		❑ Self-Esteem ❑ Security ❑ Ambitions ❑ Personal Relations ❑ Sex Relations ❑ Pride/Shame ❑ Fear

List Major "Character Defects" in preparation for STEPS 6 & 7

AMENDS		STEP 8
		❑ Now ❑ Later ❑ Never

Ask yourself: ** (AA 67.3) * (AA 62.2)	*Putting out of our minds the wrongs others had done, we resolutely looked for our own mistakes... We admitted our wrongs honestly...** Column (4)
Where had (I) been selfish, self-centred or self-seeking?**	
Where had (I) been dishonest?**	
Where had (I) been frightened?**	
Where had (I) been (responsible) to blame?**	
What decisions did I make based on self that later placed me in a position to be hurt?*	
When in the past can I remember making this decision?* (Early memory.)	
Where was I wrong?** **What was my part?**	

Ask yourself: ** (AA 67.3) * (AA 62.2)	*Putting out of our minds the wrongs others had done, we resolutely looked for our own mistakes... We admitted our wrongs honestly...** Column (4)
Where had (I) been selfish, self-centred or self-seeking?**	
Where had (I) been dishonest?**	
Where had (I) been frightened?**	
Where had (I) been (responsible) to blame?**	
What decisions did I make based on self that later placed me in a position to be hurt?*	
When in the past can I remember making this decision?* (Early memory.)	
Where was I wrong?** **What was my part?**	

Ask yourself: ** (AA 67.3) * (AA 62.2)	*Putting out of our minds the wrongs others had done, we resolutely looked for our own mistakes... We admitted our wrongs honestly...** Column (4)
Where had (I) been selfish, self-centred or self-seeking?**	
Where had (I) been dishonest?**	
Where had (I) been frightened?**	
Where had (I) been (responsible) to blame?**	
What decisions did I make based on self that later placed me in a position to be hurt?*	
When in the past can I remember making this decision?* (Early memory.)	
Where was I wrong?** **What was my part?**	

I'm Resentful at or Fear: (1)	The Cause (2)	Affects my: (3) (Check below)
		❑ Self-Esteem ❑ Security ❑ Ambitions ❑ Personal Relations ❑ Sex Relations ❑ Pride/Shame ❑ Fear

List Major "Character Defects" in preparation for STEPS 6 & 7

AMENDS		STEP 8
		❑ Now ❑ Later ❑ Never

I'm Resentful at or Fear: (1)	The Cause (2)	Affects my: (3) (Check below)
		❑ Self-Esteem ❑ Security ❑ Ambitions ❑ Personal Relations ❑ Sex Relations ❑ Pride/Shame ❑ Fear

List Major "Character Defects" in preparation for STEPS 6 & 7

AMENDS		STEP 8
		❑ Now ❑ Later ❑ Never

I'm Resentful at or Fear: (1)	The Cause (2)	Affects my: (3) (Check below)
		❑ Self-Esteem ❑ Security ❑ Ambitions ❑ Personal Relations ❑ Sex Relations ❑ Pride/Shame ❑ Fear

List Major "Character Defects" in preparation for STEPS 6 & 7

AMENDS		STEP 8
		❑ Now ❑ Later ❑ Never

12 STEP WORKBOOK

Ask yourself: ** (AA 67.3) * (AA 62.2)	Putting out of our minds the wrongs others had done, we resolutely looked for our own mistakes... We admitted our wrongs honestly...** Column (4)
Where had (I) been selfish, self-centred or self-seeking?**	
Where had (I) been dishonest?**	
Where had (I) been frightened?**	
Where had (I) been (responsible) to blame?**	
What decisions did I make based on self that later placed me in a position to be hurt?*	
When in the past can I remember making this decision?* (Early memory.)	
Where was I wrong?** **What was my part?**	

Ask yourself: ** (AA 67.3) * (AA 62.2)	Putting out of our minds the wrongs others had done, we resolutely looked for our own mistakes... We admitted our wrongs honestly...** Column (4)
Where had (I) been selfish, self-centred or self-seeking?**	
Where had (I) been dishonest?**	
Where had (I) been frightened?**	
Where had (I) been (responsible) to blame?**	
What decisions did I make based on self that later placed me in a position to be hurt?*	
When in the past can I remember making this decision?* (Early memory.)	
Where was I wrong?** **What was my part?**	

Ask yourself: ** (AA 67.3) * (AA 62.2)	Putting out of our minds the wrongs others had done, we resolutely looked for our own mistakes... We admitted our wrongs honestly...** Column (4)
Where had (I) been selfish, self-centred or self-seeking?**	
Where had (I) been dishonest?**	
Where had (I) been frightened?**	
Where had (I) been (responsible) to blame?**	
What decisions did I make based on self that later placed me in a position to be hurt?*	
When in the past can I remember making this decision?* (Early memory.)	
Where was I wrong?** **What was my part?**	

I'm Resentful at or Fear: (1)	The Cause (2)	Affects my: (3) (Check below)
		❑ Self-Esteem ❑ Security ❑ Ambitions ❑ Personal Relations ❑ Sex Relations ❑ Pride/Shame ❑ Fear

List Major "Character Defects" in preparation for STEPS 6 & 7

AMENDS		STEP 8
		❑ Now ❑ Later ❑ Never

I'm Resentful at or Fear: (1)	The Cause (2)	Affects my: (3) (Check below)
		❑ Self-Esteem ❑ Security ❑ Ambitions ❑ Personal Relations ❑ Sex Relations ❑ Pride/Shame ❑ Fear

List Major "Character Defects" in preparation for STEPS 6 & 7

AMENDS		STEP 8
		❑ Now ❑ Later ❑ Never

I'm Resentful at or Fear: (1)	The Cause (2)	Affects my: (3) (Check below)
		❑ Self-Esteem ❑ Security ❑ Ambitions ❑ Personal Relations ❑ Sex Relations ❑ Pride/Shame ❑ Fear

List Major "Character Defects" in preparation for STEPS 6 & 7

AMENDS		STEP 8
		❑ Now ❑ Later ❑ Never

Ask yourself: ** (AA 67.3) * (AA 62.2)	Putting out of our minds the wrongs others had done, we resolutely looked for our own mistakes... We admitted our wrongs honestly...** Column (4)
Where had (I) been selfish, self-centred or self-seeking?**	
Where had (I) been dishonest?**	
Where had (I) been frightened?**	
Where had (I) been (responsible) to blame?**	
What decisions did I make based on self that later placed me in a position to be hurt?*	
When in the past can I remember making this decision?* (Early memory.)	
Where was I wrong?** **What was my part?**	

Ask yourself: ** (AA 67.3) * (AA 62.2)	Putting out of our minds the wrongs others had done, we resolutely looked for our own mistakes... We admitted our wrongs honestly...** Column (4)
Where had (I) been selfish, self-centred or self-seeking?**	
Where had (I) been dishonest?**	
Where had (I) been frightened?**	
Where had (I) been (responsible) to blame?**	
What decisions did I make based on self that later placed me in a position to be hurt?*	
When in the past can I remember making this decision?* (Early memory.)	
Where was I wrong?** **What was my part?**	

Ask yourself: ** (AA 67.3) * (AA 62.2)	Putting out of our minds the wrongs others had done, we resolutely looked for our own mistakes... We admitted our wrongs honestly...** Column (4)
Where had (I) been selfish, self-centred or self-seeking?**	
Where had (I) been dishonest?**	
Where had (I) been frightened?**	
Where had (I) been (responsible) to blame?**	
What decisions did I make based on self that later placed me in a position to be hurt?*	
When in the past can I remember making this decision?* (Early memory.)	
Where was I wrong?** **What was my part?**	

I'm Resentful at or Fear: (1)	The Cause (2)	Affects my: (3) (Check below)
		☐ Self-Esteem ☐ Security ☐ Ambitions ☐ Personal Relations ☐ Sex Relations ☐ Pride/Shame ☐ Fear

List Major "Character Defects" in preparation for STEPS 6 & 7

AMENDS		STEP 8
		☐ Now ☐ Later ☐ Never

I'm Resentful at or Fear: (1)	The Cause (2)	Affects my: (3) (Check below)
		☐ Self-Esteem ☐ Security ☐ Ambitions ☐ Personal Relations ☐ Sex Relations ☐ Pride/Shame ☐ Fear

List Major "Character Defects" in preparation for STEPS 6 & 7

AMENDS		STEP 8
		☐ Now ☐ Later ☐ Never

I'm Resentful at or Fear: (1)	The Cause (2)	Affects my: (3) (Check below)
		☐ Self-Esteem ☐ Security ☐ Ambitions ☐ Personal Relations ☐ Sex Relations ☐ Pride/Shame ☐ Fear

List Major "Character Defects" in preparation for STEPS 6 & 7

AMENDS		STEP 8
		☐ Now ☐ Later ☐ Never

Ask yourself: ** (AA 67.3) * (AA 62.2)	Putting out of our minds the wrongs others had done, we resolutely looked for our own mistakes... We admitted our wrongs honestly...** Column (4)
Where had (I) been selfish, self-centred or self-seeking?**	
Where had (I) been dishonest?**	
Where had (I) been frightened?**	
Where had (I) been (responsible) to blame?**	
What decisions did I make based on self that later placed me in a position to be hurt?*	
When in the past can I remember making this decision?* (Early memory.)	
Where was I wrong?** **What was my part?**	

Ask yourself: ** (AA 67.3) * (AA 62.2)	Putting out of our minds the wrongs others had done, we resolutely looked for our own mistakes... We admitted our wrongs honestly...** Column (4)
Where had (I) been selfish, self-centred or self-seeking?**	
Where had (I) been dishonest?**	
Where had (I) been frightened?**	
Where had (I) been (responsible) to blame?**	
What decisions did I make based on self that later placed me in a position to be hurt?*	
When in the past can I remember making this decision?* (Early memory.)	
Where was I wrong?** **What was my part?**	

Ask yourself: ** (AA 67.3) * (AA 62.2)	Putting out of our minds the wrongs others had done, we resolutely looked for our own mistakes... We admitted our wrongs honestly...** Column (4)
Where had (I) been selfish, self-centred or self-seeking?**	
Where had (I) been dishonest?**	
Where had (I) been frightened?**	
Where had (I) been (responsible) to blame?**	
What decisions did I make based on self that later placed me in a position to be hurt?*	
When in the past can I remember making this decision?* (Early memory.)	
Where was I wrong?** **What was my part?**	

I'm Resentful at or Fear: (1)	The Cause (2)	Affects my: (3) (Check below)
		☐ Self-Esteem ☐ Security ☐ Ambitions ☐ Personal Relations ☐ Sex Relations ☐ Pride/Shame ☐ Fear

List Major "Character Defects" in preparation for STEPS 6 & 7

AMENDS		STEP 8
		☐ Now ☐ Later ☐ Never

I'm Resentful at or Fear: (1)	The Cause (2)	Affects my: (3) (Check below)
		☐ Self-Esteem ☐ Security ☐ Ambitions ☐ Personal Relations ☐ Sex Relations ☐ Pride/Shame ☐ Fear

List Major "Character Defects" in preparation for STEPS 6 & 7

AMENDS		STEP 8
		☐ Now ☐ Later ☐ Never

I'm Resentful at or Fear: (1)	The Cause (2)	Affects my: (3) (Check below)
		☐ Self-Esteem ☐ Security ☐ Ambitions ☐ Personal Relations ☐ Sex Relations ☐ Pride/Shame ☐ Fear

List Major "Character Defects" in preparation for STEPS 6 & 7

AMENDS		STEP 8
		☐ Now ☐ Later ☐ Never

Ask yourself: ** (AA 67.3) * (AA 62.2)	Putting out of our minds the wrongs others had done, we resolutely looked for our own mistakes... We admitted our wrongs honestly...** Column (4)
Where had (I) been selfish, self-centred or self-seeking?**	
Where had (I) been dishonest?**	
Where had (I) been frightened?**	
Where had (I) been (responsible) to blame?**	
What decisions did I make based on self that later placed me in a position to be hurt?*	
When in the past can I remember making this decision?* (Early memory.)	
Where was I wrong?** **What was my part?**	

Ask yourself: ** (AA 67.3) * (AA 62.2)	Putting out of our minds the wrongs others had done, we resolutely looked for our own mistakes... We admitted our wrongs honestly...** Column (4)
Where had (I) been selfish, self-centred or self-seeking?**	
Where had (I) been dishonest?**	
Where had (I) been frightened?**	
Where had (I) been (responsible) to blame?**	
What decisions did I make based on self that later placed me in a position to be hurt?*	
When in the past can I remember making this decision?* (Early memory.)	
Where was I wrong?** **What was my part?**	

Ask yourself: ** (AA 67.3) * (AA 62.2)	Putting out of our minds the wrongs others had done, we resolutely looked for our own mistakes... We admitted our wrongs honestly...** Column (4)
Where had (I) been selfish, self-centred or self-seeking?**	
Where had (I) been dishonest?**	
Where had (I) been frightened?**	
Where had (I) been (responsible) to blame?**	
What decisions did I make based on self that later placed me in a position to be hurt?*	
When in the past can I remember making this decision?* (Early memory.)	
Where was I wrong?** **What was my part?**	

I'm Resentful at or Fear: (1)	The Cause (2)	Affects my: (3) (Check below)
		☐ Self-Esteem ☐ Security ☐ Ambitions ☐ Personal Relations ☐ Sex Relations ☐ Pride/Shame ☐ Fear

List Major "Character Defects" in preparation for STEPS 6 & 7

AMENDS		STEP 8
		☐ Now ☐ Later ☐ Never

I'm Resentful at or Fear: (1)	The Cause (2)	Affects my: (3) (Check below)
		☐ Self-Esteem ☐ Security ☐ Ambitions ☐ Personal Relations ☐ Sex Relations ☐ Pride/Shame ☐ Fear

List Major "Character Defects" in preparation for STEPS 6 & 7

AMENDS		STEP 8
		☐ Now ☐ Later ☐ Never

I'm Resentful at or Fear: (1)	The Cause (2)	Affects my: (3) (Check below)
		☐ Self-Esteem ☐ Security ☐ Ambitions ☐ Personal Relations ☐ Sex Relations ☐ Pride/Shame ☐ Fear

List Major "Character Defects" in preparation for STEPS 6 & 7

AMENDS		STEP 8
		☐ Now ☐ Later ☐ Never

Ask yourself: ** (AA 67.3) * (AA 62.2)	Putting out of our minds the wrongs others had done, we resolutely looked for our own mistakes... We admitted our wrongs honestly...** Column (4)
Where had (I) been selfish, self-centred or self-seeking?**	
Where had (I) been dishonest?**	
Where had (I) been frightened?**	
Where had (I) been (responsible) to blame?**	
What decisions did I make based on self that later placed me in a position to be hurt?*	
When in the past can I remember making this decision?* (Early memory.)	
Where was I wrong?** **What was my part?**	

Ask yourself: ** (AA 67.3) * (AA 62.2)	Putting out of our minds the wrongs others had done, we resolutely looked for our own mistakes... We admitted our wrongs honestly...** Column (4)
Where had (I) been selfish, self-centred or self-seeking?**	
Where had (I) been dishonest?**	
Where had (I) been frightened?**	
Where had (I) been (responsible) to blame?**	
What decisions did I make based on self that later placed me in a position to be hurt?*	
When in the past can I remember making this decision?* (Early memory.)	
Where was I wrong?** **What was my part?**	

Ask yourself: ** (AA 67.3) * (AA 62.2)	Putting out of our minds the wrongs others had done, we resolutely looked for our own mistakes... We admitted our wrongs honestly...** Column (4)
Where had (I) been selfish, self-centred or self-seeking?**	
Where had (I) been dishonest?**	
Where had (I) been frightened?**	
Where had (I) been (responsible) to blame?**	
What decisions did I make based on self that later placed me in a position to be hurt?*	
When in the past can I remember making this decision?* (Early memory.)	
Where was I wrong?** **What was my part?**	

I'm Resentful at or Fear: (1)	The Cause (2)	Affects my: (3) (Check below)
		❑ Self-Esteem ❑ Security ❑ Ambitions ❑ Personal Relations ❑ Sex Relations ❑ Pride/Shame ❑ Fear

List Major "Character Defects" in preparation for STEPS 6 & 7

AMENDS		STEP 8
		❑ Now ❑ Later ❑ Never

I'm Resentful at or Fear: (1)	The Cause (2)	Affects my: (3) (Check below)
		❑ Self-Esteem ❑ Security ❑ Ambitions ❑ Personal Relations ❑ Sex Relations ❑ Pride/Shame ❑ Fear

List Major "Character Defects" in preparation for STEPS 6 & 7

AMENDS		STEP 8
		❑ Now ❑ Later ❑ Never

I'm Resentful at or Fear: (1)	The Cause (2)	Affects my: (3) (Check below)
		❑ Self-Esteem ❑ Security ❑ Ambitions ❑ Personal Relations ❑ Sex Relations ❑ Pride/Shame ❑ Fear

List Major "Character Defects" in preparation for STEPS 6 & 7

AMENDS		STEP 8
		❑ Now ❑ Later ❑ Never

Ask yourself: ** (AA 67.3) * (AA 62.2)	Putting out of our minds the wrongs others had done, we resolutely looked for our own mistakes... We admitted our wrongs honestly...** Column (4)
Where had (I) been selfish, self-centred or self-seeking?**	
Where had (I) been dishonest?**	
Where had (I) been frightened?**	
Where had (I) been (responsible) to blame?**	
What decisions did I make based on self that later placed me in a position to be hurt?*	
When in the past can I remember making this decision?* (Early memory.)	
Where was I wrong?** **What was my part?**	

Ask yourself: ** (AA 67.3) * (AA 62.2)	Putting out of our minds the wrongs others had done, we resolutely looked for our own mistakes... We admitted our wrongs honestly...** Column (4)
Where had (I) been selfish, self-centred or self-seeking?**	
Where had (I) been dishonest?**	
Where had (I) been frightened?**	
Where had (I) been (responsible) to blame?**	
What decisions did I make based on self that later placed me in a position to be hurt?*	
When in the past can I remember making this decision?* (Early memory.)	
Where was I wrong?** **What was my part?**	

Ask yourself: ** (AA 67.3) * (AA 62.2)	Putting out of our minds the wrongs others had done, we resolutely looked for our own mistakes... We admitted our wrongs honestly...** Column (4)
Where had (I) been selfish, self-centred or self-seeking?**	
Where had (I) been dishonest?**	
Where had (I) been frightened?**	
Where had (I) been (responsible) to blame?**	
What decisions did I make based on self that later placed me in a position to be hurt?*	
When in the past can I remember making this decision?* (Early memory.)	
Where was I wrong?** **What was my part?**	

I'm Resentful at or Fear: (1)	The Cause (2)	Affects my: (3) (Check below)
		☐ Self-Esteem ☐ Security ☐ Ambitions ☐ Personal Relations ☐ Sex Relations ☐ Pride/Shame ☐ Fear

List Major "Character Defects" in preparation for STEPS 6 & 7

AMENDS		STEP 8
		☐ Now ☐ Later ☐ Never

I'm Resentful at or Fear: (1)	The Cause (2)	Affects my: (3) (Check below)
		☐ Self-Esteem ☐ Security ☐ Ambitions ☐ Personal Relations ☐ Sex Relations ☐ Pride/Shame ☐ Fear

List Major "Character Defects" in preparation for STEPS 6 & 7

AMENDS		STEP 8
		☐ Now ☐ Later ☐ Never

I'm Resentful at or Fear: (1)	The Cause (2)	Affects my: (3) (Check below)
		☐ Self-Esteem ☐ Security ☐ Ambitions ☐ Personal Relations ☐ Sex Relations ☐ Pride/Shame ☐ Fear

List Major "Character Defects" in preparation for STEPS 6 & 7

AMENDS		STEP 8
		☐ Now ☐ Later ☐ Never

Ask yourself: ** (AA 67.3) * (AA 62.2)	Putting out of our minds the wrongs others had done, we resolutely looked for our own mistakes... We admitted our wrongs honestly...** Column (4)
Where had (I) been selfish, self-centred or self-seeking?**	
Where had (I) been dishonest?**	
Where had (I) been frightened?**	
Where had (I) been (responsible) to blame?**	
What decisions did I make based on self that later placed me in a position to be hurt?*	
When in the past can I remember making this decision?* (Early memory.)	
Where was I wrong?** **What was my part?**	

Ask yourself: ** (AA 67.3) * (AA 62.2)	Putting out of our minds the wrongs others had done, we resolutely looked for our own mistakes... We admitted our wrongs honestly...** Column (4)
Where had (I) been selfish, self-centred or self-seeking?**	
Where had (I) been dishonest?**	
Where had (I) been frightened?**	
Where had (I) been (responsible) to blame?**	
What decisions did I make based on self that later placed me in a position to be hurt?*	
When in the past can I remember making this decision?* (Early memory.)	
Where was I wrong?** **What was my part?**	

Ask yourself: ** (AA 67.3) * (AA 62.2)	Putting out of our minds the wrongs others had done, we resolutely looked for our own mistakes... We admitted our wrongs honestly...** Column (4)
Where had (I) been selfish, self-centred or self-seeking?**	
Where had (I) been dishonest?**	
Where had (I) been frightened?**	
Where had (I) been (responsible) to blame?**	
What decisions did I make based on self that later placed me in a position to be hurt?*	
When in the past can I remember making this decision?* (Early memory.)	
Where was I wrong?** **What was my part?**	

I'm Resentful at or Fear: (1)	The Cause (2)	Affects my: (3) (Check below)
		❑ Self-Esteem ❑ Security ❑ Ambitions ❑ Personal Relations ❑ Sex Relations ❑ Pride/Shame ❑ Fear

List Major "Character Defects" in preparation for STEPS 6 & 7					

AMENDS		STEP 8
		❑ Now ❑ Later ❑ Never

I'm Resentful at or Fear: (1)	The Cause (2)	Affects my: (3) (Check below)
		❑ Self-Esteem ❑ Security ❑ Ambitions ❑ Personal Relations ❑ Sex Relations ❑ Pride/Shame ❑ Fear

List Major "Character Defects" in preparation for STEPS 6 & 7					

AMENDS		STEP 8
		❑ Now ❑ Later ❑ Never

I'm Resentful at or Fear: (1)	The Cause (2)	Affects my: (3) (Check below)
		❑ Self-Esteem ❑ Security ❑ Ambitions ❑ Personal Relations ❑ Sex Relations ❑ Pride/Shame ❑ Fear

List Major "Character Defects" in preparation for STEPS 6 & 7					

AMENDS		STEP 8
		❑ Now ❑ Later ❑ Never

Ask yourself: ** (AA 67.3) * (AA 62.2)	Putting out of our minds the wrongs others had done, we resolutely looked for our own mistakes... We admitted our wrongs honestly...** Column (4)
Where had (I) been selfish, self-centred or self-seeking?**	
Where had (I) been dishonest?**	
Where had (I) been frightened?**	
Where had (I) been (responsible) to blame?**	
What decisions did I make based on self that later placed me in a position to be hurt?*	
When in the past can I remember making this decision?* (Early memory.)	
Where was I wrong?** **What was my part?**	

Ask yourself: ** (AA 67.3) * (AA 62.2)	Putting out of our minds the wrongs others had done, we resolutely looked for our own mistakes... We admitted our wrongs honestly...** Column (4)
Where had (I) been selfish, self-centred or self-seeking?**	
Where had (I) been dishonest?**	
Where had (I) been frightened?**	
Where had (I) been (responsible) to blame?**	
What decisions did I make based on self that later placed me in a position to be hurt?*	
When in the past can I remember making this decision?* (Early memory.)	
Where was I wrong?** **What was my part?**	

Ask yourself: ** (AA 67.3) * (AA 62.2)	Putting out of our minds the wrongs others had done, we resolutely looked for our own mistakes... We admitted our wrongs honestly...** Column (4)
Where had (I) been selfish, self-centred or self-seeking?**	
Where had (I) been dishonest?**	
Where had (I) been frightened?**	
Where had (I) been (responsible) to blame?**	
What decisions did I make based on self that later placed me in a position to be hurt?*	
When in the past can I remember making this decision?* (Early memory.)	
Where was I wrong?** **What was my part?**	

DEEP SOUL CLEANSING

I'm Resentful at or Fear: (1)	The Cause (2)	Affects my: (3) (Check below)
		❏ Self-Esteem ❏ Security ❏ Ambitions ❏ Personal Relations ❏ Sex Relations ❏ Pride/Shame ❏ Fear

List Major "Character Defects" in preparation for STEPS 6 & 7

AMENDS		STEP 8
		❏ Now ❏ Later ❏ Never

I'm Resentful at or Fear: (1)	The Cause (2)	Affects my: (3) (Check below)
		❏ Self-Esteem ❏ Security ❏ Ambitions ❏ Personal Relations ❏ Sex Relations ❏ Pride/Shame ❏ Fear

List Major "Character Defects" in preparation for STEPS 6 & 7

AMENDS		STEP 8
		❏ Now ❏ Later ❏ Never

I'm Resentful at or Fear: (1)	The Cause (2)	Affects my: (3) (Check below)
		❏ Self-Esteem ❏ Security ❏ Ambitions ❏ Personal Relations ❏ Sex Relations ❏ Pride/Shame ❏ Fear

List Major "Character Defects" in preparation for STEPS 6 & 7

AMENDS		STEP 8
		❏ Now ❏ Later ❏ Never

12 STEP WORKBOOK

Ask yourself: ** (AA 67.3) * (AA 62.2)	Putting out of our minds the wrongs others had done, we resolutely looked for our own mistakes... We admitted our wrongs honestly...** Column (4)
Where had (I) been selfish, self-centred or self-seeking?**	
Where had (I) been dishonest?**	
Where had (I) been frightened?**	
Where had (I) been (responsible) to blame?**	
What decisions did I make based on self that later placed me in a position to be hurt?*	
When in the past can I remember making this decision?* (Early memory.)	
Where was I wrong?** What was my part?	

Ask yourself: ** (AA 67.3) * (AA 62.2)	Putting out of our minds the wrongs others had done, we resolutely looked for our own mistakes... We admitted our wrongs honestly...** Column (4)
Where had (I) been selfish, self-centred or self-seeking?**	
Where had (I) been dishonest?**	
Where had (I) been frightened?**	
Where had (I) been (responsible) to blame?**	
What decisions did I make based on self that later placed me in a position to be hurt?*	
When in the past can I remember making this decision?* (Early memory.)	
Where was I wrong?** What was my part?	

Ask yourself: ** (AA 67.3) * (AA 62.2)	Putting out of our minds the wrongs others had done, we resolutely looked for our own mistakes... We admitted our wrongs honestly...** Column (4)
Where had (I) been selfish, self-centred or self-seeking?**	
Where had (I) been dishonest?**	
Where had (I) been frightened?**	
Where had (I) been (responsible) to blame?**	
What decisions did I make based on self that later placed me in a position to be hurt?*	
When in the past can I remember making this decision?* (Early memory.)	
Where was I wrong?** What was my part?	

I'm Resentful at or Fear: (1)	The Cause (2)	Affects my: (3) (Check below)
		❑ Self-Esteem ❑ Security ❑ Ambitions ❑ Personal Relations ❑ Sex Relations ❑ Pride/Shame ❑ Fear

List Major "Character Defects" in preparation for STEPS 6 & 7

AMENDS		STEP 8
		❑ Now ❑ Later ❑ Never

I'm Resentful at or Fear: (1)	The Cause (2)	Affects my: (3) (Check below)
		❑ Self-Esteem ❑ Security ❑ Ambitions ❑ Personal Relations ❑ Sex Relations ❑ Pride/Shame ❑ Fear

List Major "Character Defects" in preparation for STEPS 6 & 7

AMENDS		STEP 8
		❑ Now ❑ Later ❑ Never

I'm Resentful at or Fear: (1)	The Cause (2)	Affects my: (3) (Check below)
		❑ Self-Esteem ❑ Security ❑ Ambitions ❑ Personal Relations ❑ Sex Relations ❑ Pride/Shame ❑ Fear

List Major "Character Defects" in preparation for STEPS 6 & 7

AMENDS		STEP 8
		❑ Now ❑ Later ❑ Never

Ask yourself: ** (AA 67.3) * (AA 62.2)	Putting out of our minds the wrongs others had done, we resolutely looked for our own mistakes... We admitted our wrongs honestly...** Column (4)
Where had (I) been selfish, self-centred or self-seeking?**	
Where had (I) been dishonest?**	
Where had (I) been frightened?**	
Where had (I) been (responsible) to blame?**	
What decisions did I make based on self that later placed me in a position to be hurt?*	
When in the past can I remember making this decision?* (Early memory.)	
Where was I wrong?** **What was my part?**	

Ask yourself: ** (AA 67.3) * (AA 62.2)	Putting out of our minds the wrongs others had done, we resolutely looked for our own mistakes... We admitted our wrongs honestly...** Column (4)
Where had (I) been selfish, self-centred or self-seeking?**	
Where had (I) been dishonest?**	
Where had (I) been frightened?**	
Where had (I) been (responsible) to blame?**	
What decisions did I make based on self that later placed me in a position to be hurt?*	
When in the past can I remember making this decision?* (Early memory.)	
Where was I wrong?** **What was my part?**	

Ask yourself: ** (AA 67.3) * (AA 62.2)	Putting out of our minds the wrongs others had done, we resolutely looked for our own mistakes... We admitted our wrongs honestly...** Column (4)
Where had (I) been selfish, self-centred or self-seeking?**	
Where had (I) been dishonest?**	
Where had (I) been frightened?**	
Where had (I) been (responsible) to blame?**	
What decisions did I make based on self that later placed me in a position to be hurt?*	
When in the past can I remember making this decision?* (Early memory.)	
Where was I wrong?** **What was my part?**	

I'm Resentful at or Fear: (1)	The Cause (2)	Affects my: (3) (Check below)
		❏ Self-Esteem ❏ Security ❏ Ambitions ❏ Personal Relations ❏ Sex Relations ❏ Pride/Shame ❏ Fear

List Major "Character Defects" in preparation for STEPS 6 & 7

AMENDS		STEP 8
		❏ Now ❏ Later ❏ Never

I'm Resentful at or Fear: (1)	The Cause (2)	Affects my: (3) (Check below)
		❏ Self-Esteem ❏ Security ❏ Ambitions ❏ Personal Relations ❏ Sex Relations ❏ Pride/Shame ❏ Fear

List Major "Character Defects" in preparation for STEPS 6 & 7

AMENDS		STEP 8
		❏ Now ❏ Later ❏ Never

I'm Resentful at or Fear: (1)	The Cause (2)	Affects my: (3) (Check below)
		❏ Self-Esteem ❏ Security ❏ Ambitions ❏ Personal Relations ❏ Sex Relations ❏ Pride/Shame ❏ Fear

List Major "Character Defects" in preparation for STEPS 6 & 7

AMENDS		STEP 8
		❏ Now ❏ Later ❏ Never

Ask yourself: ** (AA 67.3) * (AA 62.2)	Putting out of our minds the wrongs others had done, we resolutely looked for our own mistakes... We admitted our wrongs honestly...** Column (4)
Where had (I) been selfish, self-centred or self-seeking?**	
Where had (I) been dishonest?**	
Where had (I) been frightened?**	
Where had (I) been (responsible) to blame?**	
What decisions did I make based on self that later placed me in a position to be hurt?*	
When in the past can I remember making this decision?* (Early memory.)	
Where was I wrong?** **What was my part?**	

Ask yourself: ** (AA 67.3) * (AA 62.2)	Putting out of our minds the wrongs others had done, we resolutely looked for our own mistakes... We admitted our wrongs honestly...** Column (4)
Where had (I) been selfish, self-centred or self-seeking?**	
Where had (I) been dishonest?**	
Where had (I) been frightened?**	
Where had (I) been (responsible) to blame?**	
What decisions did I make based on self that later placed me in a position to be hurt?*	
When in the past can I remember making this decision?* (Early memory.)	
Where was I wrong?** **What was my part?**	

Ask yourself: ** (AA 67.3) * (AA 62.2)	Putting out of our minds the wrongs others had done, we resolutely looked for our own mistakes... We admitted our wrongs honestly...** Column (4)
Where had (I) been selfish, self-centred or self-seeking?**	
Where had (I) been dishonest?**	
Where had (I) been frightened?**	
Where had (I) been (responsible) to blame?**	
What decisions did I make based on self that later placed me in a position to be hurt?*	
When in the past can I remember making this decision?* (Early memory.)	
Where was I wrong?** **What was my part?**	

I'm Resentful at or Fear: (1)	The Cause (2)	Affects my: (3) (Check below)
		❑ Self-Esteem ❑ Security ❑ Ambitions ❑ Personal Relations ❑ Sex Relations ❑ Pride/Shame ❑ Fear

List Major "Character Defects" in preparation for STEPS 6 & 7				

AMENDS		STEP 8
		❑ Now ❑ Later ❑ Never

I'm Resentful at or Fear: (1)	The Cause (2)	Affects my: (3) (Check below)
		❑ Self-Esteem ❑ Security ❑ Ambitions ❑ Personal Relations ❑ Sex Relations ❑ Pride/Shame ❑ Fear

List Major "Character Defects" in preparation for STEPS 6 & 7				

AMENDS		STEP 8
		❑ Now ❑ Later ❑ Never

I'm Resentful at or Fear: (1)	The Cause (2)	Affects my: (3) (Check below)
		❑ Self-Esteem ❑ Security ❑ Ambitions ❑ Personal Relations ❑ Sex Relations ❑ Pride/Shame ❑ Fear

List Major "Character Defects" in preparation for STEPS 6 & 7				

AMENDS		STEP 8
		❑ Now ❑ Later ❑ Never

12 STEP WORKBOOK

Ask yourself: ** (AA 67.3) * (AA 62.2)	Putting out of our minds the wrongs others had done, we resolutely looked for our own mistakes... We admitted our wrongs honestly...** Column (4)
Where had (I) been selfish, self-centred or self-seeking?**	
Where had (I) been dishonest?**	
Where had (I) been frightened?**	
Where had (I) been (responsible) to blame?**	
What decisions did I make based on self that later placed me in a position to be hurt?*	
When in the past can I remember making this decision?* (Early memory.)	
Where was I wrong?** What was my part?	

Ask yourself: ** (AA 67.3) * (AA 62.2)	Putting out of our minds the wrongs others had done, we resolutely looked for our own mistakes... We admitted our wrongs honestly...** Column (4)
Where had (I) been selfish, self-centred or self-seeking?**	
Where had (I) been dishonest?**	
Where had (I) been frightened?**	
Where had (I) been (responsible) to blame?**	
What decisions did I make based on self that later placed me in a position to be hurt?*	
When in the past can I remember making this decision?* (Early memory.)	
Where was I wrong?** What was my part?	

Ask yourself: ** (AA 67.3) * (AA 62.2)	Putting out of our minds the wrongs others had done, we resolutely looked for our own mistakes... We admitted our wrongs honestly...** Column (4)
Where had (I) been selfish, self-centred or self-seeking?**	
Where had (I) been dishonest?**	
Where had (I) been frightened?**	
Where had (I) been (responsible) to blame?**	
What decisions did I make based on self that later placed me in a position to be hurt?*	
When in the past can I remember making this decision?* (Early memory.)	
Where was I wrong?** What was my part?	

I'm Resentful at or Fear: (1)	The Cause (2)	Affects my: (3) (Check below)
		☐ Self-Esteem ☐ Security ☐ Ambitions ☐ Personal Relations ☐ Sex Relations ☐ Pride/Shame ☐ Fear

List Major "Character Defects" in preparation for STEPS 6 & 7

AMENDS		STEP 8
		☐ Now ☐ Later ☐ Never

I'm Resentful at or Fear: (1)	The Cause (2)	Affects my: (3) (Check below)
		☐ Self-Esteem ☐ Security ☐ Ambitions ☐ Personal Relations ☐ Sex Relations ☐ Pride/Shame ☐ Fear

List Major "Character Defects" in preparation for STEPS 6 & 7

AMENDS		STEP 8
		☐ Now ☐ Later ☐ Never

I'm Resentful at or Fear: (1)	The Cause (2)	Affects my: (3) (Check below)
		☐ Self-Esteem ☐ Security ☐ Ambitions ☐ Personal Relations ☐ Sex Relations ☐ Pride/Shame ☐ Fear

List Major "Character Defects" in preparation for STEPS 6 & 7

AMENDS		STEP 8
		☐ Now ☐ Later ☐ Never

Ask yourself: ** (AA 67.3) * (AA 62.2)	Putting out of our minds the wrongs others had done, we resolutely looked for our own mistakes... We admitted our wrongs honestly...** Column (4)
Where had (I) been selfish, self-centred or self-seeking?**	
Where had (I) been dishonest?**	
Where had (I) been frightened?**	
Where had (I) been (responsible) to blame?**	
What decisions did I make based on self that later placed me in a position to be hurt?*	
When in the past can I remember making this decision?* (Early memory.)	
Where was I wrong?** **What was my part?**	

Ask yourself: ** (AA 67.3) * (AA 62.2)	Putting out of our minds the wrongs others had done, we resolutely looked for our own mistakes... We admitted our wrongs honestly...** Column (4)
Where had (I) been selfish, self-centred or self-seeking?**	
Where had (I) been dishonest?**	
Where had (I) been frightened?**	
Where had (I) been (responsible) to blame?**	
What decisions did I make based on self that later placed me in a position to be hurt?*	
When in the past can I remember making this decision?* (Early memory.)	
Where was I wrong?** **What was my part?**	

Ask yourself: ** (AA 67.3) * (AA 62.2)	Putting out of our minds the wrongs others had done, we resolutely looked for our own mistakes... We admitted our wrongs honestly...** Column (4)
Where had (I) been selfish, self-centred or self-seeking?**	
Where had (I) been dishonest?**	
Where had (I) been frightened?**	
Where had (I) been (responsible) to blame?**	
What decisions did I make based on self that later placed me in a position to be hurt?*	
When in the past can I remember making this decision?* (Early memory.)	
Where was I wrong?** **What was my part?**	

I'm Resentful at or Fear: (1)	The Cause (2)				Affects my: (3) (Check below)
					☐ Self-Esteem ☐ Security ☐ Ambitions ☐ Personal Relations ☐ Sex Relations ☐ Pride/Shame ☐ Fear
List Major "Character Defects" in preparation for STEPS 6 & 7					
AMENDS					**STEP 8**
					☐ Now ☐ Later ☐ Never

I'm Resentful at or Fear: (1)	The Cause (2)				Affects my: (3) (Check below)
					☐ Self-Esteem ☐ Security ☐ Ambitions ☐ Personal Relations ☐ Sex Relations ☐ Pride/Shame ☐ Fear
List Major "Character Defects" in preparation for STEPS 6 & 7					
AMENDS					**STEP 8**
					☐ Now ☐ Later ☐ Never

I'm Resentful at or Fear: (1)	The Cause (2)				Affects my: (3) (Check below)
					☐ Self-Esteem ☐ Security ☐ Ambitions ☐ Personal Relations ☐ Sex Relations ☐ Pride/Shame ☐ Fear
List Major "Character Defects" in preparation for STEPS 6 & 7					
AMENDS					**STEP 8**
					☐ Now ☐ Later ☐ Never

12 STEP WORKBOOK

Ask yourself: ** (AA 67.3) * (AA 62.2)	Putting out of our minds the wrongs others had done, we resolutely looked for our own mistakes... We admitted our wrongs honestly...** Column (4)
Where had (I) been selfish, self-centred or self-seeking?**	
Where had (I) been dishonest?**	
Where had (I) been frightened?**	
Where had (I) been (responsible) to blame?**	
What decisions did I make based on self that later placed me in a position to be hurt?*	
When in the past can I remember making this decision?* (Early memory.)	
Where was I wrong?** What was my part?	

Ask yourself: ** (AA 67.3) * (AA 62.2)	Putting out of our minds the wrongs others had done, we resolutely looked for our own mistakes... We admitted our wrongs honestly...** Column (4)
Where had (I) been selfish, self-centred or self-seeking?**	
Where had (I) been dishonest?**	
Where had (I) been frightened?**	
Where had (I) been (responsible) to blame?**	
What decisions did I make based on self that later placed me in a position to be hurt?*	
When in the past can I remember making this decision?* (Early memory.)	
Where was I wrong?** What was my part?	

Ask yourself: ** (AA 67.3) * (AA 62.2)	Putting out of our minds the wrongs others had done, we resolutely looked for our own mistakes... We admitted our wrongs honestly...** Column (4)
Where had (I) been selfish, self-centred or self-seeking?**	
Where had (I) been dishonest?**	
Where had (I) been frightened?**	
Where had (I) been (responsible) to blame?**	
What decisions did I make based on self that later placed me in a position to be hurt?*	
When in the past can I remember making this decision?* (Early memory.)	
Where was I wrong?** What was my part?	

I'm Resentful at or Fear: (1)	The Cause (2)	Affects my: (3) (Check below)
		☐ Self-Esteem ☐ Security ☐ Ambitions ☐ Personal Relations ☐ Sex Relations ☐ Pride/Shame ☐ Fear

List Major "Character Defects" in preparation for STEPS 6 & 7

AMENDS		STEP 8
		☐ Now ☐ Later ☐ Never

I'm Resentful at or Fear: (1)	The Cause (2)	Affects my: (3) (Check below)
		☐ Self-Esteem ☐ Security ☐ Ambitions ☐ Personal Relations ☐ Sex Relations ☐ Pride/Shame ☐ Fear

List Major "Character Defects" in preparation for STEPS 6 & 7

AMENDS		STEP 8
		☐ Now ☐ Later ☐ Never

I'm Resentful at or Fear: (1)	The Cause (2)	Affects my: (3) (Check below)
		☐ Self-Esteem ☐ Security ☐ Ambitions ☐ Personal Relations ☐ Sex Relations ☐ Pride/Shame ☐ Fear

List Major "Character Defects" in preparation for STEPS 6 & 7

AMENDS		STEP 8
		☐ Now ☐ Later ☐ Never

Ask yourself: ** (AA 67.3) * (AA 62.2)	Putting out of our minds the wrongs others had done, we resolutely looked for our own mistakes... We admitted our wrongs honestly...** Column (4)
Where had (I) been selfish, self-centred or self-seeking?**	
Where had (I) been dishonest?**	
Where had (I) been frightened?**	
Where had (I) been (responsible) to blame?**	
What decisions did I make based on self that later placed me in a position to be hurt?*	
When in the past can I remember making this decision?* (Early memory.)	
Where was I wrong?** **What was my part?**	

Ask yourself: ** (AA 67.3) * (AA 62.2)	Putting out of our minds the wrongs others had done, we resolutely looked for our own mistakes... We admitted our wrongs honestly...** Column (4)
Where had (I) been selfish, self-centred or self-seeking?**	
Where had (I) been dishonest?**	
Where had (I) been frightened?**	
Where had (I) been (responsible) to blame?**	
What decisions did I make based on self that later placed me in a position to be hurt?*	
When in the past can I remember making this decision?* (Early memory.)	
Where was I wrong?** **What was my part?**	

Ask yourself: ** (AA 67.3) * (AA 62.2)	Putting out of our minds the wrongs others had done, we resolutely looked for our own mistakes... We admitted our wrongs honestly...** Column (4)
Where had (I) been selfish, self-centred or self-seeking?**	
Where had (I) been dishonest?**	
Where had (I) been frightened?**	
Where had (I) been (responsible) to blame?**	
What decisions did I make based on self that later placed me in a position to be hurt?*	
When in the past can I remember making this decision?* (Early memory.)	
Where was I wrong?** **What was my part?**	

Sample Inventory Answers

SAMPLE INVENTORY ANSWERS

Selfish/Self-Centred
- Not seeing others' POV
- Not see others problem
- Not seeing others' needs
- Not being a friend
- Being dependant
- Being dominant
- Being grandiose
- Being miserly
- Being possessive
- Thinking we're better
- Thinking they're jealous
- React from self-loathing
- React self-righteously
- Too concerned about me
- Wanting...
- Things our way
- Special treatment
- Our "needs" met
- What others have
- Control
- To be the best
- Others to be like me
- More than my share
- To look good at another's expense
- To be liked

Self-Seeking
- Manipulating others
- Put others down
- Character assassination
- Acting superior
- Acting out to fill a void
- Engaging in gluttony
- Lusting after another
- Ignoring others' needs
- Trying to control others
- Getting revenge
- Acting out to feel good
- Holding resentment

Dishonest
- Not seeing/admitting our fault
- Having a superior attitude
- Thinking we're better
- Blaming others for our problems
- Not admitting we've done the same thing
- Not expressing feelings
- Not expressing ideas
- Not being clear
- Hiding our true motives
- Lying
- Cheating
- Stealing
- Not facing facts
- Hiding from reality
- Holding on to false beliefs
- Breaking rules or laws
- Lying to ourselves
- Exaggerating
- Minimising
- Setting ourselves up to be "wronged"
- Expecting others to be what they're not
- Being a perfectionist

Our Part
- Making sweeping generalisations
- Gathering evidence to prove ourselves right
- Our part will be a distillation of the answers to the preceding questions

OUR OWN MISTAKES

Fears

- Of...
- Peoples' opinions
- Rejection
- Abandonment
- Loneliness
- Physical injury
- Abuse
- Not being able to change ourselves or others
- Not being in control
- Our inferiority
- Our inadequacy
- Criticism
- Expressing our selves
- Getting trapped
- Exposure
- Embarrassment

Blame (Responsible)

- For harsh judgement
- For ignoring the facts
- Being careless
- Bringing the past into the present
- Not dealing with our feelings
- Blaming others for our feelings
- Not working our program
- For our own upset
- For our ignorance

Decisions Or Choices

- People are stupid
- Women are weak
- Women are dangerous
- Women are ...
- Men are better off
- Men are liars
- Men are ...
- We can't trust women
- We can't trust men
- I am stupid
- I am always right
- I am always wrong
- Nobody loves me
- I'm unlovable
- I'm ugly
- I have a bad temper
- My nose is too big
- Sex is dirty
- Marriage is ...
- Life is ...
- Heights are...
- Bugs are ...
- Pets are ...
- Whites are ...
- Blacks are ...
- Spanish are ...
- Germans are ...
- Americans are ...
- British are ...
- French are ...
- Etc. etc. etc.

Step Four
Sex Inventory

Step 4 –SEX INVENTORY

SEX – Looking at both the past and present, what sex situations have caused me anxiety, bitterness, frustration, or depression? We reviewed our (sex) conduct over the years past.

Who: _____ My conduct: _____

_____
(The following questions culled from "Big Book" of *Alcoholics Anonymous* [17] and the 12 & 12 [18].)

Where was I selfish or self-seeking?

Where was I dishonest?

Where was I inconsiderate?

Whom had I hurt and how badly?

Did I unjustifiably arouse jealousy, suspicion or bitterness? Explain.

Where was I responsible? What could I have done instead?

Did I spoil my marriage (relationship) and/or injure my children? How?

Did I jeopardise my standing in the community? How?

Did I burn with a guilt that nothing could extinguish? Or did I insist that I was the pursued and not the pursuer, and thus absolve myself? Explain.

How've I reacted to frustration in sexual matters? When denied did I become vengeful or depressed? Did I take it out on others? How?

If there was rejection or coldness at home, did I use this as a reason for promiscuity? Explain.

What decisions did I make based on this experience that has affected my relationships?

What is the earliest time I can remember making this decision?

List Major "Character Defects" in preparation for STEPS 6 & 7				
AMENDS				**STEP 8**
				❑ Now
				❑ Later
				❑ Never

Make as many copies of this form that you need to complete your inventory.

DEEP SOUL CLEANSING
Step 4 –SEX INVENTORY

SEX – Looking at both the past and present, what sex situations have caused me anxiety, bitterness, frustration, or depression? We reviewed our (sex) conduct over the years past.

Who: _____ My conduct: _____
_____

(The following questions culled from "Big Book" of *Alcoholics Anonymous* [19] and the 12 & 12[20].)

Where was I selfish or self-seeking?

Where was I dishonest?

Where was I inconsiderate?

Whom had I hurt and how badly?

Did I unjustifiably arouse jealousy, suspicion or bitterness? Explain.

Where was I responsible? What could I have done instead?

Did I spoil my marriage (relationship) *and/or injure my children? How?*

Did I jeopardise my standing in the community? How?

Did I burn with a guilt that nothing could extinguish? Or did I insist that I was the pursued and not the pursuer, and thus absolve myself? Explain.

How've I reacted to frustration in sexual matters? When denied did I become vengeful or depressed? Did I take it out on others? How?

If there was rejection or coldness at home, did I use this as a reason for promiscuity? Explain.

What decisions did I make based on this experience that has affected my relationships?

What is the earliest time I can remember making this decision?

List Major "Character Defects" in preparation for STEPS 6 & 7				

AMENDS		STEP 8
		❑ Now
		❑ Later
		❑ Never

Make as many copies of this form that you need to complete your inventory.

Step 4 –SEX INVENTORY

SEX – Looking at both the past and present, what sex situations have caused me anxiety, bitterness, frustration, or depression? We reviewed our (sex) conduct over the years past.

Who: _____   My conduct: _____

_____

(The following questions culled from "Big Book" of *Alcoholics Anonymous* [21] and the 12 & 12 [22].)

Where was I selfish or self-seeking?

Where was I dishonest?

Where was I inconsiderate?

Whom had I hurt and how badly?

Did I unjustifiably arouse jealousy, suspicion or bitterness? Explain.

Where was I responsible? What could I have done instead?

Did I spoil my marriage (relationship) and/or injure my children? How?

Did I jeopardise my standing in the community? How?

Did I burn with a guilt that nothing could extinguish? Or did I insist that I was the pursued and not the pursuer, and thus absolve myself? Explain.

How've I reacted to frustration in sexual matters? When denied did I become vengeful or depressed? Did I take it out on others? How?

If there was rejection or coldness at home, did I use this as a reason for promiscuity? Explain.

What decisions did I make based on this experience that has affected my relationships?

What is the earliest time I can remember making this decision?

List Major "Character Defects" in preparation for STEPS 6 & 7				

AMENDS		STEP 8
		☐ Now
		☐ Later
		☐ Never

Make as many copies of this form that you need to complete your inventory.

DEEP SOUL CLEANSING
Step 4 –SEX INVENTORY

SEX – Looking at both the past and present, what sex situations have caused me anxiety, bitterness, frustration, or depression? We reviewed our (sex) conduct over the years past.

Who: _____   My conduct: _____

_____
(The following questions culled from "Big Book" of *Alcoholics Anonymous* [23] *and the 12 & 12* [24]*.*)

Where was I selfish or self-seeking?

Where was I dishonest?

Where was I inconsiderate?

Whom had I hurt and how badly?

Did I unjustifiably arouse jealousy, suspicion or bitterness? Explain.

Where was I responsible? What could I have done instead?

Did I spoil my marriage (relationship) *and/or injure my children? How?*

Did I jeopardise my standing in the community? How?

Did I burn with a guilt that nothing could extinguish? Or did I insist that I was the pursued and not the pursuer, and thus absolve myself? Explain.

How've I reacted to frustration in sexual matters? When denied did I become vengeful or depressed? Did I take it out on others? How?

If there was rejection or coldness at home, did I use this as a reason for promiscuity? Explain.

What decisions did I make based on this experience that has affected my relationships?

What is the earliest time I can remember making this decision?

List Major "Character Defects" in preparation for STEPS 6 & 7				

AMENDS		STEP 8
		☐ Now
		☐ Later
		☐ Never

Make as many copies of this form that you need to complete your inventory.

Step 4 –SEX INVENTORY

SEX – Looking at both the past and present, what sex situations have caused me anxiety, bitterness, frustration, or depression? We reviewed our (sex) conduct over the years past.

Who: _____ My conduct: _____

_____

(The following questions culled from "Big Book" of *Alcoholics Anonymous* [25] and the 12 & 12[26].)

Where was I selfish or self-seeking?

Where was I dishonest?

Where was I inconsiderate?

Whom had I hurt and how badly?

Did I unjustifiably arouse jealousy, suspicion or bitterness? Explain.

Where was I responsible? What could I have done instead?

Did I spoil my marriage (relationship) *and/or injure my children? How?*

Did I jeopardise my standing in the community? How?

Did I burn with a guilt that nothing could extinguish? Or did I insist that I was the pursued and not the pursuer, and thus absolve myself? Explain.

How've I reacted to frustration in sexual matters? When denied did I become vengeful or depressed? Did I take it out on others? How?

If there was rejection or coldness at home, did I use this as a reason for promiscuity? Explain.

What decisions did I make based on this experience that has affected my relationships?

What is the earliest time I can remember making this decision?

List Major "Character Defects" in preparation for STEPS 6 & 7					
AMENDS					**STEP 8**
					❑ Now
					❑ Later
					❑ Never

Make as many copies of this form that you need to complete your inventory.

DEEP SOUL CLEANSING
Step 4 –SEX INVENTORY

SEX – Looking at both the past and present, what sex situations have caused me anxiety, bitterness, frustration, or depression? We reviewed our (sex) conduct over the years past.

Who: _____ My conduct: _____

_____
(The following questions culled from "Big Book" of *Alcoholics Anonymous* [27] and the 12 & 12 [28].)

Where was I selfish or self-seeking?

Where was I dishonest?

Where was I inconsiderate?

Whom had I hurt and how badly?

Did I unjustifiably arouse jealousy, suspicion or bitterness? Explain.

Where was I responsible? What could I have done instead?

Did I spoil my marriage (relationship) and/or injure my children? How?

Did I jeopardise my standing in the community? How?

Did I burn with a guilt that nothing could extinguish? Or did I insist that I was the pursued and not the pursuer, and thus absolve myself? Explain.

How've I reacted to frustration in sexual matters? When denied did I become vengeful or depressed? Did I take it out on others? How?

If there was rejection or coldness at home, did I use this as a reason for promiscuity? Explain.

What decisions did I make based on this experience that has affected my relationships?

What is the earliest time I can remember making this decision?

List Major "Character Defects" in preparation for STEPS 6 & 7				

AMENDS		STEP 8
		☐ Now
		☐ Later
		☐ Never

Make as many copies of this form that you need to complete your inventory.

Step 4 –SEX INVENTORY

SEX – Looking at both the past and present, what sex situations have caused me anxiety, bitterness, frustration, or depression? We reviewed our (sex) conduct over the years past.

Who: _____ My conduct: _____
_____
(The following questions culled from "Big Book" of *Alcoholics Anonymous* [29] *and the 12 & 12* [30]*.)*

Where was I selfish or self-seeking?

Where was I dishonest?

Where was I inconsiderate?

Whom had I hurt and how badly?

Did I unjustifiably arouse jealousy, suspicion or bitterness? Explain.

Where was I responsible? What could I have done instead?

Did I spoil my marriage (relationship) and/or injure my children? How?

Did I jeopardise my standing in the community? How?

Did I burn with a guilt that nothing could extinguish? Or did I insist that I was the pursued and not the pursuer, and thus absolve myself? Explain.

How've I reacted to frustration in sexual matters? When denied did I become vengeful or depressed? Did I take it out on others? How?

If there was rejection or coldness at home, did I use this as a reason for promiscuity? Explain.

What decisions did I make based on this experience that has affected my relationships?

What is the earliest time I can remember making this decision?

List Major "Character Defects" in preparation for STEPS 6 & 7				

AMENDS		STEP 8
		☐ Now
		☐ Later
		☐ Never

Make as many copies of this form that you need to complete your inventory.

Step 4 –SEX INVENTORY

SEX – Looking at both the past and present, what sex situations have caused me anxiety, bitterness, frustration, or depression? We reviewed our (sex) conduct over the years past.

Who: _____   My conduct: _____
_____

(The following questions culled from "Big Book" of *Alcoholics Anonymous* [31] and the 12 & 12[32].)

Where was I selfish or self-seeking?

Where was I dishonest?

Where was I inconsiderate?

Whom had I hurt and how badly?

Did I unjustifiably arouse jealousy, suspicion or bitterness? Explain.

Where was I responsible? What could I have done instead?

Did I spoil my marriage (relationship) *and/or injure my children? How?*

Did I jeopardise my standing in the community? How?

Did I burn with a guilt that nothing could extinguish? Or did I insist that I was the pursued and not the pursuer, and thus absolve myself? Explain.

How've I reacted to frustration in sexual matters? When denied did I become vengeful or depressed? Did I take it out on others? How?

If there was rejection or coldness at home, did I use this as a reason for promiscuity? Explain.

What decisions did I make based on this experience that has affected my relationships?

What is the earliest time I can remember making this decision?

List Major "Character Defects" in preparation for STEPS 6 & 7					
AMENDS					STEP 8
					☐ Now ☐ Later ☐ Never

Make as many copies of this form that you need to complete your inventory.

Step 4 –SEX INVENTORY

SEX – Looking at both the past and present, what sex situations have caused me anxiety, bitterness, frustration, or depression? We reviewed our (sex) conduct over the years past.

Who: _____ My conduct: _____

_____
(The following questions culled from "Big Book" of *Alcoholics Anonymous* [33] and the 12 & 12[34].)

Where was I selfish or self-seeking?

Where was I dishonest?

Where was I inconsiderate?

Whom had I hurt and how badly?

Did I unjustifiably arouse jealousy, suspicion or bitterness? Explain.

Where was I responsible? What could I have done instead?

Did I spoil my marriage (relationship) *and/or injure my children? How?*

Did I jeopardise my standing in the community? How?

Did I burn with a guilt that nothing could extinguish? Or did I insist that I was the pursued and not the pursuer, and thus absolve myself? Explain.

How've I reacted to frustration in sexual matters? When denied did I become vengeful or depressed? Did I take it out on others? How?

If there was rejection or coldness at home, did I use this as a reason for promiscuity? Explain.

What decisions did I make based on this experience that has affected my relationships?

What is the earliest time I can remember making this decision?

List Major "Character Defects" in preparation for STEPS 6 & 7				
AMENDS				**STEP 8**
				☐ Now
				☐ Later
				☐ Never

Make as many copies of this form that you need to complete your inventory.

DEEP SOUL CLEANSING

Step 4 –SEX INVENTORY

SEX – Looking at both the past and present, what sex situations have caused me anxiety, bitterness, frustration, or depression? We reviewed our (sex) conduct over the years past.

Who: _____ My conduct: _____
_____
(The following questions culled from "Big Book" of *Alcoholics Anonymous* [35] and the 12 & 12[36].)

Where was I selfish or self-seeking?

Where was I dishonest?

Where was I inconsiderate?

Whom had I hurt and how badly?

Did I unjustifiably arouse jealousy, suspicion or bitterness? Explain.

Where was I responsible? What could I have done instead?

Did I spoil my marriage (relationship) *and/or injure my children? How?*

Did I jeopardise my standing in the community? How?

Did I burn with a guilt that nothing could extinguish? Or did I insist that I was the pursued and not the pursuer, and thus absolve myself? Explain.

How've I reacted to frustration in sexual matters? When denied did I become vengeful or depressed? Did I take it out on others? How?

If there was rejection or coldness at home, did I use this as a reason for promiscuity? Explain.

What decisions did I make based on this experience that has affected my relationships?

What is the earliest time I can remember making this decision?

List Major "Character Defects" in preparation for STEPS 6 & 7				
AMENDS				**STEP 8**
				☐ Now
				☐ Later
				☐ Never

Make as many copies of this form that you need to complete your inventory.

Step 4 –SEX INVENTORY

SEX – Looking at both the past and present, what sex situations have caused me anxiety, bitterness, frustration, or depression? We reviewed our (sex) conduct over the years past.

Who: _____ My conduct: _____
_____
(The following questions culled from "Big Book" of *Alcoholics Anonymous* [37] and the 12 & 12[38].)

Where was I selfish or self-seeking?

Where was I dishonest?

Where was I inconsiderate?

Whom had I hurt and how badly?

Did I unjustifiably arouse jealousy, suspicion or bitterness? Explain.

Where was I responsible? What could I have done instead?

Did I spoil my marriage (relationship) and/or injure my children? How?

Did I jeopardise my standing in the community? How?

Did I burn with a guilt that nothing could extinguish? Or did I insist that I was the pursued and not the pursuer, and thus absolve myself? Explain.

How've I reacted to frustration in sexual matters? When denied did I become vengeful or depressed? Did I take it out on others? How?

If there was rejection or coldness at home, did I use this as a reason for promiscuity? Explain.

What decisions did I make based on this experience that has affected my relationships?

What is the earliest time I can remember making this decision?

List Major "Character Defects" in preparation for STEPS 6 & 7				
AMENDS				**STEP 8**
				☐ Now
				☐ Later
				☐ Never

Make as many copies of this form that you need to complete your inventory.

DEEP SOUL CLEANSING
Step 4 –SEX INVENTORY

SEX – Looking at both the past and present, what sex situations have caused me anxiety, bitterness, frustration, or depression? We reviewed our (sex) conduct over the years past.

Who: _____   My conduct: _____
_____
(The following questions culled from "Big Book" of *Alcoholics Anonymous* [39] and the 12 & 12[40].)

Where was I selfish or self-seeking?

Where was I dishonest?

Where was I inconsiderate?

Whom had I hurt and how badly?

Did I unjustifiably arouse jealousy, suspicion or bitterness? Explain.

Where was I responsible? What could I have done instead?

Did I spoil my marriage (relationship) and/or injure my children? How?

Did I jeopardise my standing in the community? How?

Did I burn with a guilt that nothing could extinguish? Or did I insist that I was the pursued and not the pursuer, and thus absolve myself? Explain.

How've I reacted to frustration in sexual matters? When denied did I become vengeful or depressed? Did I take it out on others? How?

If there was rejection or coldness at home, did I use this as a reason for promiscuity? Explain.

What decisions did I make based on this experience that has affected my relationships?

What is the earliest time I can remember making this decision?

List Major "Character Defects" in preparation for STEPS 6 & 7				
AMENDS				**STEP 8**
				☐ Now
				☐ Later
				☐ Never

Make as many copies of this form that you need to complete your inventory.

Step 4 –SEX INVENTORY

SEX – Looking at both the past and present, what sex situations have caused me anxiety, bitterness, frustration, or depression? We reviewed our (sex) conduct over the years past.

Who: _____ My conduct: _____

_____
(The following questions culled from "Big Book" of *Alcoholics Anonymous* [41] and the 12 & 12[42].)

Where was I selfish or self-seeking?

Where was I dishonest?

Where was I inconsiderate?

Whom had I hurt and how badly?

Did I unjustifiably arouse jealousy, suspicion or bitterness? Explain.

Where was I responsible? What could I have done instead?

Did I spoil my marriage (relationship) and/or injure my children? How?

Did I jeopardise my standing in the community? How?

Did I burn with a guilt that nothing could extinguish? Or did I insist that I was the pursued and not the pursuer, and thus absolve myself? Explain.

How've I reacted to frustration in sexual matters? When denied did I become vengeful or depressed? Did I take it out on others? How?

If there was rejection or coldness at home, did I use this as a reason for promiscuity? Explain.

What decisions did I make based on this experience that has affected my relationships?

What is the earliest time I can remember making this decision?

List Major "Character Defects" in preparation for STEPS 6 & 7				
AMENDS				**STEP 8**
				☐ Now
				☐ Later
				☐ Never

Make as many copies of this form that you need to complete your inventory.

DEEP SOUL CLEANSING
Step 4 –SEX INVENTORY

SEX – Looking at both the past and present, what sex situations have caused me anxiety, bitterness, frustration, or depression? We reviewed our (sex) conduct over the years past.

Who: _____   My conduct: _____

_____

(The following questions culled from "Big Book" of *Alcoholics Anonymous* [43] and the 12 & 12 [44].)

Where was I selfish or self-seeking?

Where was I dishonest?

Where was I inconsiderate?

Whom had I hurt and how badly?

Did I unjustifiably arouse jealousy, suspicion or bitterness? Explain.

Where was I responsible? What could I have done instead?

Did I spoil my marriage (relationship) *and/or injure my children? How?*

Did I jeopardise my standing in the community? How?

Did I burn with a guilt that nothing could extinguish? Or did I insist that I was the pursued and not the pursuer, and thus absolve myself? Explain.

How've I reacted to frustration in sexual matters? When denied did I become vengeful or depressed? Did I take it out on others? How?

If there was rejection or coldness at home, did I use this as a reason for promiscuity? Explain.

What decisions did I make based on this experience that has affected my relationships?

What is the earliest time I can remember making this decision?

List Major "Character Defects" in preparation for STEPS 6 & 7				

AMENDS		STEP 8
		❑ Now
		❑ Later
		❑ Never

Make as many copies of this form that you need to complete your inventory.

274

Step 4 –SEX INVENTORY

SEX – Looking at both the past and present, what sex situations have caused me anxiety, bitterness, frustration, or depression? We reviewed our (sex) conduct over the years past.

Who: _____   My conduct: _____

_____

(The following questions culled from "Big Book" of *Alcoholics Anonymous* [45] and the 12 & 12 [46].)

Where was I selfish or self-seeking?

Where was I dishonest?

Where was I inconsiderate?

Whom had I hurt and how badly?

Did I unjustifiably arouse jealousy, suspicion or bitterness? Explain.

Where was I responsible? What could I have done instead?

Did I spoil my marriage (relationship) and/or injure my children? How?

Did I jeopardise my standing in the community? How?

Did I burn with a guilt that nothing could extinguish? Or did I insist that I was the pursued and not the pursuer, and thus absolve myself? Explain.

How've I reacted to frustration in sexual matters? When denied did I become vengeful or depressed? Did I take it out on others? How?

If there was rejection or coldness at home, did I use this as a reason for promiscuity? Explain.

What decisions did I make based on this experience that has affected my relationships?

What is the earliest time I can remember making this decision?

List Major "Character Defects" in preparation for STEPS 6 & 7				

AMENDS		**STEP 8**
		❏ Now
		❏ Later
		❏ Never

Make as many copies of this form that you need to complete your inventory.

Step Four
Harm to Others

Step 4 –HARM TO OTHERS (of any kind)

HARMS TO OTHERS – This is where you put those acts of stealing, or violence, any harm done to others that was not covered in your resentments etc.

Who: _____ My conduct: _____

_____

_____

(The following questions are culled from both the "Big Book" *Alcoholics Anonymous* [47] and the *Twelve Steps and Twelve Traditions.* [48])

Where was I selfish or self-seeking?

Where was I dishonest?

Where was I inconsiderate?

Where was I to blame (responsible)?

What could I have done instead?

What people were hurt and how badly?

Did I spoil my marriage (relationship) and/or injure my children?

Did I jeopardise my standing in the community? How?

What decisions did I make based on this experience that has affected my relationships?

What is the earliest time I can remember making this decision?

List Major "Character Defects" in preparation for STEPS 6 & 7				

AMENDS		**STEP 8**
		☐ Now
		☐ Later
		☐ Never

Make as many copies of this form that you need to complete your inventory.

DEEP SOUL CLEANSING
Step 4 –HARM TO OTHERS (of any kind)

HARMS TO OTHERS – This is where you put those acts of stealing, or violence, any harm done to others that was not covered in your resentments etc.

Who: _____ My conduct: _____

_____

_____

(The following questions are culled from both the "Big Book" *Alcoholics Anonymous* [49] and the *Twelve Steps and Twelve Traditions.* [50])

Where was I selfish or self-seeking?

Where was I dishonest?

Where was I inconsiderate?

Where was I to blame (responsible)?

What could I have done instead?

What people were hurt and how badly?

Did I spoil my marriage (relationship) and/or injure my children?

Did I jeopardise my standing in the community? How?

What decisions did I make based on this experience that has affected my relationships?

What is the earliest time I can remember making this decision?

List Major "Character Defects" in preparation for STEPS 6 & 7				
AMENDS				**STEP 8**
				☐ Now
				☐ Later
				☐ Never

Make as many copies of this form that you need to complete your inventory.

Step 4 –HARM TO OTHERS (of any kind)

HARMS TO OTHERS – This is where you put those acts of stealing, or violence, any harm done to others that was not covered in your resentments etc.

Who: _____ My conduct: _____

_____

_____

(The following questions are culled from both the "Big Book" *Alcoholics Anonymous* [51] and the *Twelve Steps and Twelve Traditions.* [52])

Where was I selfish or self-seeking?

Where was I dishonest?

Where was I inconsiderate?

Where was I to blame (responsible)*?*

What could I have done instead?

What people were hurt and how badly?

Did I spoil my marriage (relationship) *and/or injure my children?*

Did I jeopardise my standing in the community? How?

What decisions did I make based on this experience that has affected my relationships?

What is the earliest time I can remember making this decision?

List Major "Character Defects" in preparation for STEPS 6 & 7				

AMENDS		STEP 8
		❑ Now
		❑ Later
		❑ Never

Make as many copies of this form that you need to complete your inventory.

DEEP SOUL CLEANSING

Step 4 –HARM TO OTHERS (of any kind)

HARMS TO OTHERS – This is where you put those acts of stealing, or violence, any harm done to others that was not covered in your resentments etc.

Who: _____ My conduct: _____

_____

_____

(The following questions are culled from both the "Big Book" *Alcoholics Anonymous* [53] and the *Twelve Steps and Twelve Traditions.* [54])

Where was I selfish or self-seeking?

Where was I dishonest?

Where was I inconsiderate?

Where was I to blame (responsible)*?*

What could I have done instead?

What people were hurt and how badly?

Did I spoil my marriage (relationship) *and/or injure my children?*

Did I jeopardise my standing in the community? How?

What decisions did I make based on this experience that has affected my relationships?

What is the earliest time I can remember making this decision?

List Major "Character Defects" in preparation for STEPS 6 & 7				

AMENDS		STEP 8
		❑ Now
		❑ Later
		❑ Never

Make as many copies of this form that you need to complete your inventory.

Step 4 –HARM TO OTHERS (of any kind)

HARMS TO OTHERS – This is where you put those acts of stealing, or violence, any harm done to others that was not covered in your resentments etc.

Who: _____ My conduct: _____

_____

_____

(The following questions are culled from both the "Big Book" *Alcoholics Anonymous* [55] and the *Twelve Steps and Twelve Traditions.* [56])

Where was I selfish or self-seeking?

Where was I dishonest?

Where was I inconsiderate?

Where was I to blame (responsible)?

What could I have done instead?

What people were hurt and how badly?

Did I spoil my marriage (relationship) and/or injure my children?

Did I jeopardise my standing in the community? How?

What decisions did I make based on this experience that has affected my relationships?

What is the earliest time I can remember making this decision?

List Major "Character Defects" in preparation for STEPS 6 & 7				

AMENDS		STEP 8
		☐ Now
		☐ Later
		☐ Never

Make as many copies of this form that you need to complete your inventory.

DEEP SOUL CLEANSING

Step 4 –HARM TO OTHERS (of any kind)

HARMS TO OTHERS – This is where you put those acts of stealing, or violence, any harm done to others that was not covered in your resentments etc.

Who: _____ My conduct: _____

_____

_____

(The following questions are culled from both the "Big Book" *Alcoholics Anonymous* [57] and the *Twelve Steps and Twelve Traditions*. [58])

Where was I selfish or self-seeking?

Where was I dishonest?

Where was I inconsiderate?

Where was I to blame (responsible)?

What could I have done instead?

What people were hurt and how badly?

Did I spoil my marriage (relationship) and/or injure my children?

Did I jeopardise my standing in the community? How?

What decisions did I make based on this experience that has affected my relationships?

What is the earliest time I can remember making this decision?

List Major "Character Defects" in preparation for STEPS 6 & 7				
AMENDS				**STEP 8**
				☐ Now ☐ Later ☐ Never

Make as many copies of this form that you need to complete your inventory.

Step 4 –HARM TO OTHERS (of any kind)

HARMS TO OTHERS – This is where you put those acts of stealing, or violence, any harm done to others that was not covered in your resentments etc.

Who: _____ My conduct: _____

_____

_____

(The following questions are culled from both the "Big Book" *Alcoholics Anonymous* [59] and the *Twelve Steps and Twelve Traditions.* [60])

Where was I selfish or self-seeking?

Where was I dishonest?

Where was I inconsiderate?

Where was I to blame (responsible)*?*

What could I have done instead?

What people were hurt and how badly?

Did I spoil my marriage (relationship) *and/or injure my children?*

Did I jeopardise my standing in the community? How?

What decisions did I make based on this experience that has affected my relationships?

What is the earliest time I can remember making this decision?

List Major "Character Defects" in preparation for STEPS 6 & 7					
AMENDS					**STEP 8**
					☐ Now
					☐ Later
					☐ Never

Make as many copies of this form that you need to complete your inventory.

DEEP SOUL CLEANSING
Step 4 –HARM TO OTHERS (of any kind)

HARMS TO OTHERS – This is where you put those acts of stealing, or violence, any harm done to others that was not covered in your resentments etc.

Who: _____ My conduct: _____

_____

_____

(The following questions are culled from both the "Big Book" *Alcoholics Anonymous* [61] and the *Twelve Steps and Twelve Traditions.* [62])

Where was I selfish or self-seeking?

Where was I dishonest?

Where was I inconsiderate?

Where was I to blame (responsible)?

What could I have done instead?

What people were hurt and how badly?

Did I spoil my marriage (relationship) and/or injure my children?

Did I jeopardise my standing in the community? How?

What decisions did I make based on this experience that has affected my relationships?

What is the earliest time I can remember making this decision?

List Major "Character Defects" in preparation for STEPS 6 & 7				
AMENDS				**STEP 8**
				❑ Now
				❑ Later
				❑ Never

Make as many copies of this form that you need to complete your inventory.

Step 4 –HARM TO OTHERS (of any kind)

HARMS TO OTHERS – This is where you put those acts of stealing, or violence, any harm done to others that was not covered in your resentments etc.

Who: _____   My conduct: _____

_____

_____

(The following questions are culled from both the "Big Book" *Alcoholics Anonymous* [63] and the *Twelve Steps and Twelve Traditions.* [64])

Where was I selfish or self-seeking?

Where was I dishonest?

Where was I inconsiderate?

Where was I to blame (responsible)*?*

What could I have done instead?

What people were hurt and how badly?

Did I spoil my marriage (relationship) *and/or injure my children?*

Did I jeopardise my standing in the community? How?

What decisions did I make based on this experience that has affected my relationships?

What is the earliest time I can remember making this decision?

List Major "Character Defects" in preparation for STEPS 6 & 7				

AMENDS		STEP 8
		☐ Now
		☐ Later
		☐ Never

Make as many copies of this form that you need to complete your inventory.

DEEP SOUL CLEANSING
Step 4 –HARM TO OTHERS (of any kind)

HARMS TO OTHERS – This is where you put those acts of stealing, or violence, any harm done to others that was not covered in your resentments etc.

Who: _____ My conduct: _____

_____

_____

(The following questions are culled from both the "Big Book" *Alcoholics Anonymous* [65] and the *Twelve Steps and Twelve Traditions.* [66])

Where was I selfish or self-seeking?

Where was I dishonest?

Where was I inconsiderate?

Where was I to blame (responsible)?

What could I have done instead?

What people were hurt and how badly?

Did I spoil my marriage (relationship) and/or injure my children?

Did I jeopardise my standing in the community? How?

What decisions did I make based on this experience that has affected my relationships?

What is the earliest time I can remember making this decision?

List Major "Character Defects" in preparation for STEPS 6 & 7				
AMENDS				**STEP 8**
				❑ Now ❑ Later ❑ Never

Make as many copies of this form that you need to complete your inventory.

Step 4 –HARM TO OTHERS (of any kind)

HARMS TO OTHERS – This is where you put those acts of stealing, or violence, any harm done to others that was not covered in your resentments etc.

Who: _____ My conduct: _____

_____

(The following questions are culled from both the "Big Book" *Alcoholics Anonymous* [67] and the *Twelve Steps and Twelve Traditions.* [68])

Where was I selfish or self-seeking?

Where was I dishonest?

Where was I inconsiderate?

Where was I to blame (responsible)?

What could I have done instead?

What people were hurt and how badly?

Did I spoil my marriage (relationship) and/or injure my children?

Did I jeopardise my standing in the community? How?

What decisions did I make based on this experience that has affected my relationships?

What is the earliest time I can remember making this decision?

List Major "Character Defects" in preparation for STEPS 6 & 7				

AMENDS		STEP 8
		❏ Now
		❏ Later
		❏ Never

Make as many copies of this form that you need to complete your inventory.

DEEP SOUL CLEANSING

Step 4 –HARM TO OTHERS (of any kind)

HARMS TO OTHERS – This is where you put those acts of stealing, or violence, any harm done to others that was not covered in your resentments etc.

Who: _____ My conduct: _____

_____

_____

(The following questions are culled from both the "Big Book" *Alcoholics Anonymous* [69] and the *Twelve Steps and Twelve Traditions*. [70])

Where was I selfish or self-seeking?

Where was I dishonest?

Where was I inconsiderate?

Where was I to blame (responsible)?

What could I have done instead?

What people were hurt and how badly?

Did I spoil my marriage (relationship) and/or injure my children?

Did I jeopardise my standing in the community? How?

What decisions did I make based on this experience that has affected my relationships?

What is the earliest time I can remember making this decision?

List Major "Character Defects" in preparation for STEPS 6 & 7				

AMENDS		STEP 8
		☐ Now ☐ Later ☐ Never

Make as many copies of this form that you need to complete your inventory.

Step 4 –HARM TO OTHERS (of any kind)

HARMS TO OTHERS – This is where you put those acts of stealing, or violence, any harm done to others that was not covered in your resentments etc.

Who: _____ My conduct: _____

_____

_____

(The following questions are culled from both the "Big Book" *Alcoholics Anonymous* [71] and the *Twelve Steps and Twelve Traditions*. [72])

Where was I selfish or self-seeking?

Where was I dishonest?

Where was I inconsiderate?

Where was I to blame (responsible)?

What could I have done instead?

What people were hurt and how badly?

Did I spoil my marriage (relationship) and/or injure my children?

Did I jeopardise my standing in the community? How?

What decisions did I make based on this experience that has affected my relationships?

What is the earliest time I can remember making this decision?

List Major "Character Defects" in preparation for STEPS 6 & 7					
AMENDS					**STEP 8**
					☐ Now
					☐ Later
					☐ Never

Make as many copies of this form that you need to complete your inventory.

DEEP SOUL CLEANSING

Step 4 –HARM TO OTHERS (of any kind)

HARMS TO OTHERS – This is where you put those acts of stealing, or violence, any harm done to others that was not covered in your resentments etc.

Who: _____ My conduct: _____

_____

_____

(The following questions are culled from both the "Big Book" *Alcoholics Anonymous* [73] and the *Twelve Steps and Twelve Traditions.* [74])

Where was I selfish or self-seeking?

Where was I dishonest?

Where was I inconsiderate?

Where was I to blame (responsible)*?*

What could I have done instead?

What people were hurt and how badly?

Did I spoil my marriage (relationship) *and/or injure my children?*

Did I jeopardise my standing in the community? How?

What decisions did I make based on this experience that has affected my relationships?

What is the earliest time I can remember making this decision?

List Major "Character Defects" in preparation for STEPS 6 & 7				

AMENDS		STEP 8
		☐ Now
		☐ Later
		☐ Never

Make as many copies of this form that you need to complete your inventory.

Step 4 –HARM TO OTHERS (of any kind)

HARMS TO OTHERS – This is where you put those acts of stealing, or violence, any harm done to others that was not covered in your resentments etc.

Who: _____ My conduct: _____

_____

_____

(The following questions are culled from both the "Big Book" *Alcoholics Anonymous* [75] and the *Twelve Steps and Twelve Traditions.* [76])

Where was I selfish or self-seeking?

Where was I dishonest?

Where was I inconsiderate?

Where was I to blame (responsible)*?*

What could I have done instead?

What people were hurt and how badly?

Did I spoil my marriage (relationship) *and/or injure my children?*

Did I jeopardise my standing in the community? How?

What decisions did I make based on this experience that has affected my relationships?

What is the earliest time I can remember making this decision?

List Major "Character Defects" in preparation for STEPS 6 & 7				
AMENDS				**STEP 8**
				☐ Now ☐ Later ☐ Never

Make as many copies of this form that you need to complete your inventory.

Step Four
Work and Money

Step 4 – ABOUT MONEY and/or WORK

Employer or Business Deal: _____

My Conduct: _____

_____

(The following questions are culled from the *Twelve Steps and Twelve Traditions.* [77])

Did fear and inferiority about my fitness for my job destroy my confidence and fill me with conflict? Explain.

Did I try to cover up those feelings of inadequacy by bluffing, cheating, lying, or evading responsibility? Examples.

Did I gripe that others failed to recognise my truly exceptional abilities? Examples.

Did I overvalue myself and play the "big shot"? How?

Did I have such unprincipled ambition that I double-crossed and/or undercut my associates? Explain.

Was I irresponsible, wasteful and extravagant? How?

Did I recklessly borrow money, caring little whether it was repaid or not? (Mine or the companies) Explain.

Was I a pinchpenny, refusing to support my family properly? How?

Did I try to cut corners financially? Where?

What about the "quick money" deals, the stock market, and the races? How about gambling? (In or out of business) Examples.

Did I juggle credit accounts ("robbing Peter to pay Paul")? How?

Did I manipulate the food budget or other spending allowances? Examples.

What Character defects contributed to my financial instability?(Enter below)

List Major "Character Defects" in preparation for STEPS 6 & 7				
AMENDS				**STEP 8**
				❑ Now
				❑ Later
				❑ Never

Make as many copies of this form that you need to complete your inventory.

Step 4 – ABOUT MONEY and/or WORK

Employer or Business Deal: _____

My Conduct: _____
_____

(The following questions are culled from the *Twelve Steps and Twelve Traditions*. [78])

Did fear and inferiority about my fitness for my job destroy my confidence and fill me with conflict? Explain.

Did I try to cover up those feelings of inadequacy by bluffing, cheating, lying, or evading responsibility? Examples.

Did I gripe that others failed to recognise my truly exceptional abilities? Examples.

Did I overvalue myself and play the "big shot"? How?

Did I have such unprincipled ambition that I double-crossed and/or undercut my associates? Explain.

Was I irresponsible, wasteful and extravagant? How?

Did I recklessly borrow money, caring little whether it was repaid or not? (Mine or the companies) Explain.

Was I a pinchpenny, refusing to support my family properly? How?

Did I try to cut corners financially? Where?

What about the "quick money" deals, the stock market, and the races? How about gambling? (In or out of business) Examples.

Did I juggle credit accounts ("robbing Peter to pay Paul")? How?

Did I manipulate the food budget or other spending allowances? Examples.

What Character defects contributed to my financial instability?(Enter below)

List Major "Character Defects" in preparation for STEPS 6 & 7				

AMENDS		STEP 8
		☐ Now
		☐ Later
		☐ Never

Make as many copies of this form that you need to complete your inventory.

Step 4 – ABOUT MONEY and/or WORK

Employer or Business Deal: _____

My Conduct: _____

_____

(The following questions are culled from the *Twelve Steps and Twelve Traditions*. [79])

Did fear and inferiority about my fitness for my job destroy my confidence and fill me with conflict? Explain.

Did I try to cover up those feelings of inadequacy by bluffing, cheating, lying, or evading responsibility? Examples.

Did I gripe that others failed to recognise my truly exceptional abilities? Examples.

Did I overvalue myself and play the "big shot"? How?

Did I have such unprincipled ambition that I double-crossed and/or undercut my associates? Explain.

Was I irresponsible, wasteful and extravagant? How?

Did I recklessly borrow money, caring little whether it was repaid or not? (Mine or the companies) Explain.

Was I a pinchpenny, refusing to support my family properly? How?

Did I try to cut corners financially? Where?

What about the "quick money" deals, the stock market, and the races? How about gambling? (In or out of business) Examples.

Did I juggle credit accounts ("robbing Peter to pay Paul")? How?

Did I manipulate the food budget or other spending allowances? Examples.

What Character defects contributed to my financial instability?(Enter below)

List Major "Character Defects" in preparation for STEPS 6 & 7				

AMENDS		STEP 8
		❑ Now ❑ Later ❑ Never

Make as many copies of this form that you need to complete your inventory.

Step 4 – ABOUT MONEY and/or WORK

Employer or Business Deal: _____

My Conduct: _____

_____

(The following questions are culled from the *Twelve Steps and Twelve Traditions.* [80])

Did fear and inferiority about my fitness for my job destroy my confidence and fill me with conflict? Explain.

Did I try to cover up those feelings of inadequacy by bluffing, cheating, lying, or evading responsibility? Examples.

Did I gripe that others failed to recognise my truly exceptional abilities? Examples.

Did I overvalue myself and play the "big shot"? How?

Did I have such unprincipled ambition that I double-crossed and/or undercut my associates? Explain.

Was I irresponsible, wasteful and extravagant? How?

Did I recklessly borrow money, caring little whether it was repaid or not? (Mine or the companies) Explain.

Was I a pinchpenny, refusing to support my family properly? How?

Did I try to cut corners financially? Where?

What about the "quick money" deals, the stock market, and the races? How about gambling? (In or out of business) Examples.

Did I juggle credit accounts ("robbing Peter to pay Paul")? How?

Did I manipulate the food budget or other spending allowances? Examples.

What Character defects contributed to my financial instability?(Enter below)

List Major "Character Defects" in preparation for STEPS 6 & 7				

AMENDS		STEP 8
		☐ Now
		☐ Later
		☐ Never

Make as many copies of this form that you need to complete your inventory.

Step 4 – ABOUT MONEY and/or WORK

Employer or Business Deal: _____

My Conduct: _____

_____

(The following questions are culled from the *Twelve Steps and Twelve Traditions*. [81])

Did fear and inferiority about my fitness for my job destroy my confidence and fill me with conflict? Explain.

Did I try to cover up those feelings of inadequacy by bluffing, cheating, lying, or evading responsibility? Examples.

Did I gripe that others failed to recognise my truly exceptional abilities? Examples.

Did I overvalue myself and play the "big shot"? How?

Did I have such unprincipled ambition that I double-crossed and/or undercut my associates? Explain.

Was I irresponsible, wasteful and extravagant? How?

Did I recklessly borrow money, caring little whether it was repaid or not? (Mine or the companies) Explain.

Was I a pinchpenny, refusing to support my family properly? How?

Did I try to cut corners financially? Where?

What about the "quick money" deals, the stock market, and the races? How about gambling? (In or out of business) Examples.

Did I juggle credit accounts ("robbing Peter to pay Paul")? How?

Did I manipulate the food budget or other spending allowances? Examples.

What Character defects contributed to my financial instability?(Enter below)

List Major "Character Defects" in preparation for STEPS 6 & 7				

AMENDS		STEP 8
		☐ Now
		☐ Later
		☐ Never

Make as many copies of this form that you need to complete your inventory.

Step 4 – ABOUT MONEY and/or WORK

Employer or Business Deal: _____

My Conduct: _____

_____

(The following questions are culled from the *Twelve Steps and Twelve Traditions.* [82])

Did fear and inferiority about my fitness for my job destroy my confidence and fill me with conflict? Explain.

Did I try to cover up those feelings of inadequacy by bluffing, cheating, lying, or evading responsibility? Examples.

Did I gripe that others failed to recognise my truly exceptional abilities? Examples.

Did I overvalue myself and play the "big shot"? How?

Did I have such unprincipled ambition that I double-crossed and/or undercut my associates? Explain.

Was I irresponsible, wasteful and extravagant? How?

Did I recklessly borrow money, caring little whether it was repaid or not? (Mine or the companies) Explain.

Was I a pinchpenny, refusing to support my family properly? How?

Did I try to cut corners financially? Where?

What about the "quick money" deals, the stock market, and the races? How about gambling? (In or out of business) Examples.

Did I juggle credit accounts ("robbing Peter to pay Paul")? How?

Did I manipulate the food budget or other spending allowances? Examples.

What Character defects contributed to my financial instability?(Enter below)

List Major "Character Defects" in preparation for STEPS 6 & 7				

AMENDS		STEP 8
		❑ Now
		❑ Later
		❑ Never

Make as many copies of this form that you need to complete your inventory.

Step 4 – ABOUT MONEY and/or WORK

Employer or Business Deal: _____

My Conduct: _____

_____

(The following questions are culled from the *Twelve Steps and Twelve Traditions.* [83])

Did fear and inferiority about my fitness for my job destroy my confidence and fill me with conflict? Explain.

Did I try to cover up those feelings of inadequacy by bluffing, cheating, lying, or evading responsibility? Examples.

Did I gripe that others failed to recognise my truly exceptional abilities? Examples.

Did I overvalue myself and play the "big shot"? How?

Did I have such unprincipled ambition that I double-crossed and/or undercut my associates? Explain.

Was I irresponsible, wasteful and extravagant? How?

Did I recklessly borrow money, caring little whether it was repaid or not? (Mine or the companies) Explain.

Was I a pinchpenny, refusing to support my family properly? How?

Did I try to cut corners financially? Where?

What about the "quick money" deals, the stock market, and the races? How about gambling? (In or out of business) Examples.

Did I juggle credit accounts ("robbing Peter to pay Paul")? How?

Did I manipulate the food budget or other spending allowances? Examples.

What Character defects contributed to my financial instability?(Enter below)

List Major "Character Defects" in preparation for STEPS 6 & 7				

AMENDS				STEP 8
				❑ Now
				❑ Later
				❑ Never

Make as many copies of this form that you need to complete your inventory.

Step 4 – ABOUT MONEY and/or WORK

Employer or Business Deal: _____

My Conduct: _____

_____

(The following questions are culled from the *Twelve Steps and Twelve Traditions.* [84])

Did fear and inferiority about my fitness for my job destroy my confidence and fill me with conflict? Explain.

Did I try to cover up those feelings of inadequacy by bluffing, cheating, lying, or evading responsibility? Examples.

Did I gripe that others failed to recognise my truly exceptional abilities? Examples.

Did I overvalue myself and play the "big shot"? How?

Did I have such unprincipled ambition that I double-crossed and/or undercut my associates? Explain.

Was I irresponsible, wasteful and extravagant? How?

Did I recklessly borrow money, caring little whether it was repaid or not? (Mine or the companies) Explain.

Was I a pinchpenny, refusing to support my family properly? How?

Did I try to cut corners financially? Where?

What about the "quick money" deals, the stock market, and the races? How about gambling? (In or out of business) Examples.

Did I juggle credit accounts ("robbing Peter to pay Paul")? How?

Did I manipulate the food budget or other spending allowances? Examples.

What Character defects contributed to my financial instability?(Enter below)

List Major "Character Defects" in preparation for STEPS 6 & 7				

AMENDS		STEP 8
		❏ Now
		❏ Later
		❏ Never

Make as many copies of this form that you need to complete your inventory.

Step 4 – ABOUT MONEY and/or WORK

Employer or Business Deal: _____

My Conduct: _____

_____

(The following questions are culled from the *Twelve Steps and Twelve Traditions*. [85])

Did fear and inferiority about my fitness for my job destroy my confidence and fill me with conflict? Explain.

Did I try to cover up those feelings of inadequacy by bluffing, cheating, lying, or evading responsibility? Examples.

Did I gripe that others failed to recognise my truly exceptional abilities? Examples.

Did I overvalue myself and play the "big shot"? How?

Did I have such unprincipled ambition that I double-crossed and/or undercut my associates? Explain.

Was I irresponsible, wasteful and extravagant? How?

Did I recklessly borrow money, caring little whether it was repaid or not? (Mine or the companies) Explain.

Was I a pinchpenny, refusing to support my family properly? How?

Did I try to cut corners financially? Where?

What about the "quick money" deals, the stock market, and the races? How about gambling? (In or out of business) Examples.

Did I juggle credit accounts ("robbing Peter to pay Paul")? How?

Did I manipulate the food budget or other spending allowances? Examples.

What Character defects contributed to my financial instability?(Enter below)

List Major "Character Defects" in preparation for STEPS 6 & 7					

AMENDS		STEP 8
		☐ Now
		☐ Later
		☐ Never

Make as many copies of this form that you need to complete your inventory.

Step 4 – ABOUT MONEY and/or WORK

Employer or Business Deal: _____

My Conduct: _____

_____

(The following questions are culled from the *Twelve Steps and Twelve Traditions.* [86])

Did fear and inferiority about my fitness for my job destroy my confidence and fill me with conflict? Explain.

Did I try to cover up those feelings of inadequacy by bluffing, cheating, lying, or evading responsibility? Examples.

Did I gripe that others failed to recognise my truly exceptional abilities? Examples.

Did I overvalue myself and play the "big shot"? How?

Did I have such unprincipled ambition that I double-crossed and/or undercut my associates? Explain.

Was I irresponsible, wasteful and extravagant? How?

Did I recklessly borrow money, caring little whether it was repaid or not? (Mine or the companies) Explain.

Was I a pinchpenny, refusing to support my family properly? How?

Did I try to cut corners financially? Where?

What about the "quick money" deals, the stock market, and the races? How about gambling? (In or out of business) Examples.

Did I juggle credit accounts ("robbing Peter to pay Paul")? How?

Did I manipulate the food budget or other spending allowances? Examples.

What Character defects contributed to my financial instability?(Enter below)

List Major "Character Defects" in preparation for STEPS 6 & 7				

AMENDS		STEP 8
		☐ Now
		☐ Later
		☐ Never

Make as many copies of this form that you need to complete your inventory.

Step 4 – ABOUT MONEY and/or WORK

Employer or Business Deal: _____

My Conduct: _____

_____

(The following questions are culled from the *Twelve Steps and Twelve Traditions.* [87])

Did fear and inferiority about my fitness for my job destroy my confidence and fill me with conflict? Explain.

Did I try to cover up those feelings of inadequacy by bluffing, cheating, lying, or evading responsibility? Examples.

Did I gripe that others failed to recognise my truly exceptional abilities? Examples.

Did I overvalue myself and play the "big shot"? How?

Did I have such unprincipled ambition that I double-crossed and/or undercut my associates? Explain.

Was I irresponsible, wasteful and extravagant? How?

Did I recklessly borrow money, caring little whether it was repaid or not? (Mine or the companies) Explain.

Was I a pinchpenny, refusing to support my family properly? How?

Did I try to cut corners financially? Where?

What about the "quick money" deals, the stock market, and the races? How about gambling? (In or out of business) Examples.

Did I juggle credit accounts ("robbing Peter to pay Paul")? How?

Did I manipulate the food budget or other spending allowances? Examples.

What Character defects contributed to my financial instability?(Enter below)

List Major "Character Defects" in preparation for STEPS 6 & 7				

AMENDS		STEP 8
		☐ Now
		☐ Later
		☐ Never

Make as many copies of this form that you need to complete your inventory.

Step 4 – ABOUT MONEY and/or WORK

Employer or Business Deal: _____

My Conduct: _____

_____

(The following questions are culled from the *Twelve Steps and Twelve Traditions.* [88])

Did fear and inferiority about my fitness for my job destroy my confidence and fill me with conflict? Explain.

Did I try to cover up those feelings of inadequacy by bluffing, cheating, lying, or evading responsibility? Examples.

Did I gripe that others failed to recognise my truly exceptional abilities? Examples.

Did I overvalue myself and play the "big shot"? How?

Did I have such unprincipled ambition that I double-crossed and/or undercut my associates? Explain.

Was I irresponsible, wasteful and extravagant? How?

Did I recklessly borrow money, caring little whether it was repaid or not? (Mine or the companies) Explain.

Was I a pinchpenny, refusing to support my family properly? How?

Did I try to cut corners financially? Where?

What about the "quick money" deals, the stock market, and the races? How about gambling? (In or out of business) Examples.

Did I juggle credit accounts ("robbing Peter to pay Paul")? How?

Did I manipulate the food budget or other spending allowances? Examples.

What Character defects contributed to my financial instability?(Enter below)

List Major "Character Defects" in preparation for STEPS 6 & 7				
AMENDS				**STEP 8**
				❏ Now
				❏ Later
				❏ Never

Make as many copies of this form that you need to complete your inventory.

Step 4 – ABOUT MONEY and/or WORK

Employer or Business Deal: _____

My Conduct: _____

_____

(The following questions are culled from the *Twelve Steps and Twelve Traditions*. [89])

Did fear and inferiority about my fitness for my job destroy my confidence and fill me with conflict? Explain.

Did I try to cover up those feelings of inadequacy by bluffing, cheating, lying, or evading responsibility? Examples.

Did I gripe that others failed to recognise my truly exceptional abilities? Examples.

Did I overvalue myself and play the "big shot"? How?

Did I have such unprincipled ambition that I double-crossed and/or undercut my associates? Explain.

Was I irresponsible, wasteful and extravagant? How?

Did I recklessly borrow money, caring little whether it was repaid or not? (Mine or the companies) Explain.

Was I a pinchpenny, refusing to support my family properly? How?

Did I try to cut corners financially? Where?

What about the "quick money" deals, the stock market, and the races? How about gambling? (In or out of business) Examples.

Did I juggle credit accounts ("robbing Peter to pay Paul")? How?

Did I manipulate the food budget or other spending allowances? Examples.

What Character defects contributed to my financial instability?(Enter below)

List Major "Character Defects" in preparation for STEPS 6 & 7				

AMENDS		STEP 8
		☐ Now
		☐ Later
		☐ Never

Make as many copies of this form that you need to complete your inventory.

Step 4 – ABOUT MONEY and/or WORK

Employer or Business Deal: _____

My Conduct: _____
_____

(The following questions are culled from the *Twelve Steps and Twelve Traditions*. [90])

Did fear and inferiority about my fitness for my job destroy my confidence and fill me with conflict? Explain.

Did I try to cover up those feelings of inadequacy by bluffing, cheating, lying, or evading responsibility? Examples.

Did I gripe that others failed to recognise my truly exceptional abilities? Examples.

Did I overvalue myself and play the "big shot"? How?

Did I have such unprincipled ambition that I double-crossed and/or undercut my associates? Explain.

Was I irresponsible, wasteful and extravagant? How?

Did I recklessly borrow money, caring little whether it was repaid or not? (Mine or the companies) Explain.

Was I a pinchpenny, refusing to support my family properly? How?

Did I try to cut corners financially? Where?

What about the "quick money" deals, the stock market, and the races? How about gambling? (In or out of business) Examples.

Did I juggle credit accounts ("robbing Peter to pay Paul")? How?

Did I manipulate the food budget or other spending allowances? Examples.

What Character defects contributed to my financial instability?(Enter below)

List Major "Character Defects" in preparation for STEPS 6 & 7				

AMENDS		STEP 8
		❑ Now
		❑ Later
		❑ Never

Make as many copies of this form that you need to complete your inventory.

Step 4 – ABOUT MONEY and/or WORK

Employer or Business Deal: _____

My Conduct: _____

_____

(The following questions are culled from the *Twelve Steps and Twelve Traditions.* [91])

Did fear and inferiority about my fitness for my job destroy my confidence and fill me with conflict? Explain.

Did I try to cover up those feelings of inadequacy by bluffing, cheating, lying, or evading responsibility? Examples.

Did I gripe that others failed to recognise my truly exceptional abilities? Examples.

Did I overvalue myself and play the "big shot"? How?

Did I have such unprincipled ambition that I double-crossed and/or undercut my associates? Explain.

Was I irresponsible, wasteful and extravagant? How?

Did I recklessly borrow money, caring little whether it was repaid or not? (Mine or the companies) Explain.

Was I a pinchpenny, refusing to support my family properly? How?

Did I try to cut corners financially? Where?

What about the "quick money" deals, the stock market, and the races? How about gambling? (In or out of business) Examples.

Did I juggle credit accounts ("robbing Peter to pay Paul")? How?

Did I manipulate the food budget or other spending allowances? Examples.

What Character defects contributed to my financial instability?(Enter below)

List Major "Character Defects" in preparation for STEPS 6 & 7				

AMENDS		STEP 8
		☐ Now
		☐ Later
		☐ Never

Make as many copies of this form that you need to complete your inventory.

Step Five

Step Five

STEP FIVE – THE ADMISSION – CONFESSION

"Admitted To God, To Ourselves and To Another Human Being the Exact Nature of Our Wrongs"

READ IN PREPARATION:

"Big Book" of *Alcoholics Anonymous* –   Page 72-75

Twelve Steps and Twelve Traditions – Step Five   Pages 56-63

Step Six

STEP SIX – GETTING READY – WILLINGNESS

"Were Entirely Ready To Have God Remove All These Defects Of Character." [92]

READ IN PREPARATION:

"Big Book" of *Alcoholics Anonymous* –   Page 76.1

Twelve Steps and Twelve Traditions – Step Six   Pages 64-70

List Major "Character Defects" STEPS 6 & 7					

LIST OF CHARACTER DEFECTS

Abandonment

Abusive

Addictions

Aggravation

Agitation

Airhead

Alcoholism

ANGER

Annoyance

Arrogance

Belligerent

Blame

Bigotry

Bored

Coldness

Condescending

Confusion

Controlling

Cowardice

Cynicism

Deceit

Depression

Devious

Disbelief

Dishonesty

Dislike

Dismay

Dissatisfaction

Doubt

Egocentricity

ENVY

Evasiveness

False-humility

False-Pride

Fear

Frustration

GLUTTONY

Gossip

Grandiosity

GREED

Hate

Hero-Worship

Hypersensitive

Hypocrisy

Impatience

Inconsiderate

Indignation

Insecurity

Insincere

Intolerance

Irritation

Jealousy

Judgement

Lazy

Lying

LUST

Manipulative

Mind-Reading

Negativity

Obsession

Offensive

Over-eating

Over reactive

Over sensitive

Panicky

Patronising

Paranoia

People pleasing

Perfectionism

Phoney

Playing dumb

Possessiveness

Prejudice

PRIDE

Procrastination

Rage

Rebellious

Rejection

Resentment

Resistant

Righteous-Indignation

Self-Centeredness

Self-Condemnation

Self-Hate

Self-Importance

Self-Indulgence

Selfishness

Self-Justification

Self-Obsession

Self-Pity

Self-Righteousness

Self-Seeking

Shame

SLOTH

Sensitivity

Spite

Stoic

Suspicion

Touchy

Two-faced

Ungrateful

Unwillingness

Vengeful

Victim

Vindictiveness

Violent

Withdrawn

Step Seven

STEP SEVEN – ASKING FOR REMOVAL – HUMILITY

*"**Humbly Asked** (God) **To Remove Our Shortcomings.**"* [93]

READ IN PREPARATION:

Read in preparation, in the book Twelve Steps and Twelve Traditions – Step Seven

Pages 71-78

List Major "Character Defects" STEPS 6 & 7					

"My creator, I am now willing that you should have all of me good and bad. I pray that you now remove from me every single defect of character,
(including _____) *which stand*(s)
in the way of my usefulness to you and my fellows. Grant me strength as I go out from here to do your bidding.

Amen"

[94]

List Major "Character Defects" STEPS 6 & 7				
List Major "Character Defects" STEPS 6 & 7				

List Major "Character Defects" STEPS 6 & 7					

List Major "Character Defects" STEPS 6 & 7

Step Eight

STEPS EIGHT – BECOMING WILLING TO MEND – FORGIVENESS

"Made a List of All People We Have Harmed, and Became Willing To Make Amends To Them All." [95]

READ IN PREPARATION:

"Big Book" of *Alcoholics Anonymous* –	Page 76-84
Twelve Steps and Twelve Traditions – Step Eight	Pages 79-84

Let us take note that we have imbedded the Amends beneath columns 1, 2, and 3, and below each of the other Inventory sections. This should make it simpler to follow through and not conveniently "forget" anyone. However, there are extra pages of Amends, here and in the Personal Inventory Workbook. These extra pages are for any additional amends necessary due to the fallout of our behaviour.

AMENDS (Person, Place or Thing)		☐ Now ☐ Later ☐ Never
AMENDS		☐ Now ☐ Later ☐ Never
AMENDS		☐ Now ☐ Later ☐ Never
AMENDS		☐ Now ☐ Later ☐ Never
AMENDS		☐ Now ☐ Later ☐ Never
AMENDS		☐ Now ☐ Later ☐ Never
AMENDS		☐ Now ☐ Later ☐ Never

Step Nine

STEP NINE – MENDING RELATIONSHIPS – RESTITUTION

"Made Direct Amends To Such People Wherever Possible, Except When To Do So Would Injure Them or Others." [96]

READ IN PREPARATION:

"Big Book" of *Alcoholics Anonymous* –   Page 76-84

Twelve Steps and Twelve Traditions – Step Nine   Pages 85-89

For Step Nine we discuss with our Sponsors those direct amends we feel we want or need to make to or about the "Person, Place or Thing," if any.

AMENDS (Person, Place or Thing)		❑ Now ❑ Later ❑ Never
AMENDS		❑ Now ❑ Later ❑ Never
AMENDS		❑ Now ❑ Later ❑ Never
AMENDS		❑ Now ❑ Later ❑ Never
AMENDS		❑ Now ❑ Later ❑ Never
AMENDS		❑ Now ❑ Later ❑ Never
AMENDS (Person, Place or Thing)		❑ Now ❑ Later ❑ Never
AMENDS		❑ Now ❑ Later ❑ Never
AMENDS		❑ Now ❑ Later ❑ Never
AMENDS (Person, Place or Thing)		❑ Now ❑ Later ❑ Never

AMENDS		Now
(Person, Place or Thing)		Later
		Never
AMENDS		Now
		Later
		Never
AMENDS		Now
		Later
		Never
AMENDS		Now
		Later
		Never
AMENDS		Now
		Later
		Never
AMENDS		Now
		Later
		Never
AMENDS		Now
		Later
		Never
AMENDS		Now
(Person, Place or Thing)		Later
		Never
AMENDS		Now
		Later
		Never
AMENDS		Now
		Later
		Never
AMENDS		Now
		Later
		Never
AMENDS		Now
		Later
		Never
AMENDS		Now
		Later
		Never
AMENDS		Now
(Person, Place or Thing)		Later
		Never
AMENDS		Now
		Later
		Never

AMENDS		☐ Now
		☐ Later
		☐ Never
AMENDS		☐ Now
		☐ Later
		☐ Never
AMENDS		☐ Now
		☐ Later
		☐ Never
AMENDS		☐ Now
(Person, Place or Thing)		☐ Later
		☐ Never
AMENDS		☐ Now
		☐ Later
		☐ Never
AMENDS		☐ Now
		☐ Later
		☐ Never
AMENDS		☐ Now
		☐ Later
		☐ Never
AMENDS		☐ Now
		☐ Later
		☐ Never
AMENDS		☐ Now
		☐ Later
		☐ Never
AMENDS		☐ Now
(Person, Place or Thing)		☐ Later
		☐ Never
AMENDS		☐ Now
		☐ Later
		☐ Never
AMENDS		☐ Now
		☐ Later
		☐ Never
AMENDS		☐ Now
		☐ Later
		☐ Never
AMENDS		☐ Now
(Person, Place or Thing)		☐ Later
		☐ Never
AMENDS		☐ Now
		☐ Later
		☐ Never
AMENDS		☐ Now
(Person, Place or Thing)		☐ Later
		☐ Never

AMENDS		Now
		Later
(Person, Place or Thing)		Never
AMENDS		Now
		Later
		Never
AMENDS		Now
		Later
		Never
AMENDS		Now
		Later
		Never
AMENDS		Now
		Later
		Never
AMENDS		Now
		Later
(Person, Place or Thing)		Never
AMENDS		Now
		Later
		Never
AMENDS		Now
		Later
		Never
AMENDS		Now
		Later
		Never
AMENDS		Now
		Later
		Never
AMENDS		Now
		Later
		Never
AMENDS		Now
		Later
(Person, Place or Thing)		Never
AMENDS		Now
		Later
		Never
AMENDS		Now
		Later
		Never
AMENDS		Now
		Later
		Never
AMENDS		Now
		Later
(Person, Place or Thing)		Never

AMENDS		□ Now
		□ Later
		□ Never
AMENDS		□ Now
(Person, Place or Thing)		□ Later
		□ Never
AMENDS		□ Now
		□ Later
		□ Never
AMENDS		□ Now
		□ Later
		□ Never
AMENDS		□ Now
		□ Later
		□ Never
AMENDS		□ Now
		□ Later
		□ Never
AMENDS		□ Now
		□ Later
		□ Never
AMENDS		□ Now
(Person, Place or Thing)		□ Later
		□ Never
AMENDS		□ Now
		□ Later
		□ Never
AMENDS		□ Now
		□ Later
		□ Never
AMENDS		□ Now
		□ Later
		□ Never
AMENDS		□ Now
(Person, Place or Thing)		□ Later
		□ Never
AMENDS		□ Now
		□ Later
		□ Never
AMENDS		□ Now
		□ Later
		□ Never
AMENDS		□ Now
		□ Later
		□ Never
AMENDS		□ Now
(Person, Place or Thing)		□ Later
		□ Never

AMENDS		Now
		Later
(Person, Place or Thing)		Never
AMENDS		Now
		Later
		Never
AMENDS		Now
		Later
		Never
AMENDS		Now
		Later
(Person, Place or Thing)		Never
AMENDS		Now
		Later
		Never
AMENDS		Now
		Later
		Never
AMENDS		Now
		Later
		Never
AMENDS		Now
		Later
		Never
AMENDS		Now
		Later
		Never
AMENDS		Now
		Later
(Person, Place or Thing)		Never
AMENDS		Now
		Later
(Person, Place or Thing)		Never
AMENDS		Now
		Later
		Never
AMENDS		Now
		Later
		Never
AMENDS		Now
		Later
		Never
AMENDS		Now
		Later
		Never
AMENDS		Now
		Later
(Person, Place or Thing)		Never

AMENDS		Now / Later / Never

AMENDS (Person, Place or Thing) — ☐ Now ☐ Later ☐ Never

AMENDS — ☐ Now ☐ Later ☐ Never

AMENDS — ☐ Now ☐ Later ☐ Never

AMENDS (Person, Place or Thing) — ☐ Now ☐ Later ☐ Never

AMENDS — ☐ Now ☐ Later ☐ Never

AMENDS — ☐ Now ☐ Later ☐ Never

AMENDS — ☐ Now ☐ Later ☐ Never

AMENDS — ☐ Now ☐ Later ☐ Never

AMENDS (Person, Place or Thing) — ☐ Now ☐ Later ☐ Never

AMENDS — ☐ Now ☐ Later ☐ Never

AMENDS — ☐ Now ☐ Later ☐ Never

AMENDS (Person, Place or Thing) — ☐ Now ☐ Later ☐ Never

AMENDS — ☐ Now ☐ Later ☐ Never

AMENDS — ☐ Now ☐ Later ☐ Never

AMENDS — ☐ Now ☐ Later ☐ Never

AMENDS (Person, Place or Thing) — ☐ Now ☐ Later ☐ Never

AMENDS		☐ Now ☐ Later ☐ Never
AMENDS		☐ Now ☐ Later ☐ Never
AMENDS		☐ Now ☐ Later ☐ Never
(Person, Place or Thing)		
AMENDS		☐ Now ☐ Later ☐ Never
AMENDS		☐ Now ☐ Later ☐ Never
AMENDS		☐ Now ☐ Later ☐ Never
AMENDS		☐ Now ☐ Later ☐ Never
AMENDS		☐ Now ☐ Later ☐ Never
(Person, Place or Thing)		
AMENDS		☐ Now ☐ Later ☐ Never
AMENDS		☐ Now ☐ Later ☐ Never
AMENDS		☐ Now ☐ Later ☐ Never
AMENDS		☐ Now ☐ Later ☐ Never
AMENDS		☐ Now ☐ Later ☐ Never
(Person, Place or Thing)		
AMENDS		☐ Now ☐ Later ☐ Never
AMENDS		☐ Now ☐ Later ☐ Never

STEP NINE

AMENDS		☐ Now
		☐ Later
(Person, Place or Thing)		☐ Never
AMENDS		☐ Now
		☐ Later
		☐ Never
AMENDS		☐ Now
		☐ Later
		☐ Never
AMENDS		☐ Now
		☐ Later
(Person, Place or Thing)		☐ Never
AMENDS		☐ Now
		☐ Later
		☐ Never
AMENDS		☐ Now
		☐ Later
		☐ Never
AMENDS		☐ Now
		☐ Later
		☐ Never
AMENDS		☐ Now
		☐ Later
(Person, Place or Thing)		☐ Never
AMENDS		☐ Now
		☐ Later
		☐ Never
AMENDS		☐ Now
		☐ Later
(Person, Place or Thing)		☐ Never
AMENDS		☐ Now
		☐ Later
		☐ Never
AMENDS		☐ Now
		☐ Later
		☐ Never
AMENDS		☐ Now
		☐ Later
		☐ Never
AMENDS		☐ Now
		☐ Later
		☐ Never
AMENDS		☐ Now
		☐ Later
		☐ Never
AMENDS		☐ Now
		☐ Later
(Person, Place or Thing)		☐ Never

AMENDS		Now
		Later
(Person, Place or Thing)		Never
AMENDS		Now
		Later
		Never
AMENDS		Now
		Later
		Never
AMENDS		Now
		Later
		Never
AMENDS		Now
		Later
		Never
AMENDS		Now
		Later
(Person, Place or Thing)		Never
AMENDS		Now
		Later
		Never
AMENDS		Now
		Later
		Never
AMENDS		Now
		Later
		Never
AMENDS		Now
		Later
		Never
AMENDS		Now
		Later
		Never
AMENDS		Now
		Later
(Person, Place or Thing)		Never
AMENDS		Now
		Later
		Never
AMENDS		Now
		Later
		Never
AMENDS		Now
		Later
		Never
AMENDS		Now
		Later
(Person, Place or Thing)		Never

AMENDS		Now
		Later
(Person, Place or Thing)		Never
AMENDS		Now
		Later
		Never
AMENDS		Now
		Later
(Person, Place or Thing)		Never
AMENDS		Now
		Later
		Never
AMENDS		Now
		Later
		Never
AMENDS		Now
		Later
		Never
AMENDS		Now
		Later
		Never
AMENDS		Now
		Later
(Person, Place or Thing)		Never
AMENDS		Now
		Later
		Never
AMENDS		Now
		Later
		Never
AMENDS		Now
		Later
(Person, Place or Thing)		Never
AMENDS		Now
		Later
		Never
AMENDS		Now
		Later
(Person, Place or Thing)		Never
AMENDS		Now
		Later
		Never
AMENDS		Now
		Later
		Never

The Promises

"If we are painstaking about this phase of our development, we will be amazed before we are half way through. We are going to know a new freedom and a new happiness. We will not regret the past nor wish to shut the door on it. We will comprehend the word serenity and we will know peace. No matter how far down the scale we have gone, we will see how our experience can benefit others. That feeling of uselessness and self-pity will disappear. We will lose interest in selfish things and gain interest in our fellows. Self-seeking will slip away. Our whole attitude and outlook upon life will change. Fear of people and of economic insecurity will leave us. We will intuitively know how to handle situations that used to baffle us. We will suddenly realise that God is doing for us what we could not do for ourselves.

"Are these extravagant promises? We think not. They are being fulfilled among us – sometimes quickly, sometimes slowly. They will always materialise if we work for them." 97

Step Ten

STEP TEN – DISTURBANCE CONTROL – STEWARDSHIP

We—*"Continued To Take Personal Inventory And When We Were Wrong Promptly Admitted It."* [98]

READ IN PREPARATION:

"Big Book" of *Alcoholics Anonymous* –   Pages 84-85

And; *Twelve Steps and Twelve Traditions* – Step Ten
                                                      Pages 90-97

Resentment (1) and/or Fear:	The Cause (2)	Affects Our: (Column 3)
Person, Place or Thing		❑ Self-Esteem ❑ Security ❑ Ambitions ❑ Personal Relations ❑ Sex Relations ❑ Pride/Shame ❑ Fear
Ask Ourselves: ** (AA 67.3) * (AA 62.2)	Putting out of our mind the wrong others had done, we resolutely looked for our own mistakes… We admitted our wrongs honestly…** (Column 4)	
Where had we been selfish, self-centred or self-seeking?**		
Where had we been dishonest?**		
Where had we been frightened?**		
For what had we been responsible?**		
What decisions did I make based on self that later placed me in a position to be hurt?*		
When in the past did we make this decision? * (Earliest memory.)		
Where were we wrong**, **what was our part?**		

STEPS 6 & 7	List of Character Defects		

STEP 9 - Amend	Step 9
	❑ Now ❑ Later ❑ Never

12 STEP WORKBOOK

Food		Money	
Breakfast		Item	Amount
Lunch			
Dinner			
Snack			
Exercise			
Litres Water Hours Sleep		Total Spent Today	

When we retire at night we constructively review our day. We remember we have ceased fighting anything and anyone—love and tolerance of others is our code.

We Draw Up a Balance Sheet

The "Negative Side"	✔	The "Positive Side"	✔
Were we resentful?		Have we stayed clean of our addiction today?	
Were we selfish?		Were we kind?	
Were we dishonest?		Were we loving toward all?	
Were we afraid?		What did we pack into life?	
Have we kept something to ourselves?		Did we pray and meditate?	
Were we thinking of ourselves most of the time?		Did we call someone we could help today?	
Were we "disturbed" today?		Did we think of how we could help others?	
Do we owe an apology? And if so to whom?		Did we study literature today?	
What could we have done better?		Did we go to a meeting today?	
Did we blame our feelings on someone else?		Did we call our sponsor today?	
Do we need to take detailed inventory on something?		Did we do anything that is improved over our past?	

Journal

Step Eleven

STEP ELEVEN – BUILDING PEACE – CONSCIOUSNESS

"Sought Through Prayer and Meditation To Improve Our Conscious Contact With God, As We Understood Him, Praying Only For Knowledge Of His Will For Us, and the Power To Carry That Out." [99]

READ IN PREPARATION:

"Big Book" of *Alcoholics Anonymous* –   Page 85-88

Twelve Steps and Twelve Traditions – Step Eleven Pages 98-108

> ### *"THE PRAYER OF ST. FRANCIS OF ASSISI*
>
> *"Lord, make me a channel of thy peace—*
>
> *That where there is hatred, I may bring love—*
>
> *That where there is wrong, I may bring the spirit of forgiveness—*
>
> *That where there is discord, I may bring harmony—*
>
> *That where there is error, I may bring truth—*
>
> *That where there is doubt, I may bring faith—*
>
> *That where there is despair, I may bring hope—*
>
> *That where there are shadows, I may bring light—*
>
> *That where there is sadness, I may bring joy.*
>
> *Lord, grant that I may seek rather to comfort than to be comforted—*
>
> *To understand, than to be understood,*
>
> *To love, than to be loved.*
>
> *For it is by self-forgetting that one finds.*
>
> *It is by forgiving that one is forgiven.*
>
> *It is by dying that one awakens to Eternal Life."* [100]

Step Twelve

Step Twelve

STEP TWELVE – GET IT...GIVE IT... LIVE IT... – SERVICE

"Having Had a Spiritual Awakening As the Result of These Steps, We Tried To Carry This Message To Other Alcoholics, and To Practice These Principles In All Our Affairs." [101]

READ IN PREPARATION:

"Big Book" of *Alcoholics Anonymous* –   Pages   89-103

Twelve Steps and Twelve Traditions – Step Twelve Pages 109-130

References

THE REFERENCES

The page number is before the decimal and paragraph number after.

[1] Alcoholics Anonymous – Page 133.1
[2] Language of the Heart – Page 224.3
[3] Language of the Heart – Page 225.9
[4] Language of the Heart – Page 98.2
[5] Alcoholics Anonymous – Preface – Page xii.2
[6] Alcoholics Anonymous – Page 557.1 – 4th Edition
[7] Experience, Strength, & Hope – Page(s) 342.3
[8] Came to Believe… – Page(s) – 120.3
[9] Alcoholics Anonymous – Page 59 – 60
[10] Came to Believe… – Page(s) – 64.7
[11] Alcoholics Anonymous – Page 59.4
[12] Alcoholics Anonymous – Page 59.4
[13] Alcoholics Anonymous – Page 59.4
[14] Alcoholics Anonymous – Page 63.2
[15] Alcoholics Anonymous – Page 59.4
[16] Alcoholics Anonymous – Page 59.4
[17] Alcoholics Anonymous – Page 67.2 and 68.5 – 69.3
[18] Twelve Steps and Twelve Traditions – Page 52.2 and 53.4 – 54.1 – British Addition
[19] Alcoholics Anonymous – Page 67.2 and 68.5 – 69.3
[20] Twelve Steps and Twelve Traditions – Page 52.2 and 53.4 – 54.1 – British Addition
[21] Alcoholics Anonymous – Page 67.2 and 68.5 – 69.3
[22] Twelve Steps and Twelve Traditions – Page 52.2 and 53.4 – 54.1 – British Addition
[23] Alcoholics Anonymous – Page 67.2 and 68.5 – 69.3
[24] Twelve Steps and Twelve Traditions – Page 52.2 and 53.4 – 54.1 – British Addition
[25] Alcoholics Anonymous – Page 67.2 and 68.5 – 69.3
[26] Twelve Steps and Twelve Traditions – Page 52.2 and 53.4 – 54.1 – British Addition
[27] Alcoholics Anonymous – Page 67.2 and 68.5 – 69.3
[28] Twelve Steps and Twelve Traditions – Page 52.2 and 53.4 – 54.1 – British Addition
[29] Alcoholics Anonymous – Page 67.2 and 68.5 – 69.3
[30] Twelve Steps and Twelve Traditions – Page 52.2 and 53.4 – 54.1 – British Addition
[31] Alcoholics Anonymous – Page 67.2 and 68.5 – 69.3
[32] Twelve Steps and Twelve Traditions – Page 52.2 and 53.4 – 54.1 – British Addition
[33] Alcoholics Anonymous – Page 67.2 and 68.5 – 69.3
[34] Twelve Steps and Twelve Traditions – Page 52.2 and 53.4 – 54.1 – British Addition
[35] Alcoholics Anonymous – Page 67.2 and 68.5 – 69.3
[36] Twelve Steps and Twelve Traditions – Page 52.2 and 53.4 – 54.1 – British Addition
[37] Alcoholics Anonymous – Page 67.2 and 68.5 – 69.3
[38] Twelve Steps and Twelve Traditions – Page 52.2 and 53.4 – 54.1 – British Addition
[39] Alcoholics Anonymous – Page 67.2 and 68.5 – 69.3
[40] Twelve Steps and Twelve Traditions – Page 52.2 and 53.4 – 54.1 – British Addition
[41] Alcoholics Anonymous – Page 67.2 and 68.5 – 69.3
[42] Twelve Steps and Twelve Traditions – Page 52.2 and 53.4 – 54.1 – British Addition
[43] Alcoholics Anonymous – Page 67.2 and 68.5 – 69.3
[44] Twelve Steps and Twelve Traditions – Page 52.2 and 53.4 – 54.1 – British Addition
[45] Alcoholics Anonymous – Page 67.2 and 68.5 – 69.3
[46] Twelve Steps and Twelve Traditions – Page 52.2 and 53.4 – 54.1 – British Addition
[47] Alcoholics Anonymous – Page 62, 69
[48] Twelve Steps and Twelve Traditions – Pages 52.3 – 53.2 – British Addition
[49] Alcoholics Anonymous – Page 62, 69
[50] Twelve Steps and Twelve Traditions – Pages 52.3 – 53.2 – British Addition
[51] Alcoholics Anonymous – Page 62, 69
[52] Twelve Steps and Twelve Traditions – Pages 52.3 – 53.2 – British Addition
[53] Alcoholics Anonymous – Page 62, 69
[54] Twelve Steps and Twelve Traditions – Pages 52.3 – 53.2 – British Addition
[55] Alcoholics Anonymous – Page 62, 69
[56] Twelve Steps and Twelve Traditions – Pages 52.3 – 53.2 – British Addition

THE REFERENCES

[57] Alcoholics Anonymous – Page 62, 69

[58] Twelve Steps and Twelve Traditions – Pages 52.3 – 53.2 – British Addition

[59] Alcoholics Anonymous – Page 62, 69

[60] Twelve Steps and Twelve Traditions – Pages 52.3 – 53.2 – British Addition

[61] Alcoholics Anonymous – Page 62, 69

[62] Twelve Steps and Twelve Traditions – Pages 52.3 – 53.2 – British Addition

[63] Alcoholics Anonymous – Page 62, 69

[64] Twelve Steps and Twelve Traditions – Pages 52.3 – 53.2 – British Addition

[65] Alcoholics Anonymous – Page 62, 69

[66] Twelve Steps and Twelve Traditions – Pages 52.3 – 53.2 – British Addition

[67] Alcoholics Anonymous – Page 62, 69

[68] Twelve Steps and Twelve Traditions – Pages 52.3 – 53.2 – British Addition

[69] Alcoholics Anonymous – Page 62, 69

[70] Twelve Steps and Twelve Traditions – Pages 52.3 – 53.2 – British Addition

[71] Alcoholics Anonymous – Page 62, 69

[72] Twelve Steps and Twelve Traditions – Pages 52.3 – 53.2 – British Addition

[73] Alcoholics Anonymous – Page 62, 69

[74] Twelve Steps and Twelve Traditions – Pages 52.3 – 53.2 – British Addition

[75] Alcoholics Anonymous – Page 62, 69

[76] Twelve Steps and Twelve Traditions – Pages 52.3 – 53.2 – British Addition

[77] Twelve Steps and Twelve Traditions – Pages 52.3 – 53.2 – British Addition

[78] Twelve Steps and Twelve Traditions – Pages 52.3 – 53.2 – British Addition

[79] Twelve Steps and Twelve Traditions – Pages 52.3 – 53.2 – British Addition

[80] Twelve Steps and Twelve Traditions – Pages 52.3 – 53.2 – British Addition

[81] Twelve Steps and Twelve Traditions – Pages 52.3 – 53.2 – British Addition

[82] Twelve Steps and Twelve Traditions – Pages 52.3 – 53.2 – British Addition

[83] Twelve Steps and Twelve Traditions – Pages 52.3 – 53.2 – British Addition

[84] Twelve Steps and Twelve Traditions – Pages 52.3 – 53.2 – British Addition

[85] Twelve Steps and Twelve Traditions – Pages 52.3 – 53.2 – British Addition

[86] Twelve Steps and Twelve Traditions – Pages 52.3 – 53.2 – British Addition

[87] Twelve Steps and Twelve Traditions – Pages 52.3 – 53.2 – British Addition

[88] Twelve Steps and Twelve Traditions – Pages 52.3 – 53.2 – British Addition

[89] Twelve Steps and Twelve Traditions – Pages 52.3 – 53.2 – British Addition

[90] Twelve Steps and Twelve Traditions – Pages 52.3 – 53.2 – British Addition

[91] Twelve Steps and Twelve Traditions – Pages 52.3 – 53.2 – British Addition

[92] Alcoholics Anonymous – Page 59.4

[93] Alcoholics Anonymous – Page 59.4

[94] Alcoholics Anonymous – Page 76.2

[95] Alcoholics Anonymous – Page 59.4

[96] Alcoholics Anonymous – Page 59.4

[97] Alcoholics Anonymous – Page 83.4 – 85.2

[98] Alcoholics Anonymous – Page 59.4

[99] Alcoholics Anonymous – Page 59.4

[100] Twelve Steps and Twelve Traditions – Pages 101.4 – 102.2 – British Addition

[101] Alcoholics Anonymous – Page 59.4